SINCE WE'VE NO PLACE TO GO

KATE WATSON

Cover by Melody Jeffries.

To everyone who grieves—and celebrates—a little extra during the holidays.

AUTHOR'S NOTE AND CONTENT WARNING

This book contains themes of grief, illness, and mental illness. All efforts have been made to treat these topics with care. Any mistakes are my own.

This book also contains a guy who is way too cocky for his own good. Those mistakes are absolutely his.

CHAPTER ONE

LIESEL

I look at my boarding pass as if the power of my glare alone will make this airplane leave on time.

"Attention, all passengers. Blue Horizon Airlines flight 211 to Phoenix has been delayed. Blue Horizon Airlines flight 211 from Chicago to Phoenix has been delayed. The new departure time is 9 a.m."

Cool. It's cool. I've only been here since 5 a.m., and everything.

What good is arriving at the airport two hours before a flight if they can go and delay you an extra hour? Again?

I sigh and walk to the seating area to wait. The airport is decorated for Christmas. The terminal's main atrium is decked in huge garland, beautiful red bows, and white lights in the shape of flying birds so iconic, they belong in a movie (Home Alone 2, anyone?).

I'm glad I'm not in the main atrium.

But even this boarding area is too festive for my taste, and the passengers are wearing far too much red and green. Blech.

I glance around the seating area. It's completely full, but I spot a couple getting up to leave, and I wait with the determination of a predator. The couple smiles as they pass me at the end of the aisle, and I swoop in.

At the same time, a tall, athletic guy in a red Christmas cowboy hat—complete with a buckle and white fur trim—comes from the other end of the aisle. He drops to one of the two empty seats, and I walk toward the other. Not ideal, but it's the only other seat in the entire terminal.

I'm about to take the remaining seat when he sets his carry-on in the open chair.

Who does that? The airport is packed!

"Whew," he says to the passenger next to him. "That was lucky. I thought I'd missed my flight. Good thing it was delayed!"

Good thing it was delayed? This is the second delay!

I stand in front of the extra seat. He pulls up his phone. All I can see is the top of his stupid Santa-inspired Stetson.

The man doesn't look up.

I tap my foot and clear my throat.

Nothing.

"Excuse me," I say. I touch his strong shoulder, because his attention is fixed on whatever article he's reading.

"Yes?" His face flits up too fast for me to catch more than a glimpse of a beard and a face tat.

You heard me: he has a tattoo on his face.

A Rudolph the Red-Nosed Reindeer face tattoo.

I look at the chair, because the colorful Rudolph covering every remaining inch of his left cheek above his beard and beneath his hat is too distracting.

"You set your bag down in the last open seat in the boarding area. Can I sit here?"

"Oh, sure." He moves his bag underneath his chair, and I sit next to him.

And because I'm annoyed, I call my best friend. She answers on the second ring.

"Hey, I'm almost at the hospital, so I only have five minutes before work," she says. "What's up?"

"Jules, why am I like this?"

"You mean smart and gorgeous?"

"Not that smart. I've been at the airport for hours. And I'm still here."

"Flight delayed?" she asks.

"Delayed again."

"Fortune favors the prepared, sweetie."

"Not my fortune. Fortune hates me."

"It'll catch up eventually. I'm sorry about the delay. I know how much you've been looking forward to your big retreat."

"Thanks."

"What do you need from me right now? Commiseration? A pep talk?"

"A proverbial slap will do just fine," I say. The guy next to me shifts, but I physically can't care what a guy in a Santa Stetson with a Christmas face tattoo thinks.

"Okay, proverbial slap it is," she says. "Pull yourself together! Your flight was delayed. So what? Would you rather have paced around the apartment worrying about whether or not you'd be late? No. You're fine. You can wait a couple more hours to wow the entire baseball world."

"I'm not going to wow anyone."

"Not with that attitude, you're not. Now go splash some cold water on your face, find a Coconut Cream Dr. Pepper, and snap out of it."

"You want me to wash my makeup off? Are you insane?"

Juliet laughs. "I gotta go. See you when you get back. Oh, and

Nate and I sent a couple of surprises to the resort to cheer you on."

"Please tell me they're small."

"I can confidently say both are smaller than a breadbox."

"Phew," I say. "Now go nurse your face off!"

"That does not sound how you think it sounds," Juliet says.

"It really doesn't," I agree, cringing. "Have a great day at work, Nurse Jules!"

"Better. Love you!"

"Byeeee."

I feel better after talking to my friend. She's getting married in a couple of months, so our time as roommates is coming to an end. And I hate it.

So I refuse to think about it.

Refusing to think about things that cause me pain is my go-to coping tactic. I manage this with distraction, avoidance, and by always, always taking extra work home with me.

Like right now, for instance. Some people would take out a book and make their airport time their self-care time, but I don't believe in self-care, because self-care leaves time for thinking, and thinking leaves time for grieving, and I don't have time for that.

So instead, I take out my laptop and pull up a color-coded spreadsheet I've put my blood, sweat, and tears into over the last eleven months. Less the blood.

"What's that?" Face Tattoo says.

I angle it away from him. "It's something for work, but it's proprietary. Sorry."

"What do you do for work?"

"Stats," I say vaguely.

"You do stats? For what company?"

"Just some company." I shut my laptop. I try to look him in the eye, but his weird Rudolph tattoo stares back at me, and I have to avert my gaze.

"Oh, wow, are you like a spy, or something? Is that why you can't talk about it?"

"I'd be a pretty terrible spy if I opened a secret document in a crowded airport."

"But only a slightly less terrible statistician for opening a secret document in one?"

He has a point, and I already hate him a bit for it. I put my laptop away.

"Maybe you don't travel much for work, but in general, there's an unspoken traveler's code where people don't look at other people's computer screens," I say.

"You must travel a lot more than I do, because in my experience, almost everyone is paying attention to what other people are doing."

"No one cares about other people. They care about themselves, just like you do."

"Like me?"

"I mean in general," I say. "Everyone's too busy worrying about themselves to worry about other people."

"I can think of a few exceptions," he says darkly.

Okay, then.

Two TV screens hang near enough that I can turn my attention to either of them and away from Face Tattoo. One is showing a Hallmark Christmas movie, and the other is showing sports. I angle my face to the one showing sports.

Yes, it might be Christmas season, but more importantly, it's "Hot Stove Season"—the time when no baseball is played, but every team is busy making trades and getting their roster ready for the upcoming season. The sportscasters are offering predictions about what different teams will do. My team—the Chicago Firebirds—is on everyone's minds, because at the beginning of last season, we acquired the cockiest jerk in all of baseball for a monster contract. And he got injured during the last game of the league championship series.

I'm glad I don't work directly with players, because I'd have given him so many pieces of my mind, I'd be brain-dead.

"You a fan?" he asks.

I keep looking at the TV. "I live in Chicago. Everyone's a baseball fan."

"No, I mean of Coop."

"Cooper Kellogg? Not remotely. The guy is a classless, overpaid punk."

"How do you really feel, though?"

I scoff. "He signed a ten year, five hundred million dollar contract! No way is he worth fifty million a year."

"You know half of that's deferred," Face Tattoo says. "He won't get the other half until he's well into retirement."

"Are you mansplaining baseball contracts to me?"

"I'm pointing out what most fans don't realize."

"I'm not most fans."

"Ah, okay. Good for you."

I'm so tired of men thinking they know baseball better than I do. I would look at him, but between the low hat and the beard, there's nothing but Rudolph. "I know you probably think because you have an XY chromosome that a little ol' girl could never know more than you, but I work in the sport. I grew up around it. I've forgotten more about baseball than you'll ever know."

"Sounds like you have a bad memory."

THIS GUY.

"You want to talk about your boy Cooper Kellogg? There are probably a half dozen players in the league who aren't half as pretty who deserve twice the pay, deferred or not," I say.

"You think he's that good looking? It's the jaw, right? He has a great jaw."

If I were a cartoon character, steam would come off me. "Are you even a Firebirds fan?"

"You could say that."

"We should have moved Cahill to third, called up a Minor League player, and waited a year to trade for Hideo Suzuki, instead."

"Suzuki? You gotta be kidding me. Coop hit fifty-two homers last season, ten more than Suzuki!"

"Yet Suzuki batted in almost as many runs."

"So now Coop is to be blamed for other players not being able to get on base?"

I wheel on him, staring Rudolph right in the face. Face Tattoo is a lot taller than me, and he's still looking at the screen, the brat. The least he can do is look at me looking at his tattoo while I put him in his place. "Coop blew a kiss to an opposing pitcher after he hit a homer off him."

The guy snorts, eyes fixed on the TV. "That was funny."

"Then he did a backflip at home plate."

"Funny and agile. Who knew Coop could do a backflip?"

"Everyone! Because he pulls that kind of crap constantly!"

"Crap? The fans love it."

"The opposing teams don't. It puts a target on the entire Firebirds lineup."

"They were playing their biggest rivals. The pitcher was mouthing off all week to the press about how Coop wouldn't get a hit off him. So when Coop launched a bomb, he played it up for the fans. Besides, you're missing the point: he hit the home run." He shifts, tipping his head to the side so I get even more of Rudolph. "And if you're so worried about budget, keep in mind that following Coop's little stunt, he sold more jerseys than any player in the league and attendance spiked for the rest of the season. Guess who pocketed the lion's share of that money? The team."

I narrow my eyes and turn back to the TV. I never thought of it that way. The sportscasters have turned this into a piece about Cooper Kellogg's historic rise. On the cover of Sports Illustrated at seventeen, hailed as baseball's next big thing. The guy was famous before he even graduated high school. "It was disrespectful."

"Ah. You're a baseball purist."

"So?"

"So you think the game should never change, even as the world does."

"I don't mind changes," I say. "I mind hotshots."

"Coop gets people talking about baseball."

"No, he gets people talking about him." I point to the screen. "Heaven forbid a week pass where Cooper Kellogg isn't a bigger story than his team."

"People love him."

"People don't know him like I know him," I say, a jagged edge to my words.

A laugh jumps from his lips. "You know Cooper Kellogg?"

I glower, hating his line of questioning as much as his stupid tattoo. "Let's just say I have personal experience with him."

"Why does that sound like code for you hit on him, and he turned you down?"

My pulse hammers in my ears loud enough to block out all background noise. "It's. Not."

"Uh huh. Sure."

I could scream. "I'm so sick of you Cooper apologists! Like he isn't in everyone's face enough!"

"At least no one forgets about him."

The finality in his tone … the jagged edge to his words …

I look him fully in the eye, and this time, he looks at me.

And.

I.

Want.

To.

Die.

The hot ire in my chest becomes oily and weighted, pulling from my neck and ears and sinking me deep into the ground.

Bright brown eyes pierce me beneath the hat, above the beard, and past the festive face tattoo, which I can now see is fake.

"You're Cooper Kellogg," I croak.

He gives me a wry smile. "Finally caught on, did you?"

My pulse thumps so hard in my chest, it saps all the strength from my voice. "You're wearing a surprisingly effective disguise."

He cocks an eyebrow. "Not that effective."

"You have a face tattoo," I say, trying to laugh. "Believe me: it's that effective."

He taps it with his finger. "Good to know. I bought a ten pack hoping they'd do the trick. Kind of odd for a dude who 'has to make sure people are talking about him,' isn't it?"

I fiddle with an earring, twisting the diamonds. I know I hate him, and all, and I work in baseball, so this shouldn't be a big deal, but ... he's still COOPER KELLOGG.

Be cool, Liesel.

I wrinkle my nose. "I'm sorry for what I said—"

"No you're not," he says, though he's not glaring at me, which is generous of him. "You're sorry you said the quiet part out loud. People love to hate Cooper Kellogg. But no one cares why he does what he does. No one cares how he feels."

The oily guilt in my veins spreads into my limbs and cheeks. How often does stuff like this happen to him? He was sitting in an airport, having a casual conversation, and a fan started bashing him without even realizing he was right there. He did nothing to deserve that. "I'm sorry. This is your life, not just a story on the news. How do you feel?"

"Thanks for asking," he says. Then he grins, showing his teeth. "Really good. I'm so freaking rich."

I pop like a Christmas cracker.

"You are unbelievable!" I say, jumping to my feet.

He grins and takes off his hat. "That's what Sports Center tells me."

"Holy crap, you're Cooper Kellogg!" The guy across from us says. And suddenly, everyone is spotting him.

I grab my bag and storm off, unwilling to spend another second around the man.

When I turn back with my most withering glare, he's surrounded by fans and waving at me.

Oh, and he's put his carry-on back on my seat.

CHAPTER TWO

LIESEL

My phone buzzes with text after text from my brothers while I stand in line at the check-in counter at the Desert Oasis Resort, where the Firebirds baseball organization is holding meetings. They've been fired up since I texted them about my encounter in the airport.

LOGAN

Man, I hate that guy.

LUCAS

He's everything that's wrong with dudes.

And baseball.

And probably, like, toothpaste.

LOGAN

What?

LIESEL

What?

LUCAS

You know what I mean. He can make even normal stuff bad.

LOGAN

But toothpaste is toothpaste. It doesn't matter if he uses it.

LIESEL

Yeah, I'm not feeling it.

LUCAS

You'd better not feel it.

And by it, I mean him.

LIESEL

GROSS.

Like I want to *feel* Cooper Kellogg?

LOGAN

You sure about that?

LUCAS

snort

LIESEL

Don't. You. Dare.

LOGAN

GIF of kid whistling and twiddling his thumbs

LUCAS

Fine. We'll let it slide.

LOGAN

This time.

LIESEL

I will kill you both in your sleep.

LUCAS

gif of man yawning

We're going to drive to look at lights on Sunday, Lee. You coming?

LIESEL

Not sure. Juliet may have a dress fitting.

LOGAN

You said that after Halloween when we wanted to put up the tree, and we still haven't done it.

LIESEL

Sorry guys. Things are just really busy.

Checking in at the hotel. Gotta run.

I drop my phone into my bag, feeling sick.

I loved ripping on Cooper with them.

I *hate* talking about Christmas with them.

I spin one of my earrings while I wait for the front desk clerk to call me forward and pull up my reservation.

"Ms. Fischer," she says with a big smile, "I'm pleased to tell you that you've been upgraded to the Owner's Suite. All incidentals have been covered."

I shake my head and show her my ID. "No, I think you have me mistaken for someone else. I'm Liesel Fischer."

The clerk smiles. "I know who you are, Lisa."

"Liesel," I correct her. The number of times I've been called Lisa instead of Liesel reaches into the hundreds. The sweet old gossip who used to live in my apartment complex always called me Lisa, and for a while, Juliet was the only person in the entire building who knew my real name. Including her freaking fiancé.

"My mistake. But you *have* been upgraded, Ms. Fischer," she says, her tone not remotely apologetic. "Here's your key card. Your private elevator is through the hallway behind the desk."

What is happening? I push my ID back across the counter, knocking a gold garland off. I scramble to pick it back up. It's been a long day, and I'm eager to get into my room. But the Owner's Suite *can't* be my room. "You don't understand. I'm not a VIP. I'm front office staff for the Chicago Firebirds. I'm here for a staff retreat. Business meetings."

"I understand your confusion, Ms. Fischer. Mr. Cruz contacted us personally and insisted that you take the suite. He left a note to say if you have any problems or concerns, he'll be happy to ... 'send his fiancée to clear up the confusion.'"

With a resigned exhale, I nod. "Right. I'm staying at the *Cruz* Desert Oasis Resort."

My best friend is engaged to Nate Cruz, heir to one of the largest commercial real estate companies in the world. And because they inadvertently met through me, Nate has a tendency to overdo his appreciation.

Case in point? Nate gave me his white Prius last year. Literally gave it to me because my car was stolen. He just handed me the keys, signed over the title, and that was it.

Him hooking me up with a room in his family's resort is nothing. To him.

The lobby has been quiet throughout our exchange—our meetings don't start until tomorrow, and I took an early flight out to get my head in the game—but I hear footfalls behind me. The clerk hands me back my ID *again*, and I slide it into a slot at the back of my phone case.

"Ms. Fischer, we'll have someone take your bags up to your suite."

"Oh, there's no need. It's just a suitcase and a laptop bag."

"We insist," the woman says with a no-nonsense smile. I would think her smile should have a *little* nonsense, considering she's wearing light-up Christmas tree earrings. But no. She slides a gold and black keycard across the marble counter.

Smaller than a breadbox, I think. *Jules, you sneaky little liar.*

"Your private elevator is at the end of this hall," the clerk continues. "The keycard will grant you access, and it can also be used for any and all incidentals during your stay here, including spa treatments."

"I won't need a spa treatment. I'm only here for the meetings," I say.

Her smile is getting more long-suffering by the minute. "There's also a gift waiting for you in your suite."

"*Another gift?* I don't—"

"There's no shame in having friends in high places," the clerk says.

I lean closer to her and whisper, "It's not even like he's *my* friend," I say, although that's not entirely true. Nate is awesome. "He's marrying my best friend."

"Congratulations to them." Her polite grin has to be hurting her face at this point, right? "Is there anything else I can assist you with?"

I don't know why this bothers me, other than I've done nothing to deserve the Owner's Suite at the fanciest resort in Scottsdale, Arizona. I don't need this. I didn't earn this. I just know a guy.

I sigh. "Yes, do you know if my itineraries for the teams are available yet?"

"Yours is already in your room."

Of course it is.

A bellhop comes and ushers me to the side of the front desk. He makes a point of taking my things and pointing me in the direction of the private elevator.

"Hold on, please," I say when we've taken a few steps across the beautiful natural stone flooring. I stop next to one of a dozen Christmas trees decorating the lobby. I don't keep cash on me, and I'll need to give him a tip. "I'm sorry, is there an ATM around? Or I can send you money through a cash app of some kind?"

He smiles. "Mr. Cruz already took care of the tips."

I grumble. Juliet may like that she's marrying a billionaire, but I'm glad I'm not. Don't get me wrong. I have nothing against money. But I really dislike people doing things for me that I can do for myself.

While I'm in my bag, I spot my Cherry Chapstick. I've only been in Arizona for an hour, but the dryness is getting to me. I put it on my lips and notice the person who was standing behind me in line at the desk.

He must have shaved on the airplane and removed the temporary tattoo from his face. He looks much better. And much worse. I've seen so much of Cooper Kellogg's flippant face in the year I've worked for the Firebirds that I want to vomit. He's good looking—no question—but he's so brash! He's swapped his Christmasy cowboy hat for a gray baseball cap. I bet his thick, wavy brown hair sticks out of it when he wears it backwards in a way that drives women crazy.

It drives me crazy, too, but for an entirely different reason.

What is he doing here? This is supposed to be a front office staff retreat for our team and each of its affiliates. Is there a promotional event happening at the same time? Maybe he's signing his tenth endorsement of the season.

I glare thinking of our exchange in the airport. He must be laughing about how he got the best of me with his dumb stunt. He had a beard and hat and wore a fake tattoo he could have stolen from a preschool Christmas party. How was I supposed to know who he was?

"Ma'am?" the bellhop asks, drawing Cooper's attention.

He turns his face to me before I can look away, and when I meet his brown eyes, he cocks an eyebrow.

Irritation swells in me.

I glance at the bellhop. "I'm ready to go upstairs. Thank you for your patience."

"Yes, ma'am."

He escorts me up the private elevator and leaves my bags in a suite that is twice the size of my apartment and a thousand times nicer. The fixtures are all marble, gold and crystal, with Christmas decorations throughout.

Ugh. Who decorates a hotel suite for Christmas? I poke my head into room after tinsel-strewn room, almost tempted to throw the decorations in the trash. There's a grand piano in the living room! And I say "living room" to distinguish it from the family room, where the TV is.

There are Christmas trees in both.

My word.

I find the gift the clerk mentioned on the dining room table near my itinerary for the meetings. It's ornately wrapped in gold ribbon and matching wrapping paper with a note.

If anyone messes with you, I'll have Nate buy the baseball team.
XO,
Jules

I roll my eyes but laugh when I open the box and pull out a Stanley mug in the gray, blue, and red of my team. In the team's classic-inspired font, there's a customized message:

Lady in the streets, geek in the spreadsheets.

I snap a picture and send it to Juliet with a text.

LIESEL

Really?

JULIET

Just helping you project your best image to the team. You'll thank me later.

LIESEL

Oh, I'll project something, all right.

JULIET

Are you going to use it?

LIESEL

Of course I am! It's hilarious and weirdly on brand.

You guys were nice to upgrade me, btw. Have you stayed in an Owner's Suite before? This thing is insane.

JULIET

I know! Nate showed me the pictures. Opulent much?

LIESEL

Tell him I'm disappointed it doesn't have its own gym. I'm going to have to use the resort's fitness center like some common investment banker.

JULIET

It doesn't have a gym??? Ew! I'm so sorry you'll have to rub shoulders with all those basic millionaires.

LIESEL

lol

Okay, I'm going to sweat the airplane stink off of me. Thank Nate for me. You know, if my owner doesn't fire me for having a nicer suite than he has.

JULIET

Good point. You should probably use the stairs instead of the private elevator so they don't realize you're better than them.

LIESEL

You're just trying to make me take the stairs. But joke's on you. I never take them when you're not with me.

JULIET

So you're NOT worried about getting trapped in an elevator with a hot guy? Like maybe Cooper Kellogg?

LIESEL

HA HA. Very funny.

Seriously, though, should I take the stairs? Will they think I'm some snob for using the private elevator?

JULIET

You're not a snob and no one would think you are. The only reason you should take the stairs is because stairs can't break down in the middle of a power outage.

LIESEL

You really cannot get over that, can you?

JULIET

GIF of kid sticking her tongue out

Have fun!

Jules may have been kidding about the private elevator, but I'm not. It's not like I can walk out of the fanciest suite without attracting attention, can I?

Sure I can. I have a reason why I'm staying in this suite. It's not a big deal.

Or is it?

Ugh. I'm overthinking this. *Turn off, brain!*

I walk into the master bedroom—not to be confused with the other two bedrooms—and change into my workout clothes. You know how some people are doers? I'm a stew-er. I think and stew and stew and think. I hate not having a reason for the decisions I make. Worse, I hate making the wrong decision. Oh, and I also hate feeling like I'm wasting my time, so I spend disproportionate amounts of time debating what the best use of my time *is*.

Go anxiety!

The one thing I know for certain is that a workout always makes me feel better. After putting ice and water in my new tumbler, I take my phone, keycard, and earbuds and sneak out the front door and to the stairs. I'm staying on the seventeenth floor, and the map in my room said the gym is on the fourth floor. I take them quickly.

When I'm almost to the ninth floor, the door opens. A man in a gray baseball hat and athletic wear steps out, and I internalize a groan.

Cooper freaking Kellogg.

I slow down, hoping he won't notice me, but he does. He looks at my mug and then smirks before looking up at me. I wait for him to walk downstairs, but he gestures for me to go first.

"I'm fine," I say. "After you."

"No, I insist," he says. "Even if I am a rude, classless, overpaid punk."

I flare my nostrils but jog down the stairs past him. I refuse to worry about my pace the whole time. I run the stairs more than a professional athlete thanks to my ultra paranoid roommate. If he's chomping at the bit to pass me, he'll live.

At the fourth floor, I hold the door open for him—go manners!—but he winks and then continues downstairs.

He *winks*.

One conversation, one argument in an airport, and now he seems intent on messing with me. We don't even know each other. We've never met before today, because it's not like most stats nerds sit around the clubhouse chatting up players.

Who does he think he is? Walking into the fitness center, I can't help but wonder where he's going. Running outside, probably, so he can revel in fawning fans.

Okay, I'm being catty.

The weather is gorgeous out, and the Uber driver told me that nearby Pinnacle Peak has tons of pretty trails. Also, he played for the Diamondbacks before getting traded to the Firebirds last season. Maybe he used to live in this area and wants to reconnect with nature.

I start running on a treadmill that's up against floor-to-ceiling glass windows. The fitness center overlooks a gorgeous golf course. I wonder if any of the people I see down there are Cooper. But no, he wouldn't be running toward a golf course.

My feet pound on the treadmill deck, and my curiosity gets the best of me. I pull him up on Instagram.

Wow.

He's *already* taken a selfie outside the hotel with a fan and shared it to his stories. And, naturally, it's a woman. And she's gorgeous.

I'm glad I don't work directly with players. My dad and brothers have always warned me against them, but it's a warning I don't need. I would rather date the abominable snowman than a hotshot like Cooper Kellogg.

CHAPTER THREE

COOPER

"I'm such a huge fan, Coop. We're all rooting for you to make a full recovery," the very tan woman I just took a selfie with says.

"That means a lot," I say with my signature grin. She turns her attention to her phone, and I'm 99% sure she's going to give me her number. I bolt before she can.

I run hard and fast for the first half mile, wanting to get as much distance as possible between me and potential fans. But soon, my feet find a familiar rhythm that calms my racing thoughts.

It's good to be back in Phoenix. The bone-chill of Chicago makes my elbow ache enough to need *another* surgery. I grew up in a border town in New Mexico, so mild, dry winters feel familiar to me. Because we didn't have our own MLB team, my family cheered for the Diamondbacks. Getting to play for the team I love for the first seven years of my career was a dream come true. But I may have not quite been the dream *they* wanted. I wasn't a bad teammate, or anything, but I've had a target on my back since I was on the cover of Sports Illustrated in high school. And let me tell you, I've had fun with that target. Sometimes at the expense of the team, as the woman in the airport suggested.

The woman in the airport. And the lobby. And the stairwell. She's like a pretty little pest that can't stop buzzing around my head. Those blue eyes of hers saw too much. And that mouth *said* too much. She said she works in baseball, and considering the entire Firebirds organization—from Single A to the Majors to our international affiliates—has meetings here this week, it's safe to assume she works for the Firebirds at some level. She must belong to the most long-suffering department in the business, because she's insufferable.

The stuff she spouted is nothing new; in fact, it's getting old. I'd normally keep my disguise on, but I couldn't with how wound up she was.

Maybe I shouldn't have kept winding her, come to think of it. Her neck was so red when she was ranting about me, I probably should have kept quiet and at least listened politely.

Or not.

I'm not trying to make my team hated; I'm trying to make baseball fun again. Other sports have so much tradition around celebration, and baseball has a tradition of being "too good to celebrate."

Too boring, more like it.

Kids don't watch baseball to the same degree anymore. There's a reason more and more people are getting into teams like the Savannah Bananas. They make baseball fun.

And so do I.

When the Diamondbacks traded me, it was because they couldn't afford me. But not all of Arizona was sad to see me go, and it's because of my "attitude" about the sport. I'm not respectful enough. I don't venerate it like some holy institution.

I see it as a game. One I get paid a lot of money to play, and one I play to the best of my ability. I train harder than any guy on the field. And the Firebirds have been good to me, fortunately. I've tried hard to be a team player. Harder, at least.

But come on, if you run your mouth about how you're going to strike me out, yeah, when I hit a homer off you, I'm going to blow you a kiss. And do a backflip onto home plate.

I don't make the rules.

After another few miles, I reach a gated community. I look at my phone and enter the code my GM sent me. A moment later, the small walking gate unlatches and I enter an immaculately kept neighborhood that's a far cry from the tiny apartment I grew up in. The entire neighborhood looks like it's something out of a "Christmas Wars" reality show, where neighbors compete for best decorations, prettiest Christmas lights, most reindeer on a roof, you name it.

And I love it.

After another half mile, I reach a gorgeous, sprawling home and press the camera doorbell. A moment later, a little kid says in a robot voice, "Who are you and why are you here?"

"I'm Cooper Kellogg, and I'm here to see your dad," I say.

"Dad! Coop's here! Can he sign my—" There's a scuffle, and a moment later, my GM opens the door, his salt and pepper hair looking disheveled.

"Hey Doug," I say.

He shakes his head. "Sorry, Coop. Come on in." His seven year-old is hiding behind his legs. "You remember Mason, don't you?"

"I do," I say, bumping his fist with mine.

"Can you sign a baseball for me?" Mason asks before his dad can cover his mouth.

"I signed ten for you last time I saw you, didn't I?" I say.

"Don't sign anything," Doug says. "He's been selling balls with your autograph on them for a hundred bucks a pop."

"A hundred each?" I chuckle. "Not bad, kid."

Mason sighs. "Yeah, but Aiden sold a Hideo Suzuki ball for two hundred."

"Two hundred?" I huff. "Hideo Suzuki can sniff my dirty socks. And so can Aiden."

"It's simple economics," Doug says, tousling his son's hair. "Aiden was the only kid in school with a signed Hideo Suzuki ball. You sold ten of Coop's. Supply and demand, kid."

Mason sticks his tongue out at his dad.

"Careful. That'll put you on the Naughty List," Doug says.

"NO!" Mason screams, falls at his dad's feet, and starts hitting Doug's legs. "Daddy, no! Don't tell Santa!"

Doug shakes his head. "I won't tell Santa."

Mason's tears dry up and he immediately runs off.

"That kid is a bigger handful than his four older siblings combined," Doug mutters.

Doug leads me through his beautifully decorated home. Each room has a Christmas tree, and it makes me nostalgic for Christmas with my parents. As lovely as Doug's mansion-home is, it can't compare to my mom's decorating. She always made our little apartment seem grander than the Windsor Hotel on Christmas. And now that she and Dad are celebrating Christmas in the house I bought for them, she does the same on a grander scale.

Doug escorts me outside to the backyard. His home is on at least a couple of acres, and just past the pool, I see an actual baseball diamond I itch to play on. We walk over to it and stand in front of home plate. I breathe in deeply.

There's nothing more beautiful than an empty stadium. The perfectly manicured lawn, the crisp white base lines, the orderly seats. When I was ten, my travel baseball team had a tournament in Phoenix, and my dad took me to my first Spring Training game. The stadium took my breath away. We sat on the lawn, the sun beating down on us even in March. Dad got me a huge bag of cotton candy, and to this day, it's still my favorite treat. Then, something incredible happened. A player came up to bat and pointed to the outfield, just like Babe Ruth calling his home run.

But the crowd booed the guy.

I couldn't understand why they'd boo him. He was so brave! When he hit a pop fly, the crowd laughed, and I held back tears.

Dad put his arm around me and told me that it was just a game and the player had thick skin. The Jumbotron showed him holding out his arms in a shrug, but he was smiling. "It's all part of The Show," Dad said.

That guy became my hero.

He wasn't a big player. He only lasted six seasons in the majors. But he got into baseball operations, and guess what team he manages now?

The Chicago Firebirds.

The pretty pest from the airport and the lobby and the stairwell is right: I'm not a fifty million a year player. The Dodgers offered me even more.

But they didn't have Doug Turner as their GM.

"You miss it already, don't you?" Doug asks. His eyes jump down to the wicked scar that curves around my elbow on the inside of my arm.

"Yeah, but don't worry," I say. "I'm not doing anything to get in the way of making a full recovery."

He nods and guides us back through the yard and over to the covered patio, where a full spread awaits us. "I get it," he says. "It took me about a decade to get over retiring."

"You've done okay for yourself." I gesture around. "Summers in Chicago and winters in Scottsdale? I'd say being a general manager has its perks."

"Yeah, but I'd still be playing if I'd had half your skill."

"Or if you had your real knees."

He barks out a laugh and we both pile up our plates and sit

at the outdoor table. The weather is perfect—probably 70 degrees—and it's the only thing I *don't* like about December in the desert now that I've lived in snow.

It doesn't feel like Christmas.

My mom always made sure that even though it was sunny outside, our apartment felt like a winter wonderland. I still don't know how she did it, how she managed to make the mundane magical.

I know why she did it, though. Why she still does and always will.

I ask Doug about the team while we eat, but rather than talking about the holes in our roster, he turns the conversation back to me.

"How are your parents?" he asks.

"Fine," I say.

"Is your dad still working at the Builder's Bench? He promised he was going to retire this year, didn't he?"

"He has officially retired and is talking about buying an RV. He said once my elbow has healed, he wants to drive to every one of my games."

Doug chuckles. "How does your mom feel about that?"

I swallow hard. Doug doesn't know as much about my mom as he does about my dad, but I get the feeling he knows more than I want him to. Of course, it's hard not to put some pieces together when my dad attended every one of my playoff games last season and she didn't make it to one. "That'll be a game time decision," I say, and leave it at that.

"Are they flying out for Christmas?" he asks. My chest aches with a familiar pain.

"No, I'll go visit them."

Doug holds my eye for a moment too long. Then he crumples his napkin and throws it away.

"Let's talk about the coming season. The doc isn't clearing

you, so you have a full eighteen months to get ready for your next Spring Training. Right?"

My chest burns with something between guilt and humiliation. I was traded to the team to win them a World Series, and instead, in the last game of the league championship series, I tore a ligament in my elbow trying to throw out the tying run at home plate. I ripped my arm apart throwing that ball from right field, and it still wasn't enough.

The ump ruled the guy safe.

My injury can't compare to how bad I feel having failed my team. Failed Doug. It's a pain no surgery can fix. "Coop?"

I blink. "Uh, yeah, I'll miss all next season. It's healing nicely, but the doc doesn't want me risking reinjury. If that's okay."

"Of course it's okay. This is your *life* we're talking about. We brought you in for the long haul, not for a single season. We believe in you. And to that end," he says, distracting me from getting too choked up. "Let's talk about how we can put you to work. I'd like you to be my special assistant over scouting next year."

"Scouting? You want me in the front office?"

"You're too valuable to us not to squeeze a bit of extra work out of you."

"I'll do whatever you want." I hate how eager I sound, but I can't hide it. I'm known for my devil-may-care attitude, and I'm not playing a part as much as you'd think. You don't know me? Don't like me? I don't care what you think.

But if I like *you*—if I *respect* you—I need your approval like Mason needs to know he's on the Nice List.

Doug nods. "Good. I want you to focus hard on rehab. But this week, I need you at our staff retreat working with the analytics team to fix our roster. And you can't be a punk about it."

He grabs a heavy folder from the chair next to him and drops it between us like it's punctuation. A period. A command.

"That's the second time today I've been called a punk," I say. "Am I in a John Hughes movie? Is this *The Breakfast Club*?"

"Who was the first person?"

"Some woman in the airport."

Doug's lips twitch, but he shakes his head. "She has your number, Coop. You're the most passionate player on the field, day in, day out. Everyone who gets to see past the bravado likes you. The problem is most people don't get to know you well enough to see past it. But I need you talking to coaches and front office staff who aren't impressed by your on-base percentage because they're too busy analyzing how much you're costing the team."

"Ouch."

"I'm telling you like it is. You can't pull crap like giving them your autograph or blowing a kiss if I pick a player you recommended over them."

"I get it," I say. "I won't let you down."

Doug smiles. "Good man. Now let me drive you back to the resort so you can study prospects." We get up, and I take our dishes with me into the house. "You don't need to do that. I'll have my kids clean it up."

"I don't mind," I say. I scrape down the dishes and load them in the chef's kitchen as Doug watches me.

When I'm done, I follow him through the house and into the garage, where we climb into his Tesla. "You know, if people found out that you clean a rich dude's home, they'd have to change their minds about you. This would kill your reputation."

"Easy, now. I'm a showboat, not a jerk."

"You're a better guy than most people will ever know."

"As long as the right people know, I'm cool. Oh, and it's okay if you know, too."

Doug laughs under his breath. "Such a punk."

CHAPTER FOUR

COOPER

You wanna know what's fun?

How excited everyone is to work with me.

Wait, did I say fun?

I meant *not* fun. Not even a little.

This morning's opening session and strategy meeting were both fine. Some side-eyes, sure, but some smiles, too. Lunch with Marty Mercer, the Director of Scouting, was good. The guy's gruff, but he seemed to respect me, and we saw eye-to-eye on a lot of the prospects in the Firebirds farm system. But now, the two of us are stepping into a breakout room in the resort's conference center, and you could hear a pin drop. A dozen people look at me, a couple with surprise and excitement. A couple with contempt.

At the front of the room, a blonde woman is bent over her laptop, and given that there's a light coming from the projector but it's not sharing anything, I'd bet the muttering woman is having a hard time getting her laptop to connect.

I walk over to her, only because I promised Doug I'd be a team player. Not because she has a great figure, or anything.

"Need a hand?"

"Yes, please—" she stops abruptly. "What are you doing here?"

"It's you." I can't help myself. "The woman from the airport. And the lobby. And the stairwell."

"Yeah, I work here." I can practically smell the fumes wafting off her. "Not *here* here. For the Firebirds."

"I play for the Firebirds."

"Oh! Do you?" She bats her wide-set eyes pointedly. "We've established that, *buddy*. That's why you're 'so freaking rich,' remember?"

"So you repeatedly insult me to my face and I crack a joke, and somehow *I'm* the bad guy?"

"You're the bad guy for treating the sport like it's a joke."

It's my turn to fume. "Baseball purists."

I turn to find Marty. Unfortunately, he doesn't have an open spot near him, so I look for the woman's tumbler with its absurd *geek in the spreadsheets* message and pick the seat farthest from her.

An older woman stands and helps the obnoxious woman. A presentation flashes on the screen. The pretty pest sits down, and the older woman clears her throat.

"Thanks for being prompt," she says. "I'm Kathy Coleman, Director of Baseball Analytics." This is her department, so she's clearly introducing herself for my benefit. "We're excited to welcome Marty Mercer, Director of Scouting, and the team's new special assistant to the GM for scouting, Mr. Cooper Kellogg."

The excited people clap. I like them.

Pretty Pest doesn't. Which is fine, because I *don't* like her.

"We have an hour, people, so let's make the most of this. Coop is out for the season, and we need to determine the best way to fill the gap he's leaving next year, among others. And, as always, we need pitching."

"And we need to do all this on a reduced budget," Pretty Pest says looking at *me*.

Kathy gives a slow nod that screams *duh*. "We all understand the assignment, Liesel."

HA! Take that, *Liesel*.

Liesel. That's a pretty name. Too pretty for someone who wants to set fire to me with her eyes.

"Of course, jersey and season ticket sales have also increased dramatically," I say. "So that should help the budget."

"Uh, yeah. We've taken that into account," Kathy says with the same *duh* in her voice that was directed at Liesel. Liesel shoots me a triumphant look that makes me want to pull a Mason and stick my tongue out at her. "Let's dive in."

Liesel nods, and the projector starts sharing her screen.

Marty and I give each other a glance when we see their top draft pick. We talked about this kid at lunch. Marty juts his chin toward me, gesturing for me to speak.

"The kid's a ticking time bomb," I say.

"Excuse me?" Liesel asks. Why use such polite words with such a waspish tone? Sort of contradicts the whole thing. "He's a top fifteen college player. His college stats are as good as Derek Jeter's."

"Yeah, but Jeter didn't break his bat four times in a single season after striking out. And his mommy didn't hug him after games and threaten to give the Big Bad Umpire a piece of her mind."

Silence answers me.

Yeah, maybe I got a little waspish, too. "But you're right," I add hastily. "The guy's got great stats. If he can fundamentally change his personality, he could dominate."

Liesel doesn't just want to set me on fire with her gaze, she wants to scatter my ashes afterwards.

"Marty?" Kathy asks. The steely scout nods.

"Okay. The kid's off the table. Next."

Liesel presents several more draft potentials, and Marty and I have no objections, so they get green-lighted. But there are a lot of moving pieces to putting together an extended 40-man roster. Depending on what other trades and moves happen among other teams this week, we could find that our top picks in any category are gone, and suddenly we need to rethink the whole strategy. And Liesel, I'm seeing, is a master at strategy. With every new name, she updates a field in her software, and it populates a dozen different possible paths to filling the roster.

It's awesome.

Not that I'll ever tell her that.

We move on to pitchers, and Liesel puts up a couple of proposals, including calling up two minor league pitchers.

Logan and Lucas Fischer.

Liesel thinks *I'm* a punk? Those two are the Princes of Punk Town (still workshopping that name). More than that, though, their numbers don't convince me. They moved up to Triple-A ball last season, and they were good. By the end of the season, they were *really* good. But they're unproven.

And, as was previously established, they're massive freaking punks.

"The Fischer twins? Really?"

Liesel's nostrils flare. "Do you have a problem with them?"

"They're easier to read than a chapter book."

Kathy and Marty look at each other. Marty shrugs.

"They telegraph their pitches. Is this really news?" I ask.

But Liesel doesn't let either of them speak. "Then how about we look at your old buddy Colton Spencer, instead?"

"Colt Spencer?" I spit the name before I can stop myself.

"You blew the guy a kiss after you 'launched a bomb,' remember? I assumed you two were close."

"He's a jerk. Total clubhouse poison," I say.

"What would that be like?" she asks.

"I wouldn't know. My teammates *love* me."

"Okay, break time," Kathy says. She snaps and points to Liesel and me. "You two: here, now."

I hate the burning feeling in my chest. I'm doing a great job getting attention, but a terrible job *doing* my job. I exhale loudly. I didn't want this. I can't stand the idea of Doug thinking he assigned me for nothing. What is it about *Liesel* that makes me so irritated, so contrary, so …

Excited.

No, not excited. Just irritated and contrary. If she makes me feel more alive, it's the same way getting caught naked in a snowstorm would—sharp, cold, and impossible to ignore.

Judging by her tight eyes, she feels the same way about me.

"Did you two used to date, or something?" Kathy asks.

"No, we just met," Liesel says.

"I'm sorry, Kathy," I say, getting my apology in before Liesel can. "I should probably do a better job observing and chime in when you and Marty need me."

"Good idea," the older woman says. "I like strong opinions. But we have a lot to get through in a short time, and if you two don't stop sniping at each other, we're never going to make it."

"Sorry, Kathy," Liesel says. "Let's try this again."

We return to our seats, and when I get there, Marty is sitting beside me. Is he babysitting me? Who am I kidding? Of course he is. The presentation continues. I bite my tongue, only offering input when Marty elbows me.

And when the conversation circles back to pitching.

"You're serious about the Fischer twins?" I ask, holding back a groan.

"Fischer brothers," Liesel corrects.

"Fine, the Fischer brothers. You really think they're ready?"

"Their stats are solid," she says.

"Solid isn't exceptional," I say.

"Who in the minors is exceptional?"

"Betancourt. He exploded last season."

"He's played a half season of Triple-A. The Fischer brothers were strong all season long. They have a safer track record," Liesel argues.

"Betancourt has a bigger upside."

"His upside is unknowable!"

"Same as with the Fischer twins."

"Fischer *brothers.*"

"What is your obsession with them?" I ask. "Do you have a crush or something?"

Kathy coughs, and it almost sounds like a laugh.

"I'm not obsessed. I'm being accurate," Liesel says, her eyes slits. "They're triplets. They have a sister, okay?"

"And ... she plays for a team?"

"Nope. She works for one."

Realization dawns on me like the sun. "Liesel Fischer, huh?" I grin.

"Finally caught on, did you?" she asks, mirroring my snide comment from yesterday.

"The *geek in the spreadsheets* mug is a surprisingly effective disguise. But it's cool. I get it now."

"Get what?"

"Why you're not thinking rationally."

"Excuse me? I *always* think rationally."

"Do you know what that word means? Be honest."

Her face is so red, I think steam might actually be coming off it. "Do you ever get tired of carrying around that massive ego?"

"No, but thank you for your concern."

Kathy smacks her forehead with her palm. "Enough! If you're going to keep acting like children, I'll put you in timeout."

"Sorry, Kathy," I mumble.

"Sorry, Kathy," Liesel mutters.

Kathy flexes both hands. "Your recommendations are noted. Let's move on."

Liesel's neck is splotchy.

"Yes, ma'am," Liesel says, her eyes fixed on her laptop screen.

The look on her face causes a pang in me. Sure, she's the human equivalent of a lump of coal in your stocking, and she's dead wrong about her brothers, but I didn't want to humiliate her. I didn't want to make her feel bad.

When the breakout ends, we still have too many holes in our roster, including pitching. The rest of the room files out toward the ballroom for dinner, but Kathy and Marty pull Liesel and me aside.

"That didn't go how we expected," Kathy says shortly.

"I know," Liesel says, looking at her strappy heels. "I'm sorry again."

"I don't need your apologies, I need your brains," Kathy says. Then she looks at me. "Both of you. You have different experiences and perspectives, and we've all seen enough baseball movies to know that scouting and analytics need to work together. So congratulations."

Liesel and I look at each other like we're temporarily *not* enemies. "Congratulations?" I ask.

Marty and Kathy nod at each other. "You two are working together."

"What does that mean?" I ask Marty.

"It means you aren't coming to another meeting or even to dinner until you two have figured out our extended roster."

"But what if someone we choose gets picked up by another team—"

"Have a backup. And a backup to the backup. And you'd better have it figured out by tomorrow when we present to the GM, or we'll make you two roommates, while we're at it," Marty says.

I nod. "Yes sir."

"What about my presentation?" Liesel asks Kathy.

"This takes priority," Kathy says. "We'll see you tomorrow."

Kathy and Marty exit, leaving Liesel and me staring at each other.

"Look what you did!" she says.

"Me? Look what *you* did!"

She huffs and returns to her seat, where she shoves her personal items in her laptop bag. My satchel only has a baseball I got from a swag booth and some resistance bands for my rehab, so I stand and watch her with my hands in my pockets. When she's all packed, she stomps past me.

"Where are you going?" I ask, following her into the hall.

It's busy enough that she's forced to slow down. And she seems suddenly aware that we can be seen by the couple hundred people who are roaming the halls on their way to the ballroom. Especially considering we're the only people walking *away* from it.

I get right next to her as we walk. She pastes on a fake smile for the benefit of the rest of the Firebirds organization, no doubt. "Don't walk next to me," she says. "I don't want anyone getting the wrong idea."

"That we work together?"

"Right, like anyone thinks you're here to work."

"I had a press conference this morning. Everyone knows. That's why they're looking at us." I nod and smile at people as we walk. I incline my head toward her. "Believe me: no one would buy that we're together."

She stiffens. We turn a corner into yet another packed hallway. "Why? Because you typically only go for girls who are ultra tan and ultra *enhanced*?"

"No, because I don't date fans, sweetheart."

"I'm not your fan, and I'm definitely not your sweetheart."

"Judging by how closely you keep tabs on my social media,

we both know you're lying. Sorry, Sugar Plum. It's nothing personal, but I don't mix business and pleasure."

"You don't treat baseball like it's business."

I snort. "It's not. Baseball is the pleasure. Women are the work. And I don't need a job when I can play a game for money."

She takes me down corridors that get progressively more and more narrow until we pass the front desk and go into a private hallway with an exclusive elevator. "You are the most obnoxious man I've ever met," she says. "I would rather have to decorate the Christmas tree at Rockefeller Center than be stuck with you for another minute." We stare at each other in the reflection of the elevator. It's coming down from the seventeenth floor. My elevator only showed sixteen floors.

"That literally sounds like the best time of my entire life. I'm in." Judging by the twitch in her eye, my last comment broke something in her brain. "Let me guess: I've enraged you so much, you're planning to throw me off the roof," I say.

"If I were going to murder you, it wouldn't be a crime of passion. It would be slow, painful, and totally untraceable."

The numbers keep ticking down. "So where are we going?"

"My room."

"*Your* room? Where?"

"The Owner's Suite."

"Hold on. If you're the Fischer brothers' sister, that makes your dad Bruce Fischer, the umpire. Umps do well, but not *this* well. Is your mom a secret billionaire, or something?"

She winces. "No, my best friend's fiancé is, though."

The elevator dings.

"Okay. I see how it is. You're hoping to wow me with luxury so you can have your way with me."

As the doors slide open, the image stretches until I catch a final glimpse of half of my grinning face and half of her frowning one. We step onto the elevator, and I lean against the wall, while she stands primly, clutching her bag.

"My way would necessitate burying your body," she practically bites. "Now, we're here to work. So shut your trap so we don't have to room together."

"Marty was kidding."

Her blue eyes turn icy. "That's not a risk I'm willing to take."

"Okay, Scrooge."

"Okay, *Buddy*."

The elevator doors close, and up we go.

CHAPTER FIVE

LIESEL

WHAT WAS I THINKING?

My best friend got stuck on an elevator last Christmas with her nemesis, and here I am, just walking onto an elevator with mine like I haven't read this story before? *Smooth move, Fischer!* It worked out beautifully for Juliet, but then, Cooper Kellogg is no Nate Cruz.

For one thing, Cooper isn't a sexy European billionaire. He's an odious American millionaire. Yes, he may have a great jaw, but that does *not* make him sexy. Besides, he's hyperaware of how attractive he is. To other people, I mean. Not to me.

For another, Cooper doesn't care about things like justice and kindness. I mean, I haven't watched him around anyone else, but he's right: I've seen enough of his social media to know he's all about grandstanding, and he takes an inordinate number of selfies with women. Unless you play Banana Ball and have gone viral for lip syncing a Taylor Swift song on your way to the batter's box, no player should have that many female fans lined up.

He smells like spiced sandalwood, too. And let me tell you, a smell that divine does not belong on a man so decidedly *not*.

Oh, and can we talk about how Cooper argues about *everything?* Everything! My best friend loves to debate, but she thinks it's fun.

I don't.

I hate being second-guessed. I don't mind polite discourse. I don't even mind when someone disagrees with me, because they're so frequently wrong. I don't just throw opinions into the universe for fun like Cooper does. If I have an opinion on something, it's informed. I've studied the issue to an unhealthy degree. How can he feel so free to state his mind without a folder's worth of data to back him up?

Worst of all: how is it that he might be right?

Actually, even worse than that: why doesn't it upset me with him? Normally, confrontation makes me feel shaky and nauseated. Confronting Cooper makes me feel like I've been spiked with adrenaline: tense but also supercharged.

I've never argued with someone so boldly, but then, I'm not used to someone pushing me to stand up, either.

How dare he say I wasn't being rational?

He wasn't wrong, a little voice whispers.

Rational, shmational. I'm following my heart, thank you very much. Isn't that what data nerds are always told? We're heartless monsters who value stats over people? Well, not this nerd!

The elevator mercifully glides up to my suite, and Cooper doesn't say a word the whole way up. I watch his reflection watching me, though, and I don't like it.

Not a bit.

He doesn't look bold as brass, he looks contemplative in a way that makes me fidgety. I spin my earring and steel myself against even the possibility that Cooper Kellogg may have more than one side.

The bell dings, and the doors open to my lavish suite. Cooper whistles appreciatively. "Wow. It's like the North Pole and Buckingham Palace had a baby. Who's your friend and why did he hook you up with this suite again?"

We walk into the entry, and Cooper breezes past, not waiting for me. I hang my purse up, and follow him. "My friend is Nate Cruz."

Cooper goes to the next room and then to the next. "The actual owner?" I hear him play the first few bars of *Heart and Soul* on the piano next to the stupid eight-foot Christmas tree. Housekeeping has added decorative bowls of cinnamon pine cones, and it's enough to make me hate cinnamon. "Why did he book you this suite if he's marrying your friend? He doesn't secretly love you, does he?"

"No! She and I are roommates, and I was responsible for getting them together."

"Responsible?"

"I parked my car in a spot while I was in Costa Rica, and that made them always fight over another … it's a whole thing. Anyway, they're stupidly in love, so they're both always giving me gifts to show me their appreciation." I hold up my Stanley for emphasis.

My phone buzzes and buzzes again. I pull it out and groan. My brothers are texting on our siblings thread.

"Hold on," I tell Cooper.

LOGAN

Guys, what's the plan for the Stewart family Christmas Adam party?

LUCAS

NOT IT

LOGAN

Wouldn't expect otherwise, bro. Lee?

My stomach twists into knots. I glance up at Cooper, who's looking at the Christmas decorations with an expression I don't recognize on his normally bold face. Is it nostalgia? Longing?

LIESEL

I'm in another state right now and you two are off until Spring Training. Can't you take care of it?

LUCAS

Have you met us?

LIESEL

Aunt Linda and Uncle Paul always take care of dinner. We only have to organize the games and dessert. You can do that easily.

LUCAS

Come on. You did it half the time Mom was sick, Lee.

LIESEL

I didn't last year while I was in Costa Rica.

LUCAS

Yeah, and it was terrible. We bought Costco cookies and played charades. Uncle Paul was so mad. He said he didn't smoke ribs for 72 hours just to eat grocery store garbage. Costco cookies aren't garbage!

LIESEL

Okay, fine. I'll work on it this weekend.

LOGAN

You're the best. Want to do it at the house and we'll help?

LIESEL

No, I got it. Don't worry.

LUCAS

Come on, Lee. Do it at the house.

LIESEL

All my stuff's at my place.

LOGAN

What night do you want to do it? We'll come over.

LIESEL

I'll have to get back to you.

LUCAS

Do you guys remember how much Mom loved Christmas Adam?

LOGAN

She laughed every year about eating ribs.

LUCAS

How that joke never got old to her is a mystery.

I hate Christmas Adam.

"What's Christmas Adam?"

I clutch my phone to my chest. "Excuse me? How did you see my texts?"

"I didn't," he says, holding his hands out. "I'm four feet away from you, and you whispered it."

"Whispered what?"

"'I hate Christmas Adam.' What's Christmas Adam?"

Did I really say that out loud?

"It's a family tradition on my mom's side. The day before Christmas Eve, we have a big family party with her siblings and kids. We play games and have a huge spread. And we always eat ribs."

He nods slowly. "Ribs for Adam, because Adam came before Eve. I get it. That's funny, and it sounds awesome. Why would you hate it?"

I could answer his question in so many ways. Because it makes me think about my mom, and thinking about my mom causes me agonizing heartache. Because even before she was gone, I started taking on more and more of the mothering of my brothers, and this is another example of how I'll never get to leave that role. And that's to say nothing of how tired I am of people telling me how I look exactly like her. I'm weary of Uncle Paul saying how painful it is to look at me, and I'm emotionally exhausted from not measuring up to the ideal she created.

But I won't admit any of that to Cooper.

"I just don't like Christmas."

He studies me for too long, that contemplative look from the elevator returning in the angle of his head and the slight tension around his eyes. My heart rate rises, and I feel like I'm holding my breath for what's next. I cannot control my reactions around him. If he presses, I might spill *everything*.

I spin my earring, and Cooper takes notice, so I drop my hand, and his expression shifts just as quickly to that overly-confident look I know and loathe. "You must like the gifts, though. Your best friend's fiancé hooked you up."

"I like *reasonable* gifts as much as anyone," I say, holding up my new water bottle. "Here's what my friend gave me. There's no obligation in something like this. I'm not debilitated trying to think of what the perfect gift for her is after getting a Stanley. But do you know what Nate got me for Christmas last year? His *Prius.*"

"His car?"

"I know! In fairness to him, my car was stolen while I was interning in Costa Rica and he felt bad about it, but who gives someone a Prius?"

"That's weird. Why not let insurance take care of it?"

I don't disagree. Even if I were stranded in the middle of

nowhere, I'd struggle to let someone help me. I had options, though, and I was just desperate enough not to take them.

"You didn't fight me on that," Cooper says. I meet his eyes. I spaced out for a second, and during that second, he picked up on what my own best friend has missed. "You don't like that he did this, do you?"

I clutch my locket. "No, I don't. I like being able to do things for myself."

"You like being the helper, not the helped?"

"Who doesn't?"

"I get it. We're more alike than I thought."

"Ha! No, we're not. Having one thing in common doesn't change that."

But he shakes his head. "We have more than that in common. We both love baseball, we both have strong opinions about what's right for our team." He pauses, and I crane my head forward, curious to hear what else he's going to say. "And we both think I'm too attractive for my own good."

I roll my eyes so hard, I pull something in one of my eyeballs. "How do you always manage to say the dumbest possible thing that comes to mind?" I ask, rubbing my eye as I walk out of the living room.

"It's a skill."

"I'm rethinking throwing you from the roof."

I head into the dining room, with its twelve-seater table. I take the far end of the table and open my laptop, pull out my notebook, folders, and more. When I look up, he's sitting in the chair nearest me.

"What are you doing?"

"Getting ready to work." He looks at the table. "Did you want me to sit at the far end of the table so we could yell at each other the whole time?"

Kind of.

I grab two menus from a small corner table near me. I take one and hand him the other.

"Could you ask them to send up an ice pack, too? For my arm," he adds.

"Of course," I say, feeling a small flash of worry, because I cannot be responsible for breaking Cooper Kellogg. "Is it … are you feeling okay?"

"It still gets sore and stiff, but I'm strict with my rehab protocol and my doctor's happy with the improvement." His brow wrinkles for just a moment as he looks at his elbow, and the unmistakable flash of worry makes me look at my menu.

When I call in our order, Cooper goes into the kitchen for water. I'm just hanging up the hotel phone when his phone vibrates where he left it on the table. I glance at it without thinking.

"Your mom is FaceTiming," I call. "Want me to bring you the phone?"

Coop comes into the room with a half-filled glass and I slide the phone across the table to him. He takes a deep, almost steadying breath, and then he puts on a show-stopping grin and answers the call. "Hey, Mom!"

He walks into one of the other rooms and closes the door. I can't catch what either of them say, but I do pick up on their animated tones. A few minutes into their conversation, though, he must be standing next to the door, because I hear him say, "No, I have to be in Chicago for a charity event at the end of the week, so I won't be able to make it home until the twenty-third."

"Oh, shoot. I was hoping we could get more time with you!" his mom cries.

"I know. Me, too."

"I wish I could come to you." The catch in her voice makes tears spring to my eyes, which is silly. Their schedules don't match up and he'll get to see her in a week. Why am I emotional about that?

"It's okay, Mom!" Cooper reassures her. "It's okay. I'll be back home in no time. I promise. We'll have all the time in the world to catch up before I get back to work in January."

"Okay, sweet boy. I love you."

"Love you, too. Give Dad a hug for me."

When he comes back a few minutes later, he looks different. Not upset or worried, necessarily, but his usual cocksure expression is gone.

"Everything okay?" I ask.

"Of course. Why?"

"No reason. I was just checking."

"I have a headache," he says. He pulls out the chair next to me and sits with a little more distance than he had at first. "I've actually had it since yesterday in the airport when a super-fan decided to air all of her grievances with me to my face," he says, but he's smiling.

"Whatever. That was the best moment of your life. Didn't you say your greatest fear was being forgotten?"

"No, I definitely didn't say that," he says.

"You implied it."

"You inferred it."

"You know the difference between implied and inferred?" I ask.

"I'm an athlete, not an idiot."

"Same difference."

He chuckles, and I bite back a smile.

"You know," he says, "if we're going to work together, we should probably act friendly tomorrow in front of Kathy and Marty."

"I agree," I say, relieved that we're finally making headway. "No one needs to know that you secretly despise me."

"Or that you openly want me," Cooper says.

And we're back to square one.

* * *

We've ordered room service *twice* by the time our conversation circles back to my brothers.

"Why do you think they're ready?" Cooper asks, looking at my laptop. "What numbers are you seeing that convince you that they're a better bet than keeping Jessup and calling up Betancourt?"

"They're some of the top prospects in the Minors. We could at least put them on the extended roster."

Cooper's eyes flash. "You know they're not ready."

"I didn't say that."

"You know they telegraph their pitches, don't you!" I squeeze my fists, not wanting to answer. But he pushes. "Admit it! You know!"

"Yes!" I blurt. "And it drives me *crazy*! They never listen to me when I talk baseball! No matter what I say, what feedback I give them, they shut it down instantly." Now that the words are out, I can't take them back. And I don't want to. "They could hang in the majors. I *do* have the stats to back me up on that. Their mechanics are top tier. But they don't think they need to control themselves, and they don't accept feedback, and it's going to stop them from greatness."

Cooper slams his hand on the table. "Liesel Fischer. Atta girl."

I scorch him with my gaze. "Don't 'attagirl' me. Literally all they need to do is listen to me."

"But they don't."

"They're ready."

"But so is Betancourt. And Jessup is still strong, even if he's on the decline," he says.

"I like how you're pretending the guy you hate isn't even an option. He's a surer bet than any of them."

Cooper leans back in his dining room chair and a baseball materializes. He throws it into the air and catches it with his non-dominant hand. It's easy to forget he was ever injured, but he's only eight weeks out from surgery. He still has probably sixteen months of rehab and strength training to go. "You were serious about wanting that guy? He's a bigger jerk than I am."

I stand up and start pacing around the dining room. "Toss me the ball," I say.

He does, and I catch it with one hand. He raises his eyebrows.

"Oh, stop," I say. "There's nothing surprising about a woman being able to catch a baseball from ten feet away."

"You're right."

I throw the ball back to him as I walk, playing catch.

"Why are you so interested in Colt?" he asks. There's a note in his voice that couldn't possibly be jealousy, but is definitely *something.*

"I'm not *interested* in him. He's really good, and because he only started pitching in college, his arm will be good for a long time."

"He's a trash talker."

I laugh. "He's professional and even-keeled."

"He runs his mouth constantly."

"No, he doesn't!"

"Do you have a crush on him, or something?" Cooper asks.

I could shake this guy like a can of soda. "What is with you always asking if I have a crush on a guy you don't like?"

I mean it as a joke, but Coop's brow pinches together, almost like he's wondering the same thing. "Colt's a womanizer. I take pictures with fans. He does a lot more than that."

Ew. "That's gross but irrelevant. He's good, and you know it."

"He has baseball purists fooled, that's for sure." He gives a wry chuckle. "Colt can say anything he wants, but because he uses a professional tone instead of having some enthusiasm for the sport, he gets a pass. Doesn't matter that his team hates him."

"His team doesn't hate him."

He shrugs. "Sure. Because you talk to the players."

"Teams hate *you*."

"No, opposing fans hate me. Stuffy front office people hate me. People who haven't played with me …"

"That's a nearly comprehensive list of the human race."

"I'm *not* clubhouse poison."

"And neither is he."

"Only because he's been playing under his rookie contract. I guarantee, the second he signs a major contract, he'll be straight up toxic. Right now, he has to watch his mouth a little."

"Unlike someone I know."

"I *never* put down other players. If Colt had struck me out and pumped his fist, no one would have cared, because pitchers are allowed to be excited. Why? It's one of the unwritten rules about baseball. And it's those rules that make kids choose other sports."

We've been playing catch this whole time, but I hold my hands out so he doesn't throw the ball to me again. "You've talked about that in interviews. Baseball is *fine*. What is your obsession with kids choosing other sports?"

"Because baseball connects people to something bigger than themselves and their problems!" His face flushes, and his light brown eyes seem darker. "When I was a kid, I felt alone all the time. It wasn't until my dad put me in baseball that things changed for me. I found a community of people who *saw* me—most of them, anyway—and it helped me find myself. Without baseball, I wouldn't …" He trails off. "It doesn't matter," he says, standing up with his lips pressed into a thin smile but his eyes crinkled. "Baseball's awesome. I'm gonna take a break."

I watch him leave the dining room, and one thing is certain: Cooper Kellogg has a lot more layers than I realized.

And I'm more curious to unwrap those layers than I care to admit.

CHAPTER SIX

COOPER

I step outside to the balcony and rest my arms on the railing. I have a perfect view of the well-lit golf course from up here, and if it weren't so dark, I could see Pinnacle Peak in the distance.

It's weird to be in a place I used to call home and yet to not *feel* at home. My mom's call doesn't help.

I love my parents. They tried as hard as any two people could. My dad could have won every Father of the Year trophy since the day I was born. My mom did her very best, and I'd give her all the awards I could, too … if only she could show up to the ceremony.

My mom developed agoraphobia when I was in elementary school. At first, it manifested with her not wanting to be out in big places—malls and movie theaters. But slowly, her world got smaller and smaller. When her condition got to the point that she couldn't leave the house, dad quit his job as a long haul trucker to take something close to home.

The first year of her being shut in was brutal. I felt rejected and hurt and totally alone, even though my dad was around more than ever. In my little kid brain, I couldn't understand why I had to live my life on Mom's terms for her to be involved. I didn't understand why she only loved me at home but not enough to leave it. Such intense anxiety was completely foreign to me, but my sadness was obvious to my parents.

My dad and I would go on walks to the green space near our apartment complex and he'd let me talk. He tried to give me perspective about what my mom was going through, but I couldn't connect with her.

Dad became everything to me that first year after Mom's diagnosis. He signed me up for any sport I wanted and found ways to coach most of them. I was good at all of them the way naturally athletic kids are when they're young. But it wasn't until he put me in baseball that everything changed.

I hit a home run in my very first game. And I'm not talking about one of those home runs where a kid pops up and the other kids scramble and fall all over themselves trying to catch it. I hit it over the rec league's fence.

Our team went wild, and the stadium erupted. It was the most exciting thing that had ever happened to me. It was the most *seen* I'd ever felt. And when I got home that night, I was too excited to be hurt that my mom hadn't come to the game. I told her every detail about my home run, including the two pitches before, the way the other team crowded the infield, all of it.

Mom laughed and cheered every second. "Tell me again!" she begged, so I did. And when she started crying the second time I told it, I *felt* how much she loved me. I'd always "known" she cared, but in the months leading up to her diagnosis and the months since, I'd felt overlooked and unimportant to her.

But here she was, crying because she was so *happy.* She was *so happy!*

After that, we recorded the games and watched them together when Dad and I got home. But the videos were never enough for her.

"I don't want to just see it," she'd say. "I want to *feel* it! Tell me how it felt!"

So I started giving her play-by-plays of every catch and hit. The showier, the better. She ate it up with a spoon.

Soon, she had balloons and streamers waiting for me when I got home from a tournament. She would make posters and a cake and decorate the house. She would go all out to make me know how much she loved me, how much she celebrated me.

But it wasn't only the big moments where she made this effort. It was like her success in celebrating my achievements on the field made her realize how special she could make our home life. Homemade breakfast every day. Family game nights and movie nights.

It became clear how much she cared about the minutiae of every moment of my life, inside or outside our house. And that filled *me* with a need to bring my life to her. To make her feel like she wasn't missing anything by not going out into the world.

Liesel loves baseball, and I know there's something going on with that whole Christmas Adam thing that she isn't talking about. Maybe if I open up, she will.

But then I'd have to open up about something I don't talk about to anyone who doesn't already know.

The glass door slides open, and I hear Liesel make her way out to join me.

"Finally come to finish the job, huh?" I ask, gesturing to the ground below us.

"I don't think I could throw you over if I tried, and I don't like failing at things, so I'll let you live."

I sniff a laugh. She's funny. I've seen that a handful of times tonight. She's quick on her feet, too, and she can hang in an argument, no question. What's odd is that I'm not normally a disagreeable person. I'm showy, but I'm not typically a button pusher. But Liesel makes me want to become one. She's a shiny, bright red button that I want to push and push and push …

I'm an adult.

"It's 2 a.m.," Liesel says, "and we need to make some decisions. Are you … okay?"

"Fine." It's a brisk night for Arizona. I'm chilly, but Liesel doesn't seem fazed.

"We're down to my brothers or Colt and … Betancourt or Jessup. I don't care. But we need to come to a consensus. So can you tell me the real reason why you don't want Colt? If we signed him to a big enough deal, you two could play together for a long time."

I huff. I'm too tired to filter myself like I should. "He reminds me of all the rich kids I faced growing up in club sports."

"So? You played on those same teams. You were clearly one of them."

"I was *not* one of those kids." My throat hurts when I swallow. "I was a scholarship kid."

"A lot of players in the majors were."

"Not as many as there should be. You want to talk about everything that's wrong about baseball? Club and travel teams take the cake. My dad worked his butt off, but club sports have ruined meritocracy. The most talented kids don't always get the chance to play anymore because their parents aren't rich enough."

"That's true," she says, much to my relief. Her dad's a huge deal in the league. He definitely did well enough for them.

"The Colton Spencers of the world have never liked me. I was the kid who took their less-talented friend's place on the team and all because I was 'poor,' as they saw it. So much of baseball is about community, but on those teams, it was cutthroat. I was allowed to play with them, but they made sure I knew I couldn't sit with them."

"Cooper—"

"Spare me the pity," I say. I'm torn between feeling frustrated about my admission and guilt for snapping at her. I never talk about this stuff, and here I am, spilling the tea to the last woman who wants to talk to *me*. "I don't need it. You worked down in Costa Rica where the kids would have killed for a sob story like mine."

"That's true."

"Exactly. And it's not even really a sob story. Kids from America don't know hardship like kids from Third World countries. I'm being soft."

"You think because bad things happen to other people in the world, you're not allowed to feel the bad things that have happened to you?"

The lump in my throat started as a marble and has swelled to a softball. "Guys like Colt are subtle. They know how to say the right things in public so they can get away with saying all the wrong things in private. No one would believe Colt's poisonous because he carries himself right."

She tilts her head. "I haven't seen that."

"You mean you haven't watched for it." I pull up my phone and find the clip of the interview he had after I hit the home run and blew him a kiss. And backflipped onto home plate. The video of Colt's response has nearly as many views as the video of the incident itself.

I skip to Colt's answer.

"I don't want to talk about whether or not Coop was being disrespectful. I want to focus on winning the next game."

"It was a classy response. I don't see the problem," Liesel says.

"Classy? Now watch this." I rewind to the question the journalist actually asked.

"Colt, you said last week that Cooper would be too busy doing backflips to get a hit off you, but he was three for four tonight, including that famous homer where he celebrated in exactly the way you accused. How does that feel?"

"I don't want to talk about whether or not Coop was being disrespectful to me and to the game. I want to focus on winning the next game."

Liesel's mouth falls open. "Whoa. They didn't ask about *you*, they asked how he felt about being put in his place. No one even mentioned that you were disrespectful until Colt said it."

"Exactly!" Months of irritation rise off of me like steam from a hot tub. "That's what I've been saying!"

She rewinds the video and watches it again, and this time, I see the annoyance on her face. And it makes my eyes sting. "What a jerk move! How did I miss that?"

"He knows how to make a soundbite."

She gives me a flat look, but it can't erase the softness in her eyes. "So do you."

"Not like that. I don't know how to twist my words. I know how to get attention. I know how to put on a show."

"And you do it better than anyone."

I chuckle beneath my breath. She's right, and I'm not ashamed of the fact.

"Is this enough to take him off the table?" she asks.

"I can't recommend the guy when I know half his team hates him."

"What about the other half?"

"They haven't met him."

"So are you saying you can't work with him?" she asks.

"We hate each other's guts."

"Michael Jordan and Scottie Pippin didn't get along."

"That's basketball."

"Okay, Jonathan Papelbon choked Bryce Harper, and they worked it out."

I laugh weakly. "Can I be the one to choke him?"

"Ha. Would you prefer my brothers?"

I bump my head on the railing. "What do the stats say?"

"Colt Spencer and Jessup, that's what."

I groan.

"Tell me about it," she says. "This would break my mother's heart."

I lift my head up and look at Liesel. The lights from her suite are bright enough that I can make out the frown on her face. "Would?"

She puts her elbows on the railing beside me. "My mom had Lou Gehrig's Disease—ALS—for a long time. She lived just long enough to see my brothers get drafted together for the same team." Her eyes well with tears. "It was one of the happiest days of her life and the last good day she had."

"Shoot," I say, wishing I could take back half of my words and *all* of my attitude from earlier. "I'm sorry, Liesel. Now I feel like a jerk for saying you weren't being rational."

"You were a jerk," she says. "But you weren't wrong."

Our shoulders and arms are only a few inches apart, close enough that I can feel the heat radiating from her. "I get why you want to look out for them. Regardless of what happens this week, they're going to be okay. You're right that they're strong prospects, and they're part of our organization. Besides, we still have the extended roster."

Her eyes widen. "That's right. We do. That's enough, isn't it? They're good enough for that?"

"They are. No question. They'll be in the majors in no time."

This should comfort her, shouldn't it? But she buries her face in her hands, and I tug them down. Her skin is soft and warm enough that I wish I'd brought a jacket.

"Hey, don't worry. They don't know about any of these discussions. They're not missing out on anything. And—" I inhale sharply. I can't believe I'm about to say what I'm about to say, but making a woman cry wasn't on my Christmas list. "Your forecasts are compelling. I think we should recommend your brothers for the extended roster and sign Colt."

"Really?" She throws her arms around me, squeezing me like a boa constrictor. "Thank you, Coop! Kathy's going to be so relieved that we have a good solution."

I pat her shoulder, noticing that the muscles in her arms extend to her back. I like a girl who works out.

Not this girl, specifically. *A* girl.

She releases me quickly, and I'm only disappointed because I'm cold and she's somehow retained more warmth than I have.

Also, she smells like cotton candy.

"But we need to put together a customized training program for your bros and convince them to *listen*. You're a geek in the spreadsheets, right?"

She laughs nervously. "Yeah. We can do that."

"And then when the call comes—and it always comes—the Fischer twins will be ready."

"They're triplets," she says.

"Unless you're planning to suit up, I think you're going to have to get used to them being called the wrong name."

"Right, because a whole lifetime of experience hasn't prepared me for that."

I tap her forehead. "Hey, you're a big deal in the Firebirds' front office. You're important enough to make recommendations directly to the GM. Your brothers *might* be a big deal. They'll probably be a big deal. But right now, they're Liesel Fischer's brothers. The thought of you giving that up has to suck at least a little."

She gives me a look. "Don't psychoanalyze me."

I look back over the golf course. The lights are bright enough that a few people are even playing. My elbow hurts just thinking of trying to swing a club. "I could be wrong."

"You're not wrong." She inhales and exhales slowly. "I've

never had anything that's my own. I've been looking out for my brothers since my mom got sick when we were thirteen. Working for the Firebirds is the only thing that's ever really felt like it was *mine*. Sometimes ... sometimes I wish they didn't play for our affiliate. I can't fail them if they play for someone else."

"You don't seem like you're capable of failing anyone."

She snorts. "We were in the same meeting with Kathy and Marty."

I nudge her shoulder with mine. "You didn't fail. You got into a heated work discussion with a cocky jerk."

"When you put it that way ..." she teases.

I breathe in the dry, cold air, and my teeth chatter together. My elbow is starting to throb. I rotate my arm slowly. "What you're saying makes sense. It's hard when you're constantly having to keep it together for someone else. When it feels like their happiness rests solely on your shoulders."

"Yup."

"It's not true, though. We can't be the only part of the equation."

"We?"

I shake my head. That was a slip worthy of Freud. "In the broadest sense," I say. "At some point, we have to accept people for who they are and where they are. And they have to own their own happiness."

"That sounds easy," she says sarcastically.

"Oh, yeah. Simple."

She gives me a half smile, and I shiver again.

"It's 55 degrees," she says. "How are you so cold?"

"Because it's 55 degrees," I say. "This is winter."

She laughs. "This is not winter. This is barely fall weather. Do you need a blanket?"

"How do you not?"

"I don't understand the question."

"You Midwesterners have ice in your veins."

"You Southwesterners are soft."

"Say that again when you're burning to a crisp in 122 degrees."

"It's a dry heat."

"So is a forest fire."

She laughs. "If you're so cold, why have you stayed in Chicago this winter? Why not go home?"

I don't like where this question is headed. "Because my doctor and rehab is all in Chicago. The more I travel, the more I risk messing something up," I say.

"I bet you miss your parents."

"All the time," I say honestly.

I will never, ever resent my mom for her illness. It's hard, and it's left a mark on me, but I wouldn't resent her if she had cancer, and I won't resent her for mental illness, either.

But it is hard.

On all of us. But especially on her.

She's missed so much. And if it were up to me, she'd never miss out on anything again. But after almost twenty years of watching her struggle with it, I'm past trying to fix her. My only job is to love her.

Even if the only thing I've ever wished is for her to come to one of my games. Or even to my house for Christmas.

"You know," I say, hiding behind a yawn. "The one thing Chicago has over Arizona is that it's way more Christmasy."

She groans, yawning, too. "Oh no. You're a Christmas fanatic, aren't you?"

"I have a Santa cowboy hat. Is that even a question?"

"Bah humbug," she says. She stretches out her arms. "Should we get back to work?"

"Lead the way."

She does, and I follow. And for the first time tonight, I don't mind.

CHAPTER SEVEN

LIESEL

After another long day of meetings, Cooper and I have officially presented our proposal to the GM, along with backups and backups of backups. That means we've recommended signing Colton Spencer, keeping Jessup for another year, and signing my brothers to the extended roster. I don't think either Coop or I are truly thrilled about it, but what happens now is out of my hands.

Bah humbug.

Being in control is the best, and I hate the idea that I'm not. That may be the way life goes but I don't have to like it.

"You two seem to have gotten past your differences," Kathy says afterwards. "Good."

"Liesel gave a very heartfelt apology," Coop tells her. "It moved me."

Kathy shakes her head, and walks past us. "See you at six for cocktails."

When she's gone, I scowl at Coop. "You can't shut up, can you?"

"Oh no. Not even a little," he says. We leave the room together. "And it's so much harder when I *haven't slept*." He bumps his elbow into my side, and I swat it away.

"People will get the wrong idea," I hiss.

"Again with this? What do you think they'll think? That we—gasp—successfully put aside our differences? Or do you mean they'll think we *canoodled*?"

He waggles his eyebrows, and I have the urge to shave them off. "Don't say that."

"Canoodle? Why not? It's a great word."

It's the end of our second day, and I'm *spent*. Between the late night and the full day of meetings—including a two-hour long presentation on a new ticketing system that will surely rock the sports world—I could hibernate for the winter. Oh, and if that's not enough, Coop has been my shadow all day.

I go between amusement and annoyance every time he opens his mouth. Also, and this is probably the exhaustion talking, he has a *really* attractive mouth. If only it would stop long enough for me to look at it.

"Why are you so bent on vexing me?" I ask.

"Why are you so easy to vex?"

I punch his arm, and he laughs. We're near the stairs, and while I'm used to taking them with Juliet, I don't want to, not even with Coop.

I mean, especially *not* with Coop.

I'm tired. *Too* tired. And I haven't showered yet after our long night. I'm not saying I stink, but I'm saying the dry shampoo I used this morning makes me look like a frosted fruitcake.

"See you in an hour," I say when Coop opens the stairwell.

"I'll be the one in a Santa hat."

I groan but smile.

He's not that bad.

I'm just walking into my suite when I get a video call from Lucas. My brothers both play for the same Triple-A Firebirds affiliate team, so I'm sure Logan will be close by.

"Hey," Lucas says.

"Hey," I say. "Are you wearing one of your Christmas sweaters?"

"Of course I am," he says, looking at me in confusion. It probably was a silly question, but I avoid wearing mine until I have to. I really am the Grinch of the family, but I have my reasons. "Speaking of which, are you going to come over to the house and help us decorate the Christmas tree? Dad insists we can't do it without you."

I prop the phone against the poinsettia at the dining room table and unpack my laptop bag. Hopefully he can't see the frown I'm fighting off. "You can do it without me." *Please.*

"He says Mom wouldn't have done it without you."

My throat thickens. "It's December 9th. Mom always had the tree up the day after Halloween."

"Yeah, and it was a family tradition to do it *together*. You've been avoiding coming home—"

"I'm not avoiding coming home," I lie a big, huge lie. "I don't get months off for vacation when the season's over like the rest of you. And I'm Juliet's maid of honor. I'm *busy*."

Lucas nods, but he's clearly not buying it. He blows a raspberry. "So how's the staff retreat?"

"Not bad," I say.

"You're not dating any players, are you?"

"No, I'm not dating any players." I roll my eyes. "Players don't attend staff meetings, anyway."

"Unless they happen to injure their elbow and get a special assignment with the GM ..."

I blink tiredly. "You're so overprotective, it's adorable. Like a big, dumb golden retriever who thinks he's a German Shepherd."

"Lee," he says in his sternest "big brother" voice.

"I'm not dating Cooper Kellogg!"

"Really? Then why did a fan share a picture of the two of you together on social media?"

"WHAT?"

I swipe out of FaceTime and to social media. A few quick searches, and …

I gasp.

This picture is from only ten minutes ago, when Coop and I were walking through the hallway. I knew this would happen! He's giving me that mock sexy, flirty look, and I'm glaring at him, but somehow it looks … playful. Coy.

The fact that we're standing so close together when no one is actually *that* close to us is a coincidence. There were throngs of people! Throngs!

"This is *totally* out of context. He was elbowing me to make it *look* like he was joking about something he wasn't joking about. If the fan had taken another photo a second later, it would have shown me practically vomiting on his shoe."

"Are you sure?"

"I'm positive. You know I can't stand Cooper Kellogg. He's the worst," I say, but it feels like lip service after working together last night. He still has the biggest head of anyone I've ever met, but he's not a *bad* guy. He's simply a bad ambassador for the game I love so much.

To old timers, at any rate.

"So what were you two doing?"

"Work. He's helping with scouting, and I'm in analytics. That's the job. We're looking to fill Coop's spot, and that utility player I discovered from Costa Rica is at the top of our list."

He nods. "How about the rest of the lineup?"

My chest grows hot. My brothers have never pressured me

to put in a good word for them or put them on the GM's radar. But I can't tell if it's subtext on his part or a guilt complex on my part that makes me feel pressure to do everything I can to promote his career.

"I'm not sure. We have some trades and moves in the works, but it'll be the GMs call."

"Doug's the best, man. You're so lucky to work with him."

More guilt. More pressure. Is this a friendly conversation, or is he hinting at something? An image of my mom crying happy tears when my brothers were drafted springs to mind, followed by her grabbing my hand.

"You're the best sister they could have hoped for. I know you'll always take care of them."

And suddenly, the pressure and guilt are more than I can stomach. I'm not taking care of them. Yes, I managed the family's schedules better than a personal assistant. I made sure they had forms and waivers and applications for every league, every tournament, every time. I ordered groceries to keep the junk out of their diets that wouldn't help with their training.

I sacrificed a lot.

But am I still? Didn't I let Coop talk me out of my duty to my brothers—to my *mom*—so we could present two other names to the GM?

"Is that Lee?" Logan says in the background. A moment later, his handsome face appears on the screen. He's also wearing one of Mom's Christmas sweaters. She got us a new one every year, and we used to open them the day we put up the Christmas tree so we could wear them all season long.

When Mom realized her illness had progressed to the point that the end was in sight, she ordered us every Christmas sweater she could find. Dad has boxes of wrapped Christmas sweaters in the attic, and he gives us a new one every year. Her handwriting was too shaky for her to write a note, so he found an app where he was able to upload and print out her handwriting based on whatever she dictated.

So on top of the Christmas sweater, we get a new card every year, too. A new card in her computerized handwriting that makes me feel like my heart is getting ripped out again *every year.*

It's a family tradition to wear our Christmas sweaters all season long, but I never will again. I hate them. I hate remembering what I used to have. I hate missing my mom so much, I can't breathe. And now, getting confronted with reminders of her at the same time that I'm wondering if I'm failing her by hurting their careers, I can't take it anymore.

I don't want to talk to my brothers. I don't want to see either of them when I may have just made the biggest mistake of their lives.

"Sorry, I have to go," I say. "See you when I get back." My smile looks like a grimace, but I stab the screen and hang up the call before they can call me on it.

My chest is tight, and I have to pant to draw in breath. And why is it so hot in this room? And why do there have to be so many reminders of Christmas?

Of Mom?

I rush outside to the balcony, my breath bursting from me in something between sobs and hyperventilation. My eyes fly everywhere.

Name five things you can see! I cry to myself.

My shaking hands. The twinkle lights around the balcony. The green of the golf course. Pinnacle Peak in the background. The sun setting behind it.

Four things you can touch.

I close my eyes for this exercise and strain my senses to really feel each of them.

My clammy forehead. The velvety texture of my navy blazer.

The cool metal of the balcony railing. The light breeze stirring my hair.

Three things you can hear.

I tune the world out, letting my ears hear dozens of sounds. I fixate on only a few.

My shallow breathing. The ringing of a phone in the distance. The crack of a driver hitting a golf ball.

Two things you can smell.

I breathe deeply, in and out. In and out. My lungs are moving slow now, and my pulse has steadied.

I smell fresh, dry desert air, so different from home. Spiced sandalwood …

Spiced sandalwood?

My eyes open and I whip around.

Cooper is leaning against the doorframe like the roguish heartthrob of every romance reader's dreams. He's wearing a rich, dark green suit that fits him far too well. Men like him shouldn't be allowed to wear suits so perfectly tailored to their bodies. It's like giving them an arsenal no woman could defend against.

Except me.

I give him my sternest, most piercing look. "What are you doing here? How did you get in?"

He shrugs. "The clerk saw me come up last night, and when I told her my date was late for cocktail hour, she called upstairs. You didn't answer, so we agreed that I should check on you."

"You flirted with her to get up here?" I push past him to get inside my suite. "And you lied! I'm not late."

"That's what you think I lied about? Not you being my date?"

"Put those suggestive eyebrows down this instant, young man."

His grin is pure mischief.

"Okay, so you're not *technically* late, but something told me you're the kind of girl who likes to be early. When you weren't, it made me wonder if you were okay."

"I have an hour to get ready," I say. "The meetings just ended."

"The meetings ended forty-eight minutes ago. Cocktail hour starts in twelve minutes."

"WHAT? I need to shower! My hair! My makeup!"

"You look great!"

"What do you know?" I yell, my back to him. Sprinting to my room, I pull a hair tie from around my wrist and put my hair up so it won't get wet. In the bathroom with the door *firmly* locked, I throw my clothes off and hop into the shower, soaping down with the speed of a superhero. My legs are stubbly, but no one's going to be touching them, and if anyone gets his face close enough to tell, I'll kick it.

I dry off and drop my towel on the ground in front of the mirror.

I pull my dry-shampooed hair up into a sleek ponytail and then spin it around in an equally sleek bun. Most women will know this is a twenty second hairstyle, but something tells me my boss—who wore Crocs today with her pantsuit—isn't one to care.

My makeup has mostly cracked from the intense dryness, but I don't have time to wash my face. So I use a face mist, pat it, and then add a quick extra coat of mascara, because I love my eyelashes, but I look like a middle schooler without makeup. So I make them extra dark and thick. It's a good thing I dyed my naturally blonde eyebrows before I left for Arizona. I use an eyeliner stick to add a quick and dirty smoky effect that'll do the job. I don't know how to contour, but I use a highlighter stick on the bridge and tip of my nose, and I'll use my lipstick as blush in the elevator on the way down. I throw on my little black cocktail dress and slip into a pair of shimmery heels. With a minute to spare, I run out of the room.

And smack into Coop's rock hard chest.

"Why are you still here?" I say, rubbing my chin.

"Whoa," he says at the same time, putting his hands on my shoulders. The fitted black dress has a sweetheart neckline and a sheer mesh top, so even though he's technically touching fabric, it also feels like he's touching skin.

My irritation flares hotter. And ... less like irritation.

No.

Not *less* like irritation. Exactly like irritation.

I march past him, holding my phone and lipstick, but he's standing still. I go back five steps, grab his hand, and tug. "What are you doing?"

"I, uh—" He shakes his head. "Nothing." I press the elevator button and catch his reflection. He's taking me in.

A lot.

I duck my head to keep back a smile.

We step on to the elevator, and I dot lipstick on my cheekbones and blend it in. Thank goodness this elevator is so shiny.

"That was the fastest transformation I've ever seen," Coop says. "And you look way hotter than Clark Kent."

"Oh, stop." I glare at him for effect. "Don't you dare badmouth Henry Cavill in my presence."

He grins, and for a second, my heart leaps. No, the elevator stopped on the first floor, and it made *me* leap. That's all that was.

We walk together toward the ballroom, where the cocktail hour and dinner will be, and I realize I forgot something.

"Shoot," I whisper.

"Everything okay?" he asks.

"I forgot my clutch. Walking around with lipstick and a phone in my hands isn't quite the vibe I was going for."

"Use my pockets."

"No. That's a date thing."

"We've already established that you *are* my date."

"Have not," I say.

We turn a corner. "You didn't deny it upstairs."

"Because the idea of being late is the *only* fate worse than dating you."

"It's all coming up Coop," he says.

I can't help but laugh. And when he takes my lipstick and phone and puts them in his pocket, I also can't help but notice how strong and … attractive his hands are.

(And yes, I'm fully aware how strange it is to find someone's hands attractive.)

The hallways are full of people. Because the sessions are over for the day, it's easier to spot the non-baseball guests and fans. Yes, the meetings themselves are private, but it's still a big hotel with plenty of other people staying.

We get our pictures snapped by a couple dozen people, and I try to hide my face.

"Embarrassed to be seen with me?" Coop says.

"More like worried my brothers will flip their lids. I'm not allowed to date baseball players."

"That's a stupid rule."

"You don't date fans."

He gives me his most impish smile yet. "Haven't you heard, Frosted Sugar Plum? Rules are made to be broken."

"Frosted? Because I'm a bit of an ice queen?"

"Nah, because of the dry shampoo," he says.

I laugh. "Get over yourself, *Buddy*."

"You called me that earlier. Why?"

"You wore a Christmas cowboy hat in an airport with a Rudolph face tattoo."

"Yeah?"

"You're Buddy the Elf."

Laughter bursts from him. "Yes! That is so much better than I thought."

"Why did you think I was calling you 'Buddy?'"

"I was worried you were friend-zoning me."

Heat pools in my abdomen before spreading out to my limbs. But before I can respond or even process what he just said, Coop spots someone up ahead.

"Braden!" He jogs forward a dozen yards and pulls the guy into a big hug. "How are you, man? How's Las Cruces?"

"Not the same without you," he says.

I'm not sure if I should walk in without him, or not, but Coop turns to me and waves me over. "Braden, this is my friend, Liesel," Coop says, "She works for the Firebirds. Liesel, this is Braden, one of my friends from home. He's a pitching coach for the Double-A team in New Mexico where we grew up."

We shake hands, and Braden gives me a friendly smile. Coop puts his hand on my lower back as he and Braden catch up. His hand is warm and presses around my spine in a way that gives me goosebumps. If I didn't know better, I'd think Coop was putting out a vibe to his friend.

A possessive vibe.

But that's silly. He couldn't be possessive. We can barely tolerate each other.

I know, I know: he came up to my room to check on me. He's escorting me to cocktail hour. He's holding my stuff. He's touching my back in a way that makes me shiver.

But he's not being possessive. He's playing mind games with me, because that's what nemeses do. And that's all we are. Hot nemeses.

I mean, regular nemeses. Not hot. Fine looking nemeses. *Absolutely* fine looking.

We're both fine.

"Hey, I saw your mom at the grocery store the other day."

Coop makes a choking sound. Worried, I pat his back. "I'm fine," he says, making my cheeks burn hot.

Fine will never mean what it used to mean, I think.

Coop clears his throat and says to Braden, "Nah. You must be mistaken."

"That's what I thought at first. I know your mom. But then—"

"You're wrong, bro," Coop says so firmly, it ends the discussion. "We gotta go in. I'll see you inside."

I expect to see offense all over Braden's face, but instead, his eyebrows tug together and he gives an understanding smile. "Okay. I'll see you in there, Coop. Glad you're here."

"Thanks."

"What was that about?" I ask Coop when he opens the ballroom door for me.

"Nothing."

He grins broadly, with eyes crinkling in a way that almost seems purposeful. Calculated. It's like someone told him once that his smile didn't reach his eyes, so he designed one that would make sure no one could ever say it again.

And now I know how to tell when Coop is lying.

CHAPTER EIGHT

COOPER

Well, I'm drunk.

Not on alcohol, mind you. I'm an elite athlete at an event where I'm trying to impress my boss. I'm not dumb enough to get hammered.

No, I'm drunk on Liesel Fischer.

Drunk isn't even the right word, because you have to drink something to get drunk, and Liesel doesn't give me almost anything. But her playful scowls and verbal jabs are just enough to make me crave more.

Crave. That's right. I'm not drunk, I'm *hungry*. She's salty and occasionally sweet—the best combination—and I'm starving for more. It's like that week of Thanksgiving when you only eat enough to survive so you can gorge yourself on Thanksgiving dinner and enjoy every morsel.

I've only eaten long enough to survive for a long time.

I want to feast.

That's not sexual, by the way. Yeah, she's a total smoke-show in that dress, but I'm around attractive women plenty.

It's *her*. Her essence. Her sense of humor. Her *mind.*

Unfortunately, the stupid cocktail hour has pulled us from each other too often, with various affiliate owners and GMs vying for my attention, no matter how hard I try to shrug them off.

The ballroom lighting is low enough for comfort, but because it's Christmas themed, twinkling lights illuminate the faces brightly enough that I can see Liesel and the people she's talking to.

And they're all dudes. Young dudes who are probably attractive to women, but I wouldn't know, because I think they all have dumb, smarmy faces.

Including my own friend, Braden.

Who the heck chats up the girl his friend was clearly staking a claim on? I know I can't *really* stake a claim on her, because she's not mine and we low key "hate" each other (which is a cover, because it's obvious we actually love fighting with each other). If I didn't care so much about my job, I'd go over and give him a knuckle punch in the thigh just hard enough to make sure he gets it.

But no, Liesel and Braden are laughing, and she's playing with that earring and occasionally touching the skin behind her earlobe, and I wonder what it feels like. Her shoulders were soft and supple when I grabbed them in her suite. Her hands were velvety smooth when I took her lipstick and phone.

She gave me her lipstick and phone.

That's such a date move. It's a sign of *huge* trust, whether she knows it or not. Do you know why?

She has a wallet case phone. I could look at her driver's license and get her address, not that I would because I'm not a total creep. Her key card is in this, not that I need it, because the front desk clerk had no problem letting me upstairs.

But still.

For whatever reason, she's not afraid of what I could do. She's not worried I'll use the knowledge I could get here to toilet paper her place or rack up a bunch of room service charges. She trusts me. Or she's starting to, at least.

I try to make my way closer to her, weaving through the crowds, but Marty stops me. I swallow my frustration.

"I hate mixers," Marty says, taking a long drink from his glass. A server walks by, and Marty puts his glass down and grabs another. "Too many people."

I look past him to see Liesel grinning at something Braden says, but her gleaming eyes find mine.

And she plays with that earring again.

I'm hungrier than ever. *Famished.*

"Mind if I join you two?" a woman says.

Marty looks at me, holding my gaze for a beat too long. I try to beg him with my eyes to stay so *I* can go. But he says, "Sorry, I was just on my way … over there." And he walks off.

Thanks a lot, Marty.

"Sure thing." I look at Liesel before turning to the woman.

"Your girlfriend is lovely," she says.

"She wouldn't like you calling her that, but I agree."

"Lovely or your girlfriend?"

"The latter. The compliment is true, regardless."

The woman smiles. She's in her early 30s and very pretty. If I hadn't just been looking at Liesel, I'd probably flirt with her, but as it is, nothing else will satisfy my appetite.

"I'm Kayla," the woman says, holding a champagne flute in one hand and shaking my hand with the other. "I'm the new owner of the …" she pauses, "Mullet Ridge Mudflaps."

The Mullet Ridge Mudflaps are famous for a few reasons: one, their name. It's like calling them the Mullet Ridge Mullets. Two, the billionaire Carville family just bought them. And three, the team has been the worst in the minor leagues for the last ten years. I wouldn't be surprised if the previous owner *paid* the Carvilles to take it from him.

"You're Kayla Carville?" I say. "I don't mean this in a rude way, but the Mudflaps aren't a Firebirds affiliate. What are you doing here?"

"A few friends and I are here for a spa retreat. It's my bachelorette party." My eyes drop to the huge rock on her left hand.

"Congratulations."

"Thank you. When I heard there was a baseball meeting in town, I thought I'd try my luck at recruiting help."

"How's that working out for you?"

"Terribly," she says. "Everyone views me as the competition."

"Can you blame them?"

She taps her glass. "Only if I try really hard." I chuckle. "I've given you my name, but I didn't catch yours," she says.

"Cooper Kellogg."

"What do you do, Cooper?"

I grin. I'm not used to being a stranger to people, especially at a baseball event.

"I'm a player. But I injured my elbow, so I'm working with the front office this next season while I rehab."

"Are you good?"

I can't help laughing. "Ask my not-girlfriend." We both look at Liesel, who gives a tinkling laugh at something the dork she's talking to says. At least it's not Braden now. I glance back at Kayla, who's as well dressed and upscale a woman as I've ever seen. The idea of *her* owning the Mullet Ridge Mudflaps is hilarious. "I'm sorry, but you don't seem happy to be here."

"I'm not *un*happy."

"I can see that."

She purses her lips. "Let me put it this way: I don't know anything about baseball, but my dad thought buying me a team would be a good birthday present. I would have preferred a pony."

"Do you ride?"

"No. And I'm allergic to horses."

I cough a laugh. "Do we have a Ted Lasso situation on our hands? Are you looking to hire someone terrible so you can tank the team, but you'll end up coming around and showing us all you have a heart of gold?"

"Excuse me? I happen to have a heart of gold already. It's huge. Everyone loves it," she says in mock outrage. Liesel glances at us, a thin line between her eyebrows. "And no, I don't want to tank the team. I don't know what to do with the team. We're evidently the laughingstock of the league."

"Yeah. Your name has two mullets in it."

"I fail to see the problem," she deadpans.

"Ha. I see what you did there," I say. I like this woman. I don't want to flirt with her or date her, but I like her. "Well, I can tell you this much: you need a good GM and an even better coach."

"Okay."

"And pitchers. Get yourself some all star pitchers. I'll deny this if you tell my *not*-girlfriend over there, but as much as I think runs win games, pitching wins championships."

"Pitchers. Those are the guys who throw the ball at the other guys?" she asks. My eyes turn into saucers. "I'm kidding." The corner of her mouth raises. "Thank you. Now, if I were going to find good pitching …"

"I can't help you there. I just recommended Colt Spencer over the Fischer brothers. Willingly. I clearly can't be trusted."

She nods, looking deep in thought. "Well, thank you, Cooper. I appreciate you taking a minute away from ogling your date."

"Oh, don't worry. I still ogled her a lot."

She laughs, showing a smile worthy of a young Julia Roberts. "Good luck," she says, and she walks off.

And my attention turns right back to Liesel. Liesel talking to some probably-attractive-if-he-weren't-so-punchable dude.

There are a fair number of women here, but Liesel puts them to shame, which explains all the men flocking to her.

Darn it.

Things would be so much easier if she weren't so … flirt-able. Tease-able.

I've given her a wide berth all night, but I'm done being polite. I march past the people trying to grab my arm and am almost to Liesel when—

"You've been busy all night," Doug says, standing in front of me.

Special characters appear in my mind in place of all the curse words I want to say. "Hey, Doug. Yup. Busy night."

"You and Liesel did good work," he says.

"Yeah, she's really smart." I steal a glance at her. "Even if she hates me."

He claps my shoulder. "She hasn't gotten to know you yet. You'll win her over."

I look at him. "You wouldn't care if I tried something with your lead analytics manager?"

"Whoa. Who said anything about trying something? I thought you were talking about working together." Doug takes a long drink from his glass and then stares me down. "I'd care a lot. Her dad is an umpire. If you mess something up with her, he could take it out on you every time you're at the plate, to say nothing of the team."

"I guess it's a good thing I'm sitting out this next season. Gives me a lot of time before we have to test that theory."

Doug looks alarmed. But when he sees my grin, he chuckles. He doesn't know the grin is fake.

Disappointment sinks into a pit in my chest. Liesel is the first woman who's interested me in years. I first talked to her in the airport because she was watching a sports channel instead of a Christmas movie. Almost nothing is more attractive than a woman who knows baseball.

But then when she had such strong opinions—opinions that revolved around *me*—I couldn't stop myself.

Because the only thing I find more attractive than a woman who knows baseball is a woman who doesn't care who I am. Funny enough, those two don't intersect much.

Except for in Liesel.

Talk about irresistible.

Doug swirls the ice in his glass. "I gotta ask, though: what was going through your head when you recommended your ol' buddy Colton Spencer? Marty and Kathy both said you prefer that Triple-A kid, Betancourt."

I shrug, purposefully *not* looking at Liesel, but Doug chuckles, anyway. "That's what I thought."

"She has stats to back her up."

"I know. They're compelling. But is that what you want?"

A server walks by with something wrapped in bacon, and I take a couple from the tray and pop one in my mouth. I make every effort to seem casual, because I'm actually at war with myself.

I like Liesel. I respect Doug.

I want Liesel to like me. I want Doug to respect me.

But … I want to keep flirting with Liesel. I want to flirt and tease and laugh and make her laugh. I want to get her to glare at me with that half smile she's trying to cover. And I want to talk with her. Get to know her. Watch her brain work in real time. I want her to push me. Call me on my crap. Make me think.

Heck, I want to kiss her.

Without Doug finding out.

I'm not an utter fool, though, so I say something that won't get me in trouble. "Is acquiring Colton what I want?" I put another appetizer in my mouth. "I want to win. If Colton can do that for us, I can put up with him."

Doug smirks. "Thanks for taking one for the team." Someone walks by and Doug gets his attention, signaling that

I'm free to go. But Doug looks at me before I walk off. "Coop, I meant what I said. *Do not mess with her.*"

My easy grin reaches all the way to my eyes. It's a skill I learned when I brought home an honor roll certificate from school right after Mom was diagnosed. She was crying that she missed it, and I couldn't handle her disappointment. So I smiled and hugged her and tried to hold back my own tears while telling her it was okay, it didn't matter, she didn't miss a thing.

"See?" I told her. "I'm smiling! It's okay, Mom!"

"But it doesn't reach your eyes," she sobbed.

I didn't even know what that meant at nine, but I learned fast. I practiced smiles in the mirror all night, and I promised myself that I would never be the reason my mom cried again. Even that young, I knew she was trying. Her condition wouldn't let her do the things she wanted, and it broke her heart probably even more than it broke mine.

I made sure that when I came home from a game—win or lose—I acted as enthusiastic and positive as possible. The more bombastic I was, the more she cheered.

And soon, her tears were a memory, and my replays became more exciting to me than the games themselves. Because my mom enjoyed them with me.

"Don't worry about a thing, Doug," I say with my patented smile.

"Good man," Doug says. "I'll see you tomorrow."

I walk away from Doug and, more importantly, Liesel, and I keep that fake grin on my face until I'm out of sight. When it's time for dinner, I start for a table as far from Liesel as possible, even though it feels like I've crossed over from being famished to positively dying of hunger.

When I'm about to sit, I make the mistake of looking at Liesel. Her eyes are searching, and I see her smile at her own team, assuming she'll go sit with them, but she waves and keeps looking.

Until her eyes find mine.

Her expression shifts, and she shoots me a look—half wary, half challenging.

Don't go over. I tell myself. *Don't go over*!

"Is this seat taken?" I ask her.

She takes her napkin and drops it on the open chair. "Oops, sorry. It's an otherwise full table, but I don't think about others, so I like to put my stuff on chairs so people can't sit there."

"That's okay," I say, picking up her napkin and returning it to her lap, letting my finger skim her knees. "You're only human."

She shakes her head, but she has a saucy, exasperated smile on her face that makes my stomach growl.

I take the seat and move it ever so slightly closer to her.

It's dumb of me, but hey.

I'm only human.

CHAPTER NINE

LIESEL

I can't focus all throughout dinner.

Our owner is talking, giving some speech about taking the Firebirds farther than we've ever gone before, but Coop is incorrigible.

"What does that even mean?" Coop asks, almost in my ear. "Space?"

"Shush," I say out of the corner of my mouth.

"Who were those guys you were talking to?"

I would ignore him, but he's relentless.

Also … this is kind of boring.

I pick at a piece of breadstick and put it in my mouth, chewing slowly because Coop's eyes are on me, and I can tell the wait is driving him nuts. "Just stats and marketing guys from the affiliates. And your buddy, Braden."

"Braden," he scoffs.

"*You* introduced us."

He drains his water. "Biggest mistake of the week," he grumbles, the glass at his lips.

Why does me talking to his friend make him grumble? And why does his grumble make my stomach flutter?

"How so?"

"Because he's dangerous." I arch my eyebrow at him. "He is!" Coop says in a loud whisper. "He volunteers at a pet hospital on the weekend."

I cough to cover my laugh. "And how does that make him dangerous?"

"Rabies, probably. Kennel Cough. Parvo. I bet he has it all."

I have to duck my head, I'm laughing so hard. Coop pounds on my back, as if saving me from choking on a breadstick. But his hand lingers on my shoulder blade after the pounding, rubbing circles on my upper back.

"I think I'm okay now," I mutter.

He rubs one final circle—softer and infuriatingly tender—and then he pats my back again. "There. All good. She's safe, everybody," he says. I kick him under the table, and that only makes him smile.

When the servers come to clear our plates and give us our soup, I take the opportunity to look at Coop.

His eyes are all over me. I can practically see the heart shape of my face as his eyes trace it.

That. Is. Hot.

No. I mean *it* is hot. In here. It's hot in here.

You're not allowed to date a player.

I'm not dating him, I argue with my mind. *I'm flirting with him. Big difference.*

And I'm not even flirting with him! I'm fighting with him. It doesn't matter that I'm having fun doing it.

Our owner finishes his big speech, and no one claps louder than Coop.

"Great speech," he says loudly to the table. "Rousing stuff.

Didn't you all think it was rousing?" Kathy nods from the other end of the round table, and a few others do, too. "Liesel, how did you like the speech?"

I hold back a glare *and* a smile. "It was great."

"What was your favorite part?"

I hope my gaze tells him that I'm going to kill him slowly, painfully, and totally untraceably.

"I thought his idea for a unified vision throughout the affiliates was brilliant. 'For the love of the game … and the fans.' It's a nice touch."

"That *was* great. Rousing, even."

"Rousing," I agree through gritted teeth.

He grins.

I don't know how we make it through dinner. Coop manages to include others in our conversation *just* enough that I doubt anyone else can sense his focus on me. But I feel it. I feel his attention like a physical weight. Because out of everyone at the table, he's chosen to talk to Todd, a guy from the analytics department sitting on the other side of me. That means, every time he speaks to Todd, Coop leans so close, his face is practically next to mine. He drapes his arm casually around the back of my chair, almost around me, claiming my space.

It's subtle. All in the name of being friendly with Todd. But it also forces me to participate, whether I want to or not. And I am firmly "Team Not," as I have to remind myself again and again. Especially when his thumb "accidentally" grazes my shoulder or neck.

"What an interesting point, Todd. I agree that we need better entertainment on the Jumbotron during delays. Don't you agree, Liesel?"

"I agree, Todd and Cooper," I say, kicking Coop again.

For his part, Todd seems overjoyed to be talking to one of the best players in baseball. He's a data engineer, so scoreboard production is outside his wheelhouse, yet he talks with the enthusiasm of a little kid who's discovered Minecraft.

I gotta be honest: it's boring the life out of me.

But Coop listens. He asks questions. He responds to Todd in a way that makes me think he's actually engaged in the conversation. I can't imagine how he does it, considering the efforts he's making to breathe in a way that stirs the tiny hairs on my neck. It takes all of my focus not to melt along with the gelato served during dessert.

"So how long have you two known each other," Todd asks me through his horn-rimmed glasses.

I sit up straighter, ignoring the feeling of Coop's finger brushing my neck. "Uh, just this week."

"Really?" Todd asks. "I assumed you guys must be old friends. You're so comfortable with each other."

"Comfortable?" Coop laughs. "You were in the same meeting we were, Todd. She hates me. And because I'm me, I can't stop teasing her about it."

"Hate is a *little* strong," I say. "Barely tolerate is more accurate."

Todd laughs. "Then maybe I shouldn't invite you guys to the escape room if you and Liesel can't stand each other."

Coop perks up. "Escape room?" He meets my eye, and I give him a death glare I hope Todd can't see. "We'd love to!"

"Awesome!" Todd says. "It's a team builder for the data scientists and engineers. Sorry we didn't include the analytics managers, Liesel," he says with a splotchy flush.

"That's fine," I say. "I don't know if I should—"

"She's joking," Coop says, and I grind my heel into his fancy Italian shoe. I see him wince from the corner of my eye, but instead of backing away, he only leans closer. He moves his arm from the back of my chair to my shoulders and shakes me like we're old buddies. "Liesel is a logic puzzle genius. A lady in the streets, and a geek in the spreadsheets, if you know what I mean."

I.

Hate.

Him.

Todd laughs harder at this than it deserves, but then, it's not often you get to invite one of your heroes to hang out and he says yes. Todd gets a pass.

Coop doesn't.

"Okay, sounds fun!" I say. "But can we make sure no one posts about it on social media?" I ask.

Todd looks at me like I'm crazy. "We're doing a team builder with Cooper Kellogg. Of course we'll post this on social media!"

"So will I!" Coop says, laughing along with Todd.

I smile and don't move my lips when I say, "I'm going to kill you," in Coop's ear.

He mutters softly, "I can't wait."

* * *

An hour later, we've changed into casual clothes and the "party bus" Todd booked has dropped us off at the escape room, along with his team.

Coop looks irritatingly handsome in dark gray joggers, his gray baseball cap, and a baby blue Firebirds zip up hoodie that I've never seen before but want with my whole soul.

I love oversized sweatshirts. I grew up taking my brothers' clothes all the time, and I'd spray them with enough perfume that they'd get too grossed out and would never take them back. It was awesome.

Something tells me stealing something of Coop's would be even better.

"Are you ready?" he asks as we stand outside the room,

waiting for the game master to let us in. I've never done an escape room before. But he's right that I'm great at logic and puzzles, and I'm confident that will extend to an escape room.

Even if it's a "Help Buddy the Elf Save Christmas" escape room.

I shake my head knowingly.

"What?" he asks with a Cheshire grin.

"Buddy the freaking Elf," I say.

"Scrooge the freaking McDuck," he says.

A laugh bubbles from my throat. "I think you mean Ebenezer Scrooge."

"I think you're staying in the Owner's Suite."

"Shut up."

"Make me."

Todd and his team are distracted, making wagers on who's going to find the most clues, and that gives me an idea.

"Okay, how about we make a bet," I say. Coop cocks his head to the side. "If I solve more puzzles than you, you have to wear one of your Christmas face tattoos to tomorrow's meetings. And you can't say a word about it."

"Wow. You're talking real stakes here. Okay, okay. Fine, but if I win, *you* have to wear one of my jerseys tomorrow, *and* you have to tell everyone that it's because you lost a bet to me because I'm smarter than you."

"What? No way."

"Way," Coop says. "Unless you're chicken."

The game master announces that the doors will open in ten seconds, and the energy in the waiting room shifts.

We both spin around, waiting at the door. The timer flashes and starts counting down from ten. "I'm not chicken," I say, adrenaline coursing through my veins and speeding up my breathing. "I'm going to break you like a stale gingerbread house."

"Then I guess it's on like a bon bon."

The countdown beeps.

3, 2, 1—

The doors fly open, and we run into the room.

Snowy white faux wood planks cover the walls of the room, and decorative white beams connect the walls to the ceiling. It's designed to look like the elves' workshop in the North Pole. Christmas music plays quietly over the speakers, and all around the room are Christmas decorations—garlands, huge red bows, twinkle lights, and a massive Christmas tree, with dozens of presents at its base. A table too short for an adult sits in the center of the room, with twelve small chairs around it. There's an Etch A Sketch in the middle of the table.

"I guarantee that Etch A Sketch has instructions on it," I say.

"That doesn't count as solving a puzzle, you know," Coop says.

"I know," I say, even though I don't. I don't have any idea what I'm supposed to do, mostly because Coop wouldn't stop messing with me when the game master told us the rules.

Todd sees me pointing to the Etch A Sketch, and he picks it up.

"It's the first puzzle!" he says. Coop bumps my hip with his. Todd reads the message, his coworkers poised for action.

"Of the food groups, Buddy loves four:
Candy, candy corn, syrup, and more.
Find all twelve of the one that's missing,
Then underneath the mistletoe, you'll be kissing."

"The one that's missing?" one of Todd's friends asks. "The one what?"

"The food groups," I say. "What are Buddy's four food groups from the movie? Candy, candy corn, syrup …"

"Candy canes!" Coop shouts.

"And we need to find twelve!" Todd yells.

Immediately, we set to work, finding candy canes hanging from the Christmas tree, scattered among the presents, hanging from Christmas lights, and underneath the table. Each of them has a letter on it, and we spread them out on the table.

"They must spell something," I say, dropping to one of the chairs at the little table. I move them around, trying different combinations of letters to make a word.

Coop reaches over me, adjusting letters, and Todd and his team stand behind me, trying to unscramble the words out loud.

"Child."

"Holly, nope, that would be holy."

"Uh, here, hero, lair, day."

"Holiday!" I blurt, arranging the letters in the first word.

"Cheer," Coop says, figuring out the next word before I can.

"Holiday cheer," Todd says. "What's the best way to spread Christmas cheer?" he asks.

"Singing loud for all to cheer!" one of his friends says.

We all look at Todd's friend. "It's *hear,* not *cheer,*" Todd says. "You can't rhyme a word with itself." Todd looks disgusted, and his friend looks red-faced with shame.

"It's okay," Coop says, clapping the guy's back and earning a smile.

"What are we supposed to sing?" I ask.

"Or where?" Coop says.

We look at each other and both yell. "Mistletoe!"

We all dart for the mistletoe hanging from one of the beams. "What song do they sing in the movie?" Todd asks.

Coop starts singing the first line from *"Baby, It's Cold Outside,"* and soon we're all singing under the mistletoe.

But nothing happens.

"What is it?" I ask. "Why isn't anything happening?"

"Read the last line," the only other woman on the team says.

"'Then underneath the mistletoe, you'll be kissing,'" Todd says. "We need to kiss!?"

He tries to grab the girl, but she stiff-arms him in the face.

"NOPE," she says.

"Come on, Candace! It's for a clue!" Todd says.

"Not happening," Candace says.

"Liesel?" Todd says, trying to grab me next, but Coop blocks him and puts his arm behind my back, like he's about to sweep me into a dip.

"I got this," he says, as my pulse triples.

"No," I say.

"So you *are* chicken," Coop says with an impish quirk of his lips.

"I'll do it!" Candace says to Coop, looking a little too starry-eyed for my liking.

"Fine!" I say. "But this is for the *game*." I point to everyone. "And I may not be your direct boss, but if anyone records this, you're fired."

A few people laugh as Coop takes off his hat and tries to dip me. I smack his arm. "This isn't *Gone with the Wind*. No dips."

"No fun is more like it," Coop mutters, his face next to mine. He holds there, his eyes open, staring into mine with a puckish gleam.

So I press my lips on his in a peck, but Coop parts his, and that hint of heat sends a zip of electricity through my body. I push away fast.

"There. Done," I say a little too quickly. But it's because we're on a deadline. Also because I don't want to kiss him, obviously.

Coop's face is half smirk, half . . . also smirk, actually.

All smirk.

There's a click, and then a peg board drops from the ceiling. We run over to the board, where a note is dangling from one of the pegs. We all lunge for it, but Coop grabs it first.

"Five golden rings, a festive sight,
But ten rings are needed this glorious night.
Toss them true, but oh, be wise!
And the next clue will be your greatest prize.
What looks like a peg to you and me
Just may be the needed key."

"Where are the rings?" Candace asks.

"Seriously, Candace? We clearly need to find them!" Todd shouts. "Come on!"

Coop and I both snort behind our hands.

"Come on, Candace!" Coop says to me under his breath in his best Napoleon Dynamite impression. "Gosh!"

I laugh freely as I run to find rings, getting one from around a tube-shaped present and another from an ornament on the tree. Soon, we've found all ten rings, and we're standing in front of the peg board. Todd tries to put a peg directly on the board, but a buzzer sounds, and a voice like it's from the movie says, "Don't make me call security."

"You have to stay behind the line, *Todd*," Candace says, pointing to a bright red, sparkly line maybe six feet back from the pegboard. "And we should probably let Coop throw, considering he's the only person here who actually knows how to throw something."

"Loving that energy, Candace," Coop says, making me snicker. "But I just had surgery. I know for a fact, though, that Liesel here can catch a baseball from ten feet away. One-handed."

"I didn't know I could hate you more," I say with a razor-sharp grin.

"Do it!" Todd yells.

Coop gives me his widest eyes yet, and I take the rings from him. "I'll do half, you do half," I say. "Left-handed."

"Don't make me quote *The Princess Bride* to you," he says, but he takes five of the rings from me.

And we throw.

We both land our first ones quickly. Right-handed, I'm better than Coop is, but he's still weirdly good with his left hand.

"Why are you giving me that look?" he asks, tossing a ring. He misses but mine lands. "Nice one," he says.

"There's no *look*," I say. "And if there is, it's a gloating look because I'm better than you."

He grins and tosses another ring. He's not threatened by me at all. Not by my baseball knowledge or my intelligence, and not by the fact that I'm beating him in a ring toss game, even if he's not using his dominant hand.

It shouldn't be a big deal, but it is. Not much is more attractive than a guy who appreciates a competent woman.

Candace and a few others stand under the pegboard, chucking rings back to us whenever we miss one. After a minute, we've landed each of the ten rings, but nothing happens.

We look around, in case we missed something. We count the rings on the pegs. The more we scramble, the more uptight Todd gets.

"What do we do now?" he yells. "What do we do now?"

"Come on, Candace!" Coop whispers to me, and I laugh, but I'm channeling a bit of Todd, myself. What the heck do we do now?

Coop goes over to grab the instructions, and he reads it out loud again. But he's slow and steady, confidence emanating from him like heat from a fire.

"Five golden rings, a festive sight,
But ten rings are needed this glorious night.
Toss them true, but oh, be wise!

And the next clue will be your greatest prize.
What looks like a peg to you and me
Just may be the needed key."

"A key!" I say.

I run over to the pegboard, and Coop and Candace are right behind me. We tug on each of the pegs until Candace yanks one out that has a key on the end.

"What does it go to?" Todd yells.

"WE DON'T KNOW YET, *TODD*," Candace snaps. "Calm down! And everyone else, look for a keyhole."

"This door has a keyhole," Coop says.

Candace runs over, sticks the key in the door, and it opens.

"Yes!" she yells.

Candace, Todd, and their team all run into the other room, which looks like a stable. Coop is standing at the door, taking up enough space that my arm brushes his as I enter.

My arm tingles like I walked through a spiderweb. I give a small shiver.

"Cold?" he asks.

"Of course not," I say. "Midwesterners don't get cold."

"Good to know. Because if you were, I'd have to give you my hoodie."

"I'm freezing," I say.

He grins, unzips his hoodie, and puts it around my shoulders. I slide my arms in, and he turns me around to face him. Then he takes the two sides of the zipper and zips it all the way up to my chin.

And even though his hand doesn't touch a single part of my body until he reaches my chin, flames follow the movement all the way up.

He holds my gaze. "Better?"

"Much."

Then he gives me a shove, and I fall butt first into a reindeer trough.

"Cooper Kellogg!"

He winks at me, snags the next puzzle card from the seat of the giant sleigh in the middle of the room, and starts reading.

"Santa's sleigh won't drive itself,
For this one, he needs all his elves!
In pairs they'll work in perfect accord
Or the Clausometer won't move forward.
Help him fix his broken sleigh,
And get the Big Man on his way!"

We all run over to the sleigh, and one of Todd's friends pops the hood. There, we see six pairs of gear cranks, enough for twelve people. There are only nine of us. Candace calls out loudly. "We have one extra person!"

A voice sounds over a speaker. "Someone can sit out."

"You can talk to the game master?" I ask.

"Duh," Todd snaps.

Coop grabs Todd's shoulder and pulls him aside. "Todd, you need to take a break," Coop says in a soft but firm voice. I don't know if he's squeezing, but the petty part of me hopes he is. "It's just a game, but even if it weren't, real men don't snap at women. Time to pull yourself together, pal."

He's saying this quietly enough that it's not a spectacle. He's not putting Todd on the spot. But he's not letting him get away with his bad behavior, either.

Todd takes off his glasses and rubs his face. "Yeah, okay. Thanks, Coop."

Coop returns to find that everyone else has paired up, and they're spinning their gears as fast as they can.

I'm not paired up with anyone. I'll never admit this to Coop, but Candace asked if I wanted to team up with her—solidarity, sister!—but I told her I'd wait.

Not because I'm interested in Coop, or anything, but because I wanted to hear what he was saying to Todd.

That's all.

Coop gives me a smile and grabs the handle of his gear crank. "Do we just spin it?"

"I don't think so," I say, holding the puzzle card. "The Clausometer isn't moving." I read through the rhyming instructions again. "'*In pairs they'll work in perfect accord.*'" I look at our group. "Guys, I think we have to move at the exact same pace. Maybe mirror images? It says 'perfect accord.'"

"You heard the lady!" Candace says, and soon, we're all looking at our partners and syncing up. When we're all in step with our respective partner, the Clausometer starts ticking up. Whenever someone misses a beat, though, the meter drops quickly. Coop and I are both coordinated, but the data scientists are somewhat ... lacking in the physical skills department.

"Why is this so hard?" one of the guys says.

Todd looks like he's going to flip a table, but Coop shoots him a warning glance that mellows him right out. Then Coop starts singing the first line of "Let It Snow! Let It Snow! Let It Snow!"

He's turning his gear along with the beat of the song. So I chime in, and then Candace nods, like she gets what Coop is doing. Soon, we're all belting out the chorus and moving in perfect unison. Coop and I stare in each other's eyes, grinning like fools as we crank a silly gear in an escape room.

I don't remember the last time I had this much fun.

And something tells me Coop knows it.

We sing and spin until the Clausometer moves up, up, up. And then it hits the top!

"Yes!" Candace yells.

"You know, the lyric is 'we've' not 'there's,'" Todd says. "'Since *we've* no place—'"

"Enough, Todd!" the whole team yells, and Coop and I laugh as Candace reads the clue on the Clausometer.

As we rush over to the next clue, I can't help but watch Coop. And when he reaches up and turns his gray Firebirds baseball cap backwards on his head, my breath catches.

Shoot.

Shoot, shoot, shoot.

I have a crush on a baseball player.

CHAPTER TEN

LIESEL

"I definitely had one more than you!" I tell Coop on the way back to the hotel. He and I are in the backseat of the "party bus," and Candace and two of the data engineers are talking and laughing in front of us. "You forgot the Naughty List puzzle—"

"That was Paul, not you!" Coop says.

"No, it wasn't! Paul got the crossword, but I did the—" I stop myself. "Rats. It was Paul." I groan and bump my head against the back of the seat. Coop closes his eyes and rests his head on my shoulder. I shove him off, knocking his hat to the bench in the process. I scoop it up before he can and put it on my head. I get a whiff of his peppermint shampoo in the process.

Oh, wow, that's nice.

Coop takes his hat off of me and returns it to his own head, his wavy hair poking out from the bottom. "A hoodie is one thing, but no one wears my hat."

I give a disbelieving laugh. "It's a hat. You probably have a hundred."

"No, I have one. And a backup at home."

I take it off his head and put it back on mine.

He takes it back off and returns it to his own head.

"You don't understand. Finding a hat that fits me is like … Cinderella's glass slipper. It's a perfect fit. I can't let anyone wear it." He pinches my nose. "Not even you."

I don't let myself smile or blush at his implication that I'm special. I mean, I squeal inside a little, but that's because I'm tired and not thinking straight. It's almost eleven, and I hardly slept last night, what with having to fix the roster.

I yawn. "Coop, you wear a hat every game. And this is a team hat."

"Yeah, and I've tried every single hat New Era sent me. Hundreds of them. This is the only one that doesn't make my head look weird."

"Don't blame the hat," I say. "It's your weird head's fault it looks weird."

He pushes me all the way over, and I start giggling against the seat. And I can't stop.

"Whoa," he says, laughing. "Someone's getting punchy."

My laughter stops.

"What? You okay?" he asks. He pulls me up, and suddenly, tears spring to my eyes. "Liesel, are you okay? What happened?"

I shake my head, trying to shake my frown off with it. "It's nothing."

"Liesel, you went from laughing like a schoolgirl to looking like I murdered a puppy in front of your face. What's up?"

I don't want to say anything, but I'm tired and have lost my filter and too much inhibition. "I get silly when I'm tired."

"I see that."

"My brothers always had late games and tournaments, and when I'd get tired on the drive home from a game, my family would do dumb stuff to make me laugh. I'd start giggling and wouldn't be able to stop, and my mom would always say, 'Someone's getting punchy!'" I give him a sad smile and wrinkle my nose. "I haven't heard someone say that in a long time."

Coop's lips stretch into a thin line, and the street lights reflect the warmth in his eyes. He puts an arm around me and pulls me against his chest. "I'm sorry," he says.

"Thanks," I say. My throat aches with emotion, but he's holding me tenderly, and it feels nice and cozy and … distracting.

"What was your mom like?"

I'm not positive how close we are to the resort, but it took fifteen minutes to get to the escape room, and it's probably been half that time since we left.

"She was kind and funny and competitive, but not mean. And she *loved* Christmas. She started decorating the day after Halloween."

"The day after Halloween? What about Thanksgiving?"

"She was Canadian—she and Dad met in college—so she always joked that the real Thanksgiving is in October. She thought it was 'morally repugnant' that people could start decorating for Halloween on September first but had to wait until the end of November to decorate for Christmas."

"'Morally repugnant?' That's strong even for me," he teases. His right arm is slung around my shoulders, giving me my first real glimpse of his scar. It's a huge, puckered, deep purple gash, and suddenly, it makes me see this larger-than-life superstar as just another guy. A guy who can get hurt, who can bleed, who can cry. And that softens my heart the rest of the way.

"She was sick for a long time—Lou Gehrig's disease, or ALS as it's called nowadays. She used to joke that she loved baseball so much, she made sure she even got the baseball disease."

"Ouch," Coop whispers.

"She lived a lot longer than most people with it, though. We were lucky we got so much time with her."

"You weren't lucky—"

"We were," I insist. "I met kids in the hospital whose parents passed away after only a couple of years with it. We got almost ten years. They were hard, but they were *ours* and they mattered." I feel Coop nodding, but he doesn't say anything. My voice drops, almost matching the hum of the passenger van. "For the last several years of her life, she couldn't put up decorations, so I spearheaded all of it. I did the Christmas cards and all the baking. I made sure we watched all the movies on the right days, ate all the right snacks, went caroling. I planned the menu for Christmas Day and gave everyone their assignments. I went over the top making sure each Christmas was the best it could be because it could be the last. And then one day, it was." My lower lip trembles. "She fell into a coma on Christmas Day two years ago, and she never woke up."

"I'm sorry," he whispers.

"I know it's probably an insult to her memory, but I haven't been able to enjoy holidays since then. If anything, the longer we're removed from her passing, the more I hate them, especially Christmas. My dad and brothers keep trying to get me to relive all the *best traditions,* but the traditions don't matter. It's who we did them with that matters, and she's gone. So what's the point?"

I wipe away a tear as it rolls down my face. Coop's arm around my shoulder squeezes.

"What do they say?"

"Nothing. I haven't told them how I feel. I just avoid them all season long. It's too hard to be with them and pretend that everything's okay. They say that it feels like Mom is with them at Christmas but I haven't felt anything except pain. I don't want to make new memories without her. I don't even want the old memories. They hurt too much."

The tears are falling faster than I can wipe them, and when I use the sleeve of Coop's hoodie—the hoodie I'm wearing—to sop up my wet, snotty mess, I hiss. "Shoot, I'm sorry! I swear I'll wash this before I give it back."

"Don't worry about it," he says. "Take it. It's yours. Unlike a hat, hoodies really are universal."

"I'm glad to hear you say that," I tell him. "Because I wasn't planning to give this back. Employees don't get swag."

"I thought you didn't like things that weren't earned."

"Stealing is work."

He laughs, and his shaking chest makes me shake. Then he exhales slowly.

"Can I offer a different perspective about Christmas?"

"I'd really rather you not."

"Okay."

Guilt nips at my chest. No, not guilt, reality, maybe. Some part of my brain buried deep down knows what I'm doing isn't healthy. I flap my lips out like a horse. "Fine. I'll trade you the hoodie for your perspective so I can say I *earned* it."

"If you say so," he says. "It sounds like your mom created more than just Christmas rituals that require her presence to have meaning. These are etched into the soul of your family. If it hurts to remember her, that's not a bad thing. If it hurts to celebrate Christmas because you can't stop missing her, that's okay. Your family's traditions are strong enough to hold your grief. And maybe they could heal some of it. The scar will always be there, but sometimes you have to take the bandage off a wound to let it heal."

"But I don't want to *see* the wound. I want to forget about it."

"That won't make it stop hurting. It'll only make it fester."

My lips tug down deeply. "What if you're wrong?"

"Could it possibly hurt *worse* than it does now?"

I think about his question. Some days, the pain of missing my mom is so intense, it steals my breath. I can be walking through a grocery store and smell someone wearing her perfume, and the trigger has me running to the grocery store restroom to sob.

Other days are fine. Some are even good. But I always feel a little like I'm betraying her for having a good day without her, like I'm being untrue to her memory by smiling or laughing. I know that's crazy. All she wanted was for me to be happy. I know that.

Christmas just makes it hard.

Coop is probably right that participating in our rituals and traditions couldn't make me hurt worse than I already do. Seeing me grieve would hurt my dad and brothers, though. They protect me like a Momma Bear, even if I'm the one who kept the house running all those years and who still organizes our schedules around when we can see each other during baseball season.

Besides, deciding that I'll be involved at Christmas is like deciding to get the travel vaccines I needed for my internship in Costa Rica. Yeah, not getting diphtheria sounds great, but you're still scheduling your own pain.

I don't want to.

"I liked you better when I thought you were a dumb jock," I say.

"Nah," Coop says. I can hear the smile in the way he talks. "This is all part of the Cooper Kellogg appeal," he teases.

"Believe me: opening your mouth ruins the Cooper Kellogg appeal."

He laughs hard. "In other words, you think I'm hot, but annoying. I'll take it."

The van pulls into the resort, and we all file out. Coop offers me his hand, and I'm tired enough to take it.

We walk into the hotel with the rest of the group and say goodbye to them. Coop walks me over to my private elevator.

He tugs on one of the strings of his—*my*—hoodie. "Do you need anything for tomorrow?"

"Like what?" I ask.

"You know," he says flatly.

I moan. I forgot about our bet. Our stupid bet!

"We counted 'em up, and a girl like you can't get mad at math."

"Watch me."

"A deal's a deal, Liese."

"Liese, huh?" I say as my elevator approaches. "Everyone calls me Lee. Well, except for the old building gossip who thought my name was Lisa. And I guess half my apartment complex still thinks that's my name—"

"Are you trying to avoid admitting what we both know is coming?"

"Maybe."

My elevator opens, and I step on, glaring at him as the doors close.

The last thing I hear him say is, "Sweet dreams, Sugar Plum. You're going to look hot in my jersey."

CHAPTER ELEVEN

COOPER

When Liesel and I see each other the next morning, I can't tell which is stronger: my elation or her irritation.

But, then, like our wager last night, it's probably a tie.

"Mm, mm, mm," I say. I do a spinning motion with my finger. "Give us a little spin, Ms. Fischer. Let me see how good you look wearing my name on your back."

"I'm not spinning," she says.

"It's cool. I'll spin for you." And because I'm me, I take out my phone and film as I walk around her.

"DO NOT POST THAT."

"I won't! Not everything belongs to the fans." I grin as I record her. As satisfying as seeing my name on her back over that big number three, the hint of a smile peeking out from her scowl is even better.

She holds out her hands. "Happy now?"

"Immensely."

"No one with an abominable snowman tattoo covering his entire right cheek should look that happy."

"What do you mean? Post Malone is covered in face tats, and that guy's always smiling."

"You're like Pre-Malone. No, *Home Alone* Malone."

"Ha! I like that. Kevin!" I cry like I'm his mom.

"Give me strength," she mumbles heavenward.

We walk to the ballroom, where breakfast is served. Today's the last day of meetings, but because we don't end until six tonight, most people I've talked to are flying home tomorrow. Including me *and* Liesel.

Do I plan to take advantage of another night with her?

Yes. Yes, I do.

Unfortunately, the moment we walk into the ballroom, Doug is on me like Jack on Frost.

"What were you thinking, Coop?" Doug asks.

"What do you mean?" I assume he's talking about my face tattoo, but I'm not allowed to talk about it. So I gesture, instead.

He grabs my arm and smiles at someone who passes us.

"What's with the *Psycho* vibes, Doug?" I ask.

"You were with Liesel Fischer last night."

I have plausible deniability, so I don't get flustered. "Yeah, we joined the analytics team for a team builder. What's the problem?"

"You," he says.

"Me?" A twinge of worry hits me. But I brush it off. "Why? Nothing happened."

"Tell that to the representative from the Umpires Association."

And now the twinge is a full body assault. I squeeze my eyes shut, pained. "You don't mean what I think you mean."

"You know I do."

I open my eyes, and I spot Liesel looking at me from the

buffet line, confusion lifting her brow. I give her a weak wave and an even weaker smile, and then I join Doug at his table.

I hate the glimpse of hurt I catch in her eyes, so I text her.

COOP

You may want to take the jersey off.

LIESEL

Why? Are we okay?

COOP

Houston...

She's piling her plate with fruit, but I see her look up. The hurt I saw earlier is even deeper now. But I don't have time to apologize or text or even do anything but widen my eyes. Because the representative from the Umpires Association is right behind her, wearing a big, huge Momma Bear of a fatherly grin.

He puts his hand over her eyes, and roars, "LEE!"

She drops her plate with a squeak, grabs his beefy hands, and then spins around. "Dad?"

They hug tightly, and I swear I'm not imagining the glint of violence on Bruce Fischer's face when he meets my eye.

"Did you see that, too?" I ask Doug.

"I think they saw it from space," he says. He grips my shoulder. "I tried to warn you."

He did. And in true Cooper Kellogg fashion, I didn't listen. I turned it into a game. A show.

Unfortunately, the only audience that matters is the one person I didn't want to hurt.

Liesel.

* * *

In case things weren't already dire enough, Bruce and Liesel Fischer join Doug, me, our coach, and a couple of VPs at the large round table. Bruce positions himself on Doug's other side, and Liesel joins him. That means that I can't even look at her without him seeing. It also means I have both Doug and Bruce staring me down.

Let me tell you something about umps. They wear those huge pads, so they always look bigger and more intimidating than they really are. You could get a guy who weighs a buck fifty, and in pads, he looks like a gladiator.

Bruce Fischer *without* pads is bigger than any guy with. He could be John Cena's body double.

I'm not kidding. The dude is huge. I'm six-two, and Bruce is a bit shorter than me, but he's easily got thirty pounds on me, all of it muscle.

I may be a showboat, but I'm always respectful with umps, with a few minor exceptions when I've been upset. And sure, one involves Bruce, but people get heated all the time. He couldn't have taken it personally, right?

Anyway, I'm polite with umps 99.7% of the time. I say hi when I come up to the plate, and if the pitcher throws something that seems outside of the strike zone, I ask, "Is that as far out as we're going today?" Or "Is that the edge of your zone?"

And most umps will say, "Yup, that's the bottom of the zone," or "Nah, we got a couple inches still, Coop."

And then I thank them.

I've been in the league for long enough that Bruce has officiated plenty of my games. He's the best ump in the league, with a 96.5% accuracy rating. He's fair, and consistent, and I've never seen him penalize a guy for getting frustrated with a call. Not even me.

Doug and Bruce greet each other like old friends, and then Doug says, "Bruce, you know Cooper Kellogg, don't you?"

"Of course," Bruce says. I stand up and shake Bruce's hand, hoping for the same fair, consistent treatment he's always given.

But I'm not dealing with a major league umpire today. He squeezes my hand with his meat hooks, and then he squeezes harder.

I don't make a squeal.

"Is that as far out as we're going today, Bruce?" I ask, holding his eye even as the bones in my palm creak.

"Nope. I got another six inches buddy," he says, murder in his eyes. "It's gonna be a long day."

That's code if I've ever heard it.

He's not going to make this easy on me.

When he sits down, I have exactly two seconds to tell Liesel everything I want to with my eyes. They're wide and wild and I hope it's enough to tell her how disappointed I am that our day has been ruined.

I can only assume I'm interpreting the way she twists her earrings and presses her lips into a thin line correctly: she's resigned to her fate.

"So, Coop," Bruce says when he's spread his napkin across his lap. "Why is my daughter wearing your jersey?"

"For the same reason Coop is wearing a face tattoo and my analytics team looks like they lost a fight with a Christmas tree, Bruce," Doug says. "They all lost a bet during their team builder last night."

You really are the best GM in history, I think to Doug. Not that he can hear my thoughts, but hopefully he can feel my gratitude.

"What was the bet?" Bruce asks. He takes a bite of a breakfast burrito, and even the muscles in the guy's jaw are intimidating.

"To see who would solve the most puzzles in the escape room. We all had wagers going," Liesel says, exaggerating slightly. She points to Todd and the rest of his team. Someone's wearing reindeer antlers and Todd has on brightly bedazzled glasses. Candace—wearing a Rudolph nose—seems a lot happier about Todd's glasses than Todd does.

"So who won?" Bruce asks.

"Me," I say … and then immediately wipe the smirk off my face.

"But you're wearing a ridiculous tattoo on your cheek," one of the VPs says.

"Your point?" I ask, and everyone laughs, including Bruce. Bruce's laugh feels more like the Grinch laughing at the pain of the Whos down in Who-ville, though.

"We tied," Liesel corrects me. "Coop—er," she adds. "*Cooper* isn't as dumb as he looks."

Bruce chuckles and looks at his daughter, and her eyes meet mine for only a fraction of a second. Just long enough that I think she wants her words back. Or maybe I'm hoping. I might have laughed about that when it was just us, but now, in front of my boss and the people who control my fate, it feels mean.

She drops her gaze to her plate, picking at food without putting any of it in her mouth.

Bruce turns on me. "Oh, I don't think Coop is dumb at all. I think he knows exactly what he's doing. And like any good umpire, I'll call him when he's out of line."

"So Bruce," Doug says, not so subtly changing the topic. "What does the umpire association have for the team today? You're not expanding the strike zone, are you?"

"No, it's a presentation on the automatic strike zone software we're testing in the minors, and if we have time, I'll do a Q&A on ambiguous calls." Then he pats his daughter's back. "But mostly, I came to hear Liesel give her presentation on her new load management software."

I look at a red-faced Liesel before I can remind myself I'm not supposed to look at her. I forgot she was presenting today. I only looked at the itinerary once, on my first day, and I didn't know who she was yet.

Has it really only been two days since we met in the airport?

The airport …

She must be presenting about the spreadsheet she was working on in the airport! I want to say something. Tease her. Do a call back to our first conversation. But Bruce Fischer isn't letting me get away with anything today.

Certainly not flirting with his daughter. Or even taking her mind off the fact that her dad's embarrassing her in front of the entire Firebirds leadership team.

"Well, we're glad you're here," Doug tells Bruce. "You're on in five minutes, right? Need a hand getting things ready?"

"Oh, no, I'm fine," Bruce says. He takes a long drink of water, wipes his hands and mouth with his napkin, and then gives his daughter a kiss on her cheek.

"Knock 'em dead, Dad," Liesel says.

I don't look at Bruce, because I'm almost certain he wants to do exactly that. To me.

"I'll walk you over to the stage," Doug says, standing and following Bruce. He turns his head and shoots me a look that's half apology, half warning.

When her dad is far enough away, I want to take his seat and talk to Liesel, take every spare second we have to clear the air, but she sits stick-straight and looks down at her phone.

I sigh in disappointment.

A moment later, my phone vibrates.

It's a GIF from Liesel of a guy with hugely wide eyes.

LIESEL

AWKWARD!

I chuckle and respond with a GIF of a man sweating profusely.

COOPER

You think?

I hear her breathe a laugh.

LIESEL

So, I don't know if you know this, but my dad thinks that every single man is trying to date me.

COOPER

He's not wrong.

LIESEL

Oh, stop. I know you're not trying to date me, but he doesn't.

COOPER

He's a smart man.

LIESEL

Ha ha. Anyway, I'm sorry if he's coming on strong. He gets a little overprotective.

COOPER

I hadn't noticed.

LIESEL

I didn't know he was going to be here today.

COOPER

I think he wanted to surprise you. It's sweet.

LIESEL

Yeah, so is antifreeze, and that crap can kill you.

COOPER

Are you okay?

LIESEL

I don't know. I'm presenting something I've worked hard on to my colleagues, and my daddy's here like it's my kindergarten Christmas performance.

COOPER

He cares a lot about you to go out of his way like this. But I can see what you're saying. I'm sorry it's not what you wanted.

LIESEL

Thanks. And I'm sorry I called you dumb. I didn't mean it.

So she *did* feel bad about it. Relief floods me, but that relief is making the truth clearer than ever: I like Liesel.

The team owner stands on the stage and welcomes everyone to the final day of meetings. Then he introduces Bruce, and Bruce's eyes find Liesel's. And mine.

I might like her a little *too* much.

* * *

My interest in Liesel only increases as she presents.

I'm not gonna lie: seeing her wear my jersey in front of a huge crowd is blazing hot. But seeing her captivate an entire audience with her mind makes that blaze hotter than magma.

Her "load management program" is a system for monitoring the stress on players that will help prevent injury. She has up a spreadsheet showing this past season, with some players in green, others yellow, and others—including me— in red.

"These are, to borrow a term from *Top Gun,* danger zones," Liesel tells the audience. Her dad is sitting back at the table with Doug and me, but we're both too riveted to play his little psychological game of cat and mouse. (Or at least I am. I bet Bruce Fischer could play it in his sleep.)

"This year was our testing year—thank you to the Nashville Outlaws for being our guinea pigs." We all applaud for the Firebirds Triple-A team. "Using wearable devices, we were able to monitor sprint speed and heart rate, as well as stress and player fatigue. With sensors and GPS, we also tracked game load, including swings, pitches, and fielding efforts. We measured playing time and the effect of various recovery protocols. And perhaps most importantly, we learned how to identify signs of overuse."

She presses the clicker in her hand and advances to the next slide. It's a picture of me. "Let's take our most famous example," she says. She turns around and points to my name on her back, and I can't help reading into the gesture. She could have pointed to me, putting me in the spotlight and, maybe, in the line of people's ire or disappointment. But instead, she kept the attention on herself. "We recorded every data point available from the season. We analyzed video from the playoff series leading up to his injury. We looked at the training and recovery reports. And plugging that into our load management program, we were able to show that Coop was in the red—the imminent danger zone—before we even made it to the playoffs."

This earns a hush from half of the room and the frantic buzz of a hornet's nest from the other.

A hand raises. "But we can't just sit out our best players during the playoffs."

"No, you're absolutely right. But, we can do a better job of balancing rest and training. And we could have done a better job rotating players when the matchup was favorable."

As she continues, Doug leans over to Bruce. "You must be proud."

"You must need to give her a raise," Bruce jokes. But then he looks at his daughter with a soft expression. "She's just like her mom."

When her presentation's over, I sit in the ballroom until it clears out. Her fans have scattered to their breakouts, and even her dad's doing a Q&A with the coaches and position coaches in another room. She's taken an undue amount of time unhooking her laptop and putting away her notes, but I've gotten the feeling that she was waiting out the last of them, same as me.

The room finally clears, and I spring into action, running up to the stage and planting my left hand so I can hop up easily. She looks around nervously and then gives me a smile.

"How was it?" she asks.

"You're even smarter than you are hot," I say. "And that only makes you hotter."

She rolls her eyes. "Enough. Was it okay that I used you as a case study?"

I lift an eyebrow. "You can use me anyway you want."

"Good, because I bought some new duct tape, and I'm curious how effective it is at sealing people's mouths."

"Ooh, a little light kidnapping. Color me intrigued."

She lets out a playful laugh. And then a sigh.

"Where are you off to next?" I ask. "Do you have a breakout?"

"No, I have a couple of hours until the next one. So I'm going to get a massage."

"Tense now that Daddy's here?" I wince and shake my head. "I didn't mean that to sound rude. I would do anything to have my mom travel to see me."

She puts her laptop bag over her shoulder, and we start walking. "She doesn't come to your games?"

"Uh, no. But it's not a big deal."

"Is she ... okay?"

I get what she's asking. Her mom probably missed tons of her brothers' games due to her illness. "She has a mental illness that keeps her from traveling. But it's okay. I'm not complaining."

Liesel stops me with a hand on my arm. "That doesn't sound okay. I bet that's been hard."

I shrug. "Everyone's going through something. But the Kellogg family is doing just fine. My mom is awesome. She does everything she can."

She smiles. "It sounds like you're a good son."

"I try," I say honestly.

At the ballroom's double doors, we stop. As soon as we leave this room, we'll have to separate. We can't be seen walking together, or the fallout from my boss and her dad could be disastrous.

"Have a good massage," I say.

"Oh, I intend to. Have a good … breakout? What are you doing next?"

"Whatever Doug tells me to do."

"Well, enjoy."

"Don't have too much fun without me," I can't help saying as she opens the door.

She rolls her eyes but smiles.

CHAPTER TWELVE

LIESEL

With my feet soaking in the tub at the pedicure chair, I check my phone and see no less than twenty messages from my brothers in our group chat.

I don't check them.

Instead, I snap a selfie and send it to Jules.

LIESEL

I'm officially taking advantage of the spa! Aren't you so proud of me?

JULIET

Holy freaking fruitcake. I never believed this day could arrive. It's a Christmas miracle!

How are you liking it?

LIESEL

You're supposed to stay stiff as a board for the entire massage, right?

JULIET

Hardy har har. Were you seriously too tense?

LIESEL

I relaxed eventually. It was nice.

JULIET

How did the presentation go?

LIESEL

Really well! But one guess who showed up to watch his little girl?

JULIET

He didn't!

LIESEL

You've met Papa Fischer.

JULIET

Oh, Lee. I'm sorry.

LIESEL

At least he didn't bring my brothers.

JULIET

No kidding. They would have tried to snap Cooper Kellogg like a candy cane.

LIESEL

Why? Nothing's going on.

JULIET

Girl, stop. Like I didn't see those pictures that were posted all over social media. You both look way too hot and happy.

LIESEL

Whatever. We're on opposite sides of the picture.

JULIET

He's literally looking right at you.

LIESEL

What? No he isn't.

JULIET

Have you SEEN the pictures?

LIESEL

Hold please.

Oh. Oh oh oh oh oh oh. I didn't see the ones Todd posted! I only saw the ones on the team account!

JULIET

Yeah, the team shared his pictures in their stories.

LIESEL

That explains why my dad tried to break Coop's hand this morning.

JULIET

Coop, not Cooper? I thought you couldn't stand the guy... ;)

LIESEL

What? Sorry, the phone's breaking up.

JULIET

HAHAHAHAHAHA YOU LIKE HIM

LIESEL

Gotta go! Relaxation time.

I put my phone down with a soft groan. I can't believe the picture Juliet is talking about: I'm grinning like a goofball and Coop is smiling at me like I'm the only person in the room.

It's out of context, obviously. It probably caught him mid-smirk, and it was just a good photo. Or a bad one, as the case may be.

I pull my phone out again and look at Coop's sharp jawline and the almost boyish smile on his face. It's not his usual crooked smile tinged with mischief, and it's not the one I saw earlier that I'm sure is fake. His countenance is open, and it's easy to study his features, to appreciate the fact that he manages to look both intense and masculine yet hopeful and boyish at the same time. With his gaze riveted on me, he looks *happy.*

He looks smitten.

He's not. But he looks it.

And that makes me flush from the top of my head down to the tips of my immersed toes.

"You know, people usually come to a spa to *escape* the world," a woman with a teasing voice says in the chair next to me. She's halfway through her pedicure and wearing a plush robe, with her auburn waves pulled up into a loose top knot. I can't make out her face through her clay mask, but her blue eyes sparkle even more than the massive diamond engagement ring on her finger.

And I mean *massive*. It feels like the kind of ring a rich athlete would give his wife when she found out he'd cheated. It's somehow stunning and borderline tacky at the same time.

She wiggles her fingers. "It's a little much, isn't it? The center stone was my fiancé's grandmother's, but he insisted we add all the … *zhuzh.* Personally, I think a six carat emerald cut diamond can stand on its own, but he wanted to make sure it 'really pops.'"

"He succeeded," I say. She chuckles, her cheeks stretching into a big, gorgeous grin. "Congratulations, by the way. When's the wedding?"

"Next month. And thank you." She stretches her right hand across her body to shake mine. "I'm Kayla Carville."

"Oh, I know you! You're the new owner of the Mullet Ridge Mudflaps, right? I'm Liesel."

Kayla's eyebrows lift a little, cracking the clay mask. "I've never been to a resort and had people know me because of a sport I know nothing about. This has been an interesting week."

I laugh. I don't know who the Carville family is *outside* of their recent purchase. "You don't know anything about baseball? Why did you buy a baseball team?"

My pedicurist has arrived, and she takes one of my feet out and starts massaging my ankle and heel.

"I feel like a broken record, but my dad bought it for me. He thought it would be a better present than ... anything else in the world, apparently."

"A dad who thinks he knows what his daughter needs better than she does, huh? What would that be like?"

"Cheers to that." She points her Perrier in my direction and takes a swig like the glass holds something a lot stronger than water. "I'm thirty-two years old, I'm marrying my boyfriend of six years next month, and I'm the Chief Sustainability Officer for one of the largest agricultural companies in the world, which he knows, because I work for him. What could I possibly need with a baseball team?"

"What did he say when he ... *gave* it to you?"

"He said I didn't seem happy and that maybe having a 'hobby' would help."

A laugh explodes from my mouth. "I'm sorry, how rich are you guys that he thought a Minor League Baseball team would be a *hobby?*"

"That rich, I guess." She shakes her head. "I tried to give it to one of my younger brothers, but my dad threatened to fire them and cut them all off. They've been sending me all sorts of 'helpful' tips, but frankly, they're twerps, and I don't want to listen."

"Brothers are *always* twerps. I have two—we're actually triplets—but everyone calls them the Fischer twins, like I don't even exist."

Her eyes snap to mine. "The Fischer twins? Fischer brothers? Where do I know them from?"

"Nowhere," I assure her, because if she doesn't know baseball, she definitely won't know a couple of minor league prospects. "But let me tell you, they act like they're the younger brothers and the older brothers at the same time." I launch into my rant, and Kayla nods and matches my experiences with experiences of her own, even though her pedicure is over. Her toes are red, but each of them has a Christmas tree on it, even her little pinky toes.

"And then yesterday," I rant, "someone posted a picture of me with a colleague, and my brothers sent me a million warnings that I'm 'not allowed to date baseball players.' I'm not even dating the guy. We just work together."

"Oh, is that Cooper … something? I wrote his name down. I'm having to write everything down with this blasted team. Cooper Kellogg!" she says. I grow warm. "You were the girl he was looking at all night long! That's how I recognize you. I sneaked into that cocktail hour the other night to see if I could get advice on how to run a baseball team. Cooper was the only one nice enough to talk to me, even though he couldn't keep his eyes off you."

I'm not just warm now. I'm burning hot. "There's nothing going on."

"Tell that to his face," she says. "Sorry, bad joke. If you say there's nothing going on, there's nothing going on."

"Well, let's just say we don't see eye to eye on almost anything."

"Does that mean I shouldn't take his advice? He said something about pitching winning championships."

"Fine, he's not *always* wrong," I admit begrudgingly. "Definitely take that advice."

She smiles. "You know, a little conflict now and then is good for a relationship. It means he cares enough about you to invest time into disagreeing with you."

She looks at the gaudy ring on her finger, and I'm tempted to ask her if she's okay. But before I can, an elegant woman pops her head around the corner, and her eyes land on Kayla. "Pardon the interruption, but sweetie, your stylist is ready."

"Okay, Mom. I'll be there in a sec." Kayla turns toward me, and she fixes me with her full attention. "Liesel, talking with you has been one of the highlights of my week. Thank you for letting me interrupt you."

"Thank you!" I gush. "I'm so glad I got to meet you. If you ever need baseball help, let me know."

It's a throwaway comment, but she takes out her phone, has me enter my number, and she texts me her contact info immediately. My phone vibrates beneath my leg, and I know it's dumb, but it makes me feel special. Something tells me making people feel special is Kayla Carville's superpower.

"Is there any chance you're looking to become a baseball general manager?" she asks with no trace of sarcasm. "Or maybe a coach? I evidently need both, because ours are terrible enough that my dad bought the team for peanuts. Another present I would have happily taken over a baseball team: peanuts."

I laugh. "I'm definitely not qualified for either, but please, text or call me anytime."

"I will." She gets up, and just before rounding the corner, she says, "Good luck with the overprotective men in your life. And if Cooper becomes one of them, I expect an update."

It's official.

I adore Kayla Carville.

I'm on an emotional high when I leave the spa. I feel refreshed, seen, and understood, and not even the constant reminders of Christmas can take that away. Hello, Christmas tree. Hello, oversized poinsettias. Hello, abominable snowman face tattoo—

"Coop!" I stop myself before almost crashing into him. He fumbles with his phone, and it falls to the ground. I bend down to grab it for him, but he beats me to it. I only catch a glimpse of the video he's watching—a drunk guy stumbling around like a fool—but Coop turns off the phone and puts it in his pocket.

"Sorry about that," he says. "I wasn't watching where I was going."

"Too many 'drunk fail' videos on YouTube?"

His laugh is weaker than I'd expect. I wonder if it's because we both know people are watching us now. And by people, I mean my dad. And my brothers, thanks to every fool with a phone who posts pictures of other people online. I look around the mostly empty hallway. A few people with conference badges are on their laptops or talking on their phones, but the meetings are clearly still going on.

"What meeting did you just come from?" I ask.

"It was a scouting session with Marty, but I had to run out to take a call. How was the massage?"

"Good."

"You know, I give great massages." He reaches near my hip, grabbing the hem of his—my?— jersey. It's not one he's worn before, but it has his name on it, and if elementary school taught me anything, it's that if someone's name is written on something, it belongs to them. That only applies to the jersey. Not *me*. "Next time you need one ..."

"Why do I get the feeling you've used this line before?"

"Because you're inclined to think the worst of me." His arch expression is challenging.

"Or maybe because I know your type."

"No type. I'm one of a kind, baby."

"GROAN," I say, pushing his chest. "You are such a flirt."

"I'm not a flirt."

"Oh, really? Tell that to the thousands of women you take selfies with."

"What, so I'm not allowed to smile at fans?"

"Like smiling is *all* they get."

"Why is that so hard to believe?"

"Because you're Cooper Kellogg. You've aged on stage. The whole world knows your exploits."

"Man, you go on two dates with Jenna Ortega ..."

"You dated Jenna Ortega??"

"I just said it was two dates!"

A soft bell sounds, signaling that the breakout is at an end. Coop and I both take a step back. "I'm going to go."

"Don't look up pictures of us," he says, backwards walking slowly away.

"Which us? You and me? Or you and *Jenna Ortega*?"

His playful look makes me smile in spite of myself. A couple of people walk between us, though, and the break in eye contact helps me turn away to go to my next session.

A moment later, I get a text.

COOPER

I mean it.

LIESEL

Like I care enough to check.

I turn around and see him turn to face me at the exact same time. I drop my grin as fast as it appears, though. There are too many watchful eyes, and I don't want him thinking I care. Even if the second I'm in my seat, I do, in fact, search for the pictures of him with his famous ex.

I only want to vomit a little, though, because then I pull up the picture of us from last night, and I don't care if it's just a good angle. He's not looking at her the way he looks at me.

CHAPTER THIRTEEN

COOPER

Why did Liesel's dad have to show up and ruin everything? Why does Doug have to have such stupid opinions about umpires not putting a target on players' backs? Why did I ever go out with famous women that Liesel could find online?

All through the next session—which Liesel happens to be at, mind you—she sends me screenshots of me with different actresses, musicians, and, okay, one model. One! But it's not like anything went anywhere with any of them. They were for publicity. And curiosity, because come on, these women are famous and beautiful. But do I need to be reminded that I once went out with a woman who wrote a song about "athletes who put the word player in player?"

It wasn't even about me! It was about some NBA jerk. But did that stop everyone from speculating? Besides, I was nineteen at the time. Nineteen year-old boys think famous people must be hotter and more interesting than non-famous people.

Stupid Cooper.

As if anyone could be more interesting than Liesel.

Her dad must be a mindreader, because every time his hot daughter texts me, he gives me a menacing grin that's only used by professional wrestlers and serial killers, probably. My guess is Bruce Fischer could be either.

After the breakout, I avoid Liesel. But Bruce doesn't avoid me.

"How's the arm healing, Coop?"

"It's fine, Bruce. Slow going, but my doctor's pleased."

"Tommy John's surgery is a rough one." He puts his arm across my shoulders, steering me in the exact opposite direction of Liesel.

"My next breakout is actually that way."

"No, it isn't."

He leads me down the hallway and stops just past a twelve-foot Christmas tree. The thing may be tall, but it's not broad enough to hide him.

"What are we doing, Bruce? My parents already told me about Santa—"

"Stay away from my daughter."

"Done."

"Not just today, in general. In perpetuity."

Annoyance flares in my chest. "I don't know if you saw the press release, but I'm on the injured list for the upcoming season. Doug has me working as a special assistant over *scouting*. Scouting and analytics work together. I'm not going to stop doing my job."

"You can do your job. And when the particulars of an assignment are over, you can keep your distance."

I might be a punk, but I'm not typically a hothead. I've hid my emotions for years, not letting my mom see my disappointment, not letting her think for a minute that I've ever been hurt.

On the ball field, I might be showy and larger than life, but I'm not impetuous or out of control. Usually.

"Bruce, you've been calling my games for a long time. What problem do you have with me?"

"My biggest problem is that you clearly have eyes for my daughter, and I don't want that life for her."

"What life?"

"You know what life."

"Spell it out for me."

"You have a stupid Christmas tattoo covering half your face. I'm not sure you can read it even if I *do* spell it out for you."

"Then you should try."

Bruce's eyes sharpen like knives. "The travel that keeps you away from your family. The stress to perform because you're always in the spotlight. The attitude that you're somehow better than other people because you're famous. The *temptation* that comes from being famous. How easy it is to give into temptation because you're on the road and think no one will know."

"Where I'm standing, you're looking pretty hypocritical right now."

"I'm not famous," he growls. "I don't face—"

"The only difference between your job and mine is which side of the plate we're on. You're on the road every bit as much as I am! You face constant stress. You've had to learn how to handle it without hurting your kids. Fans know who you are. Considering you still have all your hair and look like you could break their spin instructors in half, I'm gonna assume women find you attractive. What egregious sin have I committed that I'm not even allowed to *talk* to your daughter?"

"You're brash, thoughtless, and arrogant. You came into the League guns blazing, no deference to the people who blazed the trail before you. All you cared about was yourself. You wanted to make sure no one could possibly overlook you. I know the profile. Guys who act the way you act on the field don't turn it off when the game is over and the cameras are off; they turn it up."

"How I act on the field?" My voice is too loud, but I can't stop myself. "I'm a good teammate! I work harder and train harder than every person out there."

"Because it serves *you*! Because it adds dollar signs to your paycheck and followers to your TikTok! Do you have any idea what it's like to sacrifice what *you* want for someone else? To put their needs in front of yours? That's not you. You swing for the bleachers every time. You need constant attention. You put yourself first because all you care about is being seen."

"I care about being seen because I care about who *sees* me," I growl. His assessment is so unjust, it makes my lip curl and my eyes sting. "You don't know the first thing about me."

"I know what I've seen and what you've said."

"Now I get it," I say, a jaded laugh slipping out of my throat. "Your precious pride won't allow another person a single mistake. You think because you have ultimate say on the field, you have ultimate say in the lives of the people around you. You think because you're a good ump—and you are; you're the best—that you know everything and know what's right for everyone. But there's no pitch camera in the real world to hold you accountable. There's no association that can train you or correct you when you overstep."

His nostrils flare. "I took a red-eye to see my daughter."

"Yeah, and you did it for *you*, not for her."

Bruce looks like I punched him. "What are you talking about?"

The tone sounds. "It's the closing session. Excuse me." I step out from around him, bumping into the Christmas tree and knocking off an ornament. I pick it up and hang it back on the branch. And then I walk off.

When he says my name again, I don't turn. And when I see

Liesel in the closing session I don't sit by her. I do text her, though.

COOPER

Sorry for giving you a wide berth. I don't want to make trouble for you.

I put my phone away, but then it vibrates in my pocket. I shouldn't pull it out and check. I really shouldn't.

But I do.

LIESEL

I get it.

There. I explained myself and she said she understands. That's all that's required. We're on the same page, and the chapter is now over.

I hold my phone between my hands, pretending to pay attention. Pretending like I care about the rest of the world when all I really want is to know what's on the next page.

COOPER

When's your flight?

LIESEL

9 AM on Blue Horizon. Yours?

COOPER

9:26am on JetWays

LIESEL

Are you working Friday?

COOPER

Marty says I am, so yes. You?

LIESEL

Naturally. I work there.

COOPER

You know I do, too, right? I play in the same stadium you work in.

LIESEL

Play is exactly right. The offices are a different animal.

COOPER

Animal? Is Todd going to go feral on me?

LIESEL

COME ON, CANDACE.

COOPER

There's my girl.

LIESEL

I'm not your girl.

COOPER

That's not what the name on your back says. ;)

LIESEL

I really should have taken this thing off.

COOPER

Sure. Go for it. I'm watching.

LIESEL

Perv!

COOPER

Nice try. I saw that tank top peeking out around the shoulders. Do it. I dare you.

LIESEL

Wow. I didn't know it was possible for me to *want* to wear your jersey.

COOPER

Whatever you have to tell yourself, sweetheart.

LIESEL

The owner's speaking. Shh.

COOPER

You have a cute glare.

LIESEL

I'm not answering you.

COOPER

I appreciate the clarification. I was confused, you know, on account of you answering me.

LIESEL

SHH!

COOPER

Even cuter.

LIESEL

Does this mean that my dad's chat didn't scare you off?

COOPER

What chat?

LIESEL

Uh huh.

COOPER

SHH!

* * *

I didn't get a second with Liesel at the Christmas party last night, but I did get a *lot* of meaningful glances.

A few were even from Liesel.

The rest were from Doug and Bruce.

Man, that guy wants to kill me.

But the staff retreat is officially over, and I'm waiting at the airport for my plane. And because I can, I go into the VIP lounge and reserve a small private meeting room, where I can talk on the phone without a dozen people being able to hear me.

My mom doesn't answer.

That's not too odd. She doesn't *always* answer when I call. She's homebound, but she still does plenty of things throughout the day. She does Tae Bo videos or walks on the treadmill. She cooks and makes cool crafts. When I was in middle school, she became a wizard at decorating cookies and cakes. And she's even started gardening.

I call Dad instead. He answers on the third ring.

"Hey, Son!"

"Hey, Dad."

"Your mom didn't answer?"

"What, like I can't talk to my old man?"

"'Old man?' What is this, the 70s?"

"Are you hassling me for having a knowledge of pop culture?"

"No, I'm hassling you for sounding like a boomer."

"That's it. Where's Mom?" I ask, and he laughs. "How is she?"

"She's good. She spent the morning in the garden."

Moving two years ago was a herculean task for my mom. We planned it for half a year, made the master bedroom a safe haven that was decorated exclusively using things from our old apartment, and had her watch virtual tours of the new house daily. She got to decorate it slowly, picking out the flow that would be most comfortable for her.

It took her over a month to be able to walk into the backyard, but it's become an extension of the house—of a place she associates with safety. It was part of the reason I chose that particular house. It has a sunroom with floor to ceiling windows and a yard with tall, thick fences that project security. Every tiny step out of her comfort zone matters.

"And you won't believe it," Dad says. "She bought a virtual reality headset."

"Why? She hates video games."

"I know, but she's not playing video games. She's going on world tours."

"World tours?"

"She said if I get to travel the country in my new RV, she gets to climb the Eiffel Tower."

"What?" I laugh. "Did you get the RV?"

"I did! It's beautiful. Bigger than our old apartment."

I laugh, a fuzzy feeling in my chest. Dad has always sacrificed for our family. But somehow he's managed to sacrifice time with Mom so I can feel special, too. One of the best parts about my mom is that she doesn't begrudge my dad doing things without her. "That's awesome," I say. "But what's this about Mom climbing the Eiffel Tower?"

"The headset is incredible! I can't believe how immersive it is. She got on the stair stepper while she had on the headset, and she climbed the Eiffel Tower. She loves this thing."

"I'm glad! That sounds really cool for her."

"It is. And her favorite part is the MLB app. She's been going back and watching all your games."

A wrecking ball crashes into my chest, breaking my heart.

Absolutely shattering it.

I've never blamed her for her condition. I've done my best to understand and to accommodate her in every way I can.

But this hurts.

It destroys me.

I spent my childhood wishing she was healthy enough that we could do dumb things like go look at Christmas lights or have her take me to see Santa at the mall. But more than anything, I wanted her to come to one of my games someday.

I used to dream about it. *Literally*. I had a recurring dream of her sitting in the bleachers with my dad, cheering for me louder than anyone. I would wake up filled with a mixture of panic and joy. Panic, because I didn't want her to break down like she did when I was a kid. And joy, because she was *outside of the house*.

I haven't had one of those dreams in years. I stopped looking for her at my games before I even had braces. When Braden told me the other night that he saw my mom at the grocery store, I didn't feel a moment of hope, only annoyance that he would even *think* to say something so asinine.

My mom is amazing, but she doesn't leave her safe place.

And now, she'll never have to. She'll never have an incentive to try again.

I spent so many years wishing my mom could go out, and now she's found even more reason to stay in. She can sit on her couch and have her head in the stands.

"How were the meetings?" Dad asks, but my heart isn't in the conversation.

"They were fine."

"Just fine?"

"I thought we had a good roster worked out, but I got some news about the pitcher we wanted that doesn't look good."

"That's too bad."

"Yeah, it sucks. But that's the Show for you. Hey, I've got a plane to catch. Give Mom a hug for me."

"Okay, son. Love you lots."

"You too."

I throw the phone to the table in the small lounge meeting room and run both hands over my face. My plane hasn't even started boarding yet. I have at least a half hour before it will.

I almost forgot about the text I got from my old teammate, Jake Rodgers, yesterday. Jake is the only guy I've played with who can out-bravado me. He's a fantastic player, and it's a good thing, because he's a loudmouth and an *actual* hothead. He doesn't care what anyone thinks of him, and he doesn't mind picking fights. If a pitcher even gets a fastball near his chin, the guy's storming the mound.

He's the bad boy of baseball.

I like him, but most people don't agree with me.

Including the idiot who picked a fight with him at a private party last night. None other than Colt Spencer.

I watch the video again. Jake is talking to a pretty woman with olive skin and jet black hair, and she's twirling the hair around her finger. The camera moves off them quickly—it looks like the video's from someone recording the atmosphere, not Jake—but then you see Colt storm through the shot, and the phone pans back to him. He pushes Jake away from the woman, Jake stumbles against the bar, grabs someone's shot and drains it, and then punches Colt in the face like they're in a movie. Colt lunges at Jake, but Jake jumps out of the way at the last second, causing Colt's hand to crash against the bar top. He crumples to the ground, clutching his hand and screaming.

He broke it badly enough to need surgery.

JAKE

His girlfriend told me they can't do the surgery until the swelling has gone down. It'll be at least a week until then, and anywhere from 8-16 wks recovery

What a clown.

COOP

Only you could flirt with the guy's girlfriend, get into a fight with him, get his girlfriend's number, and insult *him* about it.

JAKE

Don't sell yourself short, bro. You just gotta believe in yourself and this could be you.

Jake doesn't know we're trying to acquire Colt, and it's not like I'd tell him team secrets. He sent me the video because he and I agree that Colt is a huge tool, and he thought I'd get a good laugh out of it. I probably would, too.

If it didn't impact my team.

If it weren't going to upset Liesel.

I didn't have the chance to tell anyone about it last night, but I have twenty-six minutes until my plane starts boarding. I dial Doug.

"I'm sorry to ruin your Christmas, Doug …"

CHAPTER FOURTEEN

LIESEL

"Do you know what was even more fun than my dad coming to watch me deliver a major presentation to my entire organization in front of the owner?" I ask Juliet. I got home earlier in the day, but she got home from her shift at the hospital at ten p.m., an hour ago. "Him asking my boss on the flight home if he can trade her seats because he 'misses his baby girl so much.' Those are his exact words. *To my boss.*"

Jules clutches her stomach, whether from actual pain due to all the ice cream we've eaten or from laughing herself to pain, I'm not sure. "No, Papa Fischer! Bad!"

"I know. And you should have seen the way he acted around Coop. He was like the Joker, or something. It was so humiliating."

It's late, but my body was starting to adjust to Arizona's earlier time zone, so I can't sleep. And because Jules doesn't work tomorrow, we're halfway through watching the *Twelve Dates of Christmas* while we talk.

I don't love Christmas movies anymore, but this is one my mom and I watched together a lot. And the fact that I'm mostly talking to Juliet rather than watching makes it slightly more tolerable.

"How did you leave things with Coop?" I show her the texts, and I watch her grin grow and grow some more. Then I pull up a picture I sneakily took of him yesterday with his ridiculous face tattoo.

"What is going on here?" she asks. "Is that a Yeti tattoo?"

"Yes," I giggle, taking back my phone. "He's so much goofier than I expected, but he can also be surprisingly level-headed."

"Lee, what are you gonna do? You like Coop."

I rest my head on the couch and yawn. "I'm not allowed to like Coop."

"You're allowed to like whomever you want to like."

"Fine, I'm not allowed to *date* him. And honestly, I don't even know if I want to date him. He's still Cooper Kellogg, the guy who's dated half of the female A-list celebrity population. He's still an arrogant hotshot."

"Whatever you have to tell yourself."

"I don't have to tell myself anything!" I protest. "Why should I go down a road I already know is a dead end?"

"Because it might actually be a cul-de-sac. And everyone knows those are prime real estate."

* * *

Coop and I text so much at work the next day, we may as well share an office. I only see him once in a hallway with Doug, and we share a friendly smile.

"Hi Doug," I say. "Hi Coop."

Doug smiles and looks at Coop, who keeps his expression neutral.

"Hey, Liesel," is all he says. But when we pass, he makes sure his pinky grazes mine, and I feel the tingles for the rest of the day.

This goes on for the next two weeks.

TWO.

WEEKS.

Every day is a study in comportment, discretion, and restraint.

Especially restraint.

Doug can't know we're talking. He can't see us together.

Fortunately, he also can't read our texts or hear more than half of a phone call either of us takes.

Coop calls me a *lot*.

"Hello?" I answer while I'm running numbers on potential high school draft picks.

"Well hello, Ms. Fischer. You look beautiful today."

I glance around to make sure no one's walking by my door. "Can I help you with something?"

"Sugar Plum, you could help me with a lot."

"Why are you like this?" I ask, smiling and wrapping the phone cord around my finger like a girl in an Eighties movie.

Kathy walks by and I pull my finger out fast from the cord and give her an awkward wave, hoping she doesn't notice my flush.

"You mean smart and sexy?" he asks. "It's a blessing and a curse."

"The latter, mostly."

"So you admit I'm smart and sexy?"

"Did I?"

"You didn't deny it," he says. "But I do have something I need to talk to you about."

I open a different tab. "The high schooler out of Montana you and Marty have been looking at, right?"

"No. This is way more important."

"The fact that Doug hasn't made any announcements about our pitching? What's going on there?"

"I don't know."

"You haven't heard *anything*? Not even about my brothers?"

"The extended roster isn't set till Spring Training," he says. His voice sounds a little pinched, but he clears it. "Remember, there are a lot of moving parts."

"Well, I wish this part would stop moving and get settled already."

"Hey, your brothers will be okay. They're top prospects with a major team. Things will work out."

I exhale. I've been avoiding them since I got back, and not just because of Christmas. Because of baseball. I still feel racked with guilt that I didn't advocate more for them, but the compromise plan Coop and I settled on is better for the team: trade for Colt Spencer, keep our veteran pitcher, and add my brothers to the extended roster. That will give them chances to actually play this season when a regular pitcher gets injured or we have a double-header. Coop is right. They'll be okay.

"Okay, so what's the important thing you needed to talk to me about?"

"This 'Throwback Thursday' picture of you from ninth grade that your brothers posted on social media. You look hot in braces."

"I looked insane. And you can't follow my brothers on social media!" I hiss into the phone. "They'll know something's up!"

"Their profiles are public, and I'm following under my private account. You know, the one *you* follow."

I redden like I'm sitting in front of a space heater.

In the weeks since we've been home, our communication has only ramped up. He followed me on social media under his private account that first night back, and we've both done extensive background checks by this point. I've looked at all of his posts—literally thousands—dating from before he was even on MLB's radar. Pictures of him with his parents in what looks like a small apartment, but it's cozy. There are countless posts of Coop in front of a beautifully decorated cake celebrating this win or that tournament. I assumed his mom bought them at first, but then I saw pictures of her and Coop baking together, even decorating some of the ornate cakes and later cookies together. Celebrating everything *Coop* seems to be the theme of his mom's life.

A couple of weeks ago, I probably would have seen his mom's doting as a contributing factor for his arrogance.

Now, I know how sweet it really is.

In scores of photos, he's beaming in front of banners, balloons, and streamers, all in that same small apartment family room. There are pictures outside of the house, too. Some with his friends and teammates, some with his dad, some selfies. But the pictures with his mom are only *ever* at home.

Then, within the last two years, the pictures with her shift from that apartment to a bright, beautiful home. The furniture is identical to the furniture in the apartment at first, but the most recent pictures show some changes. What hasn't changed, though, is that big smile Coop wears when he's with her. I can't tell if he's the happiest version of himself with her or if he's determined to look like the happiest version of himself with her.

I'm gripped with curiosity daily. I press him for info when we text at night, but he isn't as forthcoming as I'd expect.

At the same time, I'm riddled with nerves, knowing Coop is liking and commenting on photos of me with my family. I'm worried my dad and brothers will notice that he's gone back through my posts. But that's dumb, isn't it? It's not like *they're* going back through my stuff to see if Coop is. And his private profile isn't under his name, anyway. It's a baseball moniker—@can_of_corn96—referring to an easily caught pop fly.

He especially likes the pics with my mom and me. Everyday, he screenshots a new picture and sends it to me with comments. He sent one, "You're her mini me!" text, but then he added, "On a scale of 1-10, how awkward is it that I have a crush on your mom?" and I laughed enough that the comment didn't sting the way it normally does.

"I can't comment on fan photos," I say as Doug walks by my office. "You have the wrong number."

"Wow. It's like that, is it?"

I snort. "It is, in fact."

"Then let me get to the point. We need to go on a date."

"Do we?"

"Like Santa needs Rudolph in the middle of a blizzard."

"I thought we weren't ... doing that," I say.

"By that, you mean dating? I've asked you out fourteen times in fourteen days," he says. "We both know *we* are on different pages."

"I thought you wanted to be careful."

"Careful, sure," he says. "I won't make out with you at home plate during the middle of work. In a broom closet, on the other hand."

"Are you trying to get me fired or yourself killed?"

"We both know Doug won't fire *you*. And I have nine years left on my contract."

"So it's a death wish then?"

"There are worse ways to go."

Coop is incorrigible.

I am intensely attracted to that part of his personality.

I never went on a single date in high school. Not one. Even with my mom encouraging me to go to dances or try to put myself out there, the threat of the Fischer Men was too much.

College wasn't much better, because my stupid brothers

were there with me, and they made sure everyone knew I was off limits.

I went on a handful of dates then. I even managed to sneak in a few kisses with some accounting majors and an engineer, but let me tell you: not one of them played a sport. And none of the guys I've dated since have, either. Athletes are trouble.

I just wonder if it's the good kind, or not.

"Keep dreaming, Buddy," I say.

"I will, Sugar Plum."

* * *

The day before Christmas Adam—December 22nd—I'm in my apartment pulling up a sugar cookie recipe, when I get a new text from Coop. It's a photo of me at my kindergarten Christmas recital. I have pigtails, an emerald green velvet dress with tights, and I'm playing the triangle.

COOPER

Little Liesel is biiiiig cute.

LIESEL

Didn't I say you're not allowed to look at Throwback Thursday posts??

COOPER

Too late. You are *working* this triangle. It's my new phone wallpaper.

LIESEL

Tell me you're lying.

COOPER

But *that* would be lying.

LIESEL

You're lucky I haven't made my wallpaper the picture of you with those jingle bells stuck in your nose.

COOPER

You *should* make that your wallpaper. That picture is solid gold.

LIESEL

Why haven't you posted it to your public page, then?

COOPER

IDK. Baby Coop was so heartbroken.

LIESEL

Aw. Your face was so red from crying. :(

COOPER

I thought it would make my mom laugh. I had big visions of walking around the house tricking her into thinking Santa was coming. She laughed at first and sent the video of me jingling and jangling to my dad. But then when she told me to get them out and they wouldn't, she panicked.

LIESEL

That's hilarious. Poor Momma. Did she take you to the hospital?

COOPER

No. That's part of why she panicked. My dad used to be a long haul trucker, so he wasn't home to take me. Her social anxiety kicked in kind of hard.

LIESEL

I'm sorry.

COOPER

It's okay. She searched for what to do and found out if she blew air hard through my mouth, they'd pop out on their own. Disgusting, but it worked.

LIESEL

Haha. That's nasty, but sweet. I want to give Baby Coop a hug.

COOPER

Nah, Baby Coop thought girls were even worse than snotty jingle bells.

Big Coop would take one, though.

LIESEL

You do not quit, do you?

COOPER

Not since I met you.

GIF of man biting his lip

LIESEL

snort

COOPER

What are you doing right now?

LIESEL

I'm about to start baking for Christmas Adam.

face palm emoji

COOPER

You're baking Christmas stuff and didn't invite me?

LIESEL

Jules and I were going to make them, but she got called in to work. #ERNurseLife

COOPER

Liesel Dance of the Sugar Plum Fairies Fischer. Invite me over now.

LIESEL

Why?

COOPER

Have you not looked through my instagram? Christmas is my middle name! And I'm a WIZARD at baking. A North Pole Elven Wizard.

Elvish?

Elverino?

LIESEL

Elverino for sure.

Isn't all that baking your mom?

COOPER

She taught me everything she knows. I'm not kidding. Send me your address.

LIESEL

You are to use this for emergency purposes only ...

Twenty-five minutes later, Coop is standing in my kitchen.

Cooper Christmas Kellogg is standing in my kitchen, wearing jeans and a gray sweatshirt that says "Wanted: The Wet Bandits," along with mugshots of Harry and Marv from *Home Alone.*

My mom got my brothers and me that same sweatshirt two Christmases ago.

If the situation weren't so dire, I would let myself panic. I would overthink inviting him over. I would feel the rising swell of grief and loss, and I would distract myself and shut the feelings out completely.

But this is Coop, not my brothers. There's no baggage with him. He doesn't remind me of my mom and everything I miss. If anything, he makes me wonder if I'm not missing something else, entirely.

Like how imposing yet natural his buff, six-two figure is in my kitchen.

"I see you're wearing my hoodie," he says, putting his hands in the oversized pockets and tugging me forward.

It would be so easy to kiss him, I think as I look at his lips.

"I wanted to make sure you remember that I own you," I say archly.

His eyebrows shoot up. "Really? That's what you think this gesture says?" he asks, raking his eyes over me.

Holy freaking fruitcake, is it ever hot in here.

"So about those cookies," I say, stepping to the counter so I can create enough space between us to breathe.

Coop joins me at the kitchen counter, close enough that our arms are touching. It's a decent sized space, and I have all the ingredients out and ready.

"All right, what do we have going on here? Classic sugar cookie recipe?"

"Yup."

"Give me an apron, and let's go to work."

"You want an apron?"

"What am I, a boxcar hobo? Of course I want an apron." He turns his baseball hat around, and I want to run my fingers through the hair that peeks out. "Do you not wear an apron when you bake?"

"Never. It's flour. Who cares?"

"I never pegged you for an outlaw, Sugar Plum."

"An outlaw? It's an apron."

"I notice you have no problem with me calling you Sugar Plum."

I close my eyes but laugh. "Can we just bake?"

He opens the small pantry closet and puts on Juliet's apron. It's red with white frills and says "Mrs. Claus" on it. (Yes, Nate has one in his apartment that says "Mr. Claus," although it lacks the frills.)

Coop grabs one of our kitchen towels, and the next thing I know, he's standing behind my back, putting his arms around me. He bends his face right next to mine, and I glance back at him, trying to remember how to breathe.

"What are you doing?"

Then he ties the towel around my waist, giving me a mock half-apron. His thumbs skim against me, and even though a layer of thick cotton separates his skin from mine, I feel the heat of his touch like it's direct contact.

"There," he says, his words puffing deliciously against my ear. "Now we're ready to bake." He pats my hips, and I sway. "Don't worry. I'm with you."

I'm not sure if that's the most comforting thing any man has ever said to me or the sexiest.

But as Coop gets to work creaming the butter and sugar, I think it may be both.

CHAPTER FIFTEEN

LIESEL

An hour later, the dough is chilling, and Coop has made two other types of cookie dough while we're waiting: melt-aways and gingersnaps.

"It doesn't feel like Christmas until I've eaten gingersnaps," he says. He rolls the dough into a ball and then hands it to me to dip in sugar. At first, the touch of his skin sent a thrill through me that zinged all the way to my chest. Now, every time we touch or graze each other, it feels familiar, but wonderfully so. Like that sigh of relief and acceptance you feel when someone hugs you.

"That's how I feel about my mom's nuts and bolts," I say.

"What are those?"

"They're like Chex Mix. You know my mom was Canadian, right? Nuts and bolts is the Canadian version. They use different cereals there—Shreddies instead of Wheat Chex and Crispix instead of the other kinds. It's my favorite snack in the world."

"I love Canadian chocolate," he says, handing me another rolled ball of dough. "Whenever I play a game in Toronto, I fill my suitcase with Canadian Smarties and Aero bars."

"Oh, Aero," I say with a sigh. "But you haven't lived until you've tried Crunchie bars. And Hickory Sticks!"

Soon, I'm telling Coop everything about Canadian goodies and my favorite parts of Canada, including Banff and Waterton National Parks and the Canadian side of Niagara Falls. And the more I talk, the easier it is to mention my mom without my throat threatening to close.

"Half of my mom's family lives in the US now, and half are scattered across Canada. But everyone gets together for Christmas Adam—that's the Stewart family way. They'll fly in just for Christmas Adam and take a flight home on Christmas Eve so they can spend the rest of the holiday with their in-laws in Edmonton or Toronto. We used to take turns flying to the different families' houses, but when my mom got sick, everyone started coming to Chicago. My uncle transferred for work so he could be nearby, and everything."

"Wow," Coop says. "I can't imagine everyone traveling like that. We've never traveled anywhere for Christmas. My parents are both only children, and so am I."

My brothers are twerps, to steal Kayla Carville's word, but I can't imagine life without them. My heart clenches imagining Coop and his parents in their little apartment by themselves year after year. That's probably patronizing to even consider, though. "That sounds lonely. But cozy."

"You just summed up my childhood," he says. He takes the sugar cookie dough out of the fridge and swaps it for the rolled gingersnaps. Then he spreads flour all over the counter and starts rolling out the dough with the efficiency of a pastry chef.

"You really *are* an elverino wizard," I laugh.

He grabs a pinch of flour and flicks it in my face.

I sneeze. "Rude."

"I can call myself an elverino wizard. It's offensive when you do it."

I grin, but it softens into something sweet and a little sad as I watch him press an angel cookie cutter into the dough. "My mom collected cute angel figurines, and that cookie cutter was her favorite. We made cookies with it a lot when I was little. I called them Guardian Angel cookies, but my brothers called them Herald cookies."

"Harold? Who's Harold?"

"Like 'Hark! The Herald Angels Sing,'" I say.

Coop sighs like I've just said something sad. He wipes his hands on the ruffly red apron. Then he puts his strong arms around me and pulls me into a hug. "Herald Cookies is such a better name than Guardian Angel cookies. I'm sorry, but I have to give it to your brothers on this one."

I laugh, resting my cheek on his chest. "Whatever. Guardian Angel cookies is cute."

"It's basic. Bush league, even," he says, smoothing my hair like I'm sobbing instead of laughing over cookie names.

"Was this just an excuse to hug me?" I ask.

Coop leans us to one side and then to the other, his arms firm around my back. "Do you even have to ask?"

No, I did not. I don't mind the confirmation, though.

The oven beeps, and Coop gives me one final squeeze before releasing me. "Thanks for letting me come bake with you. This is the first time in my life I haven't been able to bake with my mom during the Christmas season. I didn't realize how much I missed it."

"I know exactly what you mean," I say.

By ten p.m., I have three dozen gorgeously decorated sugar cookies, four dozen melt-aways, another four dozen ginger-snaps, and flour on my nose.

Oh, and Cooper Kellogg's arms around me.

"Thanks for coming," I say for the tenth time.

"Thanks for letting me invite myself over," he says for the eleventh.

I think it's my turn to thank him again, but I'm starting to get lost in his spiced sandalwood cologne. This may be the longest I've ever been hugged, and I can't seem to find the motivation to end it.

That is, until I hear the key jiggle in the lock. I back up from Coop just in time to see Juliet and Nate open the door.

Juliet's eyes fly between us. "Well, well, well," she says, grinning like a cat who just caught a mouse eating forbidden cheese.

Not forbidden. Just cheese. Regular, old, totally normal cheese.

"Hey," Coop says. "You must be Juliet and Nate. I'm Coop."

"Good to meet you," Juliet says, sprinkling innuendo in my face like its flour.

Coop drops his eyes to Juliet's gray sweatshirt—it has a calico cat sitting in a stocking, and on it is written the words, "The stockings were hung by the chimney with cats."

Coop's eyes alight. "That is the best sweater I've ever seen in my life."

"Tell me about it," I say. "It's almost enough to convince me to wear Christmas sweaters. They don't sell it anymore."

"I can't imagine why," Nate says wryly.

But Juliet has triumph written all over her face. "Told you. Best sweatshirt ever!"

Nate chuckles at his fiancée and then shakes Coop's hand and they exchange pleasantries.

"Are you just leaving?" Nate asks.

Coop gives me a regretful look that makes me lean forward on my toes toward him. "Yeah, I have to be up early for rehab."

"Coop!" I tsk. "I forgot about your elbow. Are you okay? I shouldn't have had you rolling all that dough."

"Is that what the kids are calling it these days?" Juliet asks.

"Come on, Jules," Nate says with a laugh. He pushes her into the apartment, giving Coop and me a semblance of privacy. "It's nice to meet you, Cooper. It's snowing, so be careful on your drive home."

Coop thanks Nate, who joins Juliet on the couch, and then he smiles at me. The Christmas tree lights reflect in his brown eyes, dozens of points of light twinkling as he looks at me. "My elbow was fine. I would tell you if it was acting up."

"Do you promise?" I ask, which is silly, because we're just friends. With feelings. Friends with feelings. Which is nothing like friends with benefits.

"Of course. I'll always be honest with you."

"Are you sure? I don't want you hiding the fact that you're in pain because you're worried about *my* feelings."

He rubs my shoulders over my hoodie. His hoodie. That I won fair and square.

"You're a tough cookie. I don't need to wear kid gloves around you, Liesel. I know you can handle the truth, however hard it is."

My lips curve up softly. His words are so simple, but they pertain to some of my most core values—honesty, trust, even empowering. If Coop is really promising to be honest, he's putting confidence in my ability to not only handle truth but manage it. I may have been my family's admin and my mom's backup caretaker for years, but I never feel like I can make decisions without their blessing.

Coop is saying the opposite. He'll challenge me, but he'll trust me, too. The meaning of his words pours into my chest, as warm and comforting as hot cider on a cold day. "Good."

"In the name of honesty, though," he whispers, "I should tell you that I really want to kiss you goodnight."

I breathe out. "I don't think my dad or Doug would be okay with that."

"I don't think I asked *their* permission."

My insides bubble with excitement. I want to kiss Coop

more than I've wanted anything in a long time. In three weeks, we've gone from nemeses to friends to … more.

So much more.

Kissing him would be a teenage Liesel's dream come true.

It would also complicate *everything*. Right now, we're friends. Friends who covertly flirt at work and who spend all night and weekend texting each other.

But if we kiss, what next? Are we going to date, in spite of my family's objections or Doug's? If I knew he was serious about me, if I knew this was a long term commitment, that would be one thing. But I don't know that, not for him *or* for me. The risk is too great. I'm not looking for a fling, and I'm not looking to rock the boat. Or the Christmas tree.

"I don't kiss on the first date," I say.

"You did, though."

"That was for the escape room," I say with a mock glower.

"As long as we're clear that that was a date and so was this." His eyes dance, and he takes my hand and rubs my knuckles with his thumb.

"Fine. I don't kiss on the second date, either," I say.

"If you want more dates with me, just ask, Sugar Plum. I'll add the third and fourth to my calendar right now."

I spin my earring and look at Coop's full lips, wanting so badly to throw caution to the wind. No one's here to see us—no one who wants to keep us apart, at any rate. But my dad and brothers and Doug are all lurking like shadows in my mind.

I haven't quite decided how much I care …

"How about we see each other at the charity event tomorrow before you get on the plane?" I ask.

"It's a date."

"Good night, Coop."

"Sweet dreams, Sugar Plum."

I close the door behind him and then walk into the family

room. I throw myself onto the couch, my head dangling upside down.

"Well, roast my chestnuts on an open fire," Juliet says. "Lee has it bad for Mrs. Claus." I look up to my friend cuddling with her fiancé.

"What?" I laugh. "*Mrs. Claus?*"

Juliet gives me a knowing look. "He's still wearing my apron."

CHAPTER SIXTEEN

COOPER

The second Liesel walks into the Feeding Futures warehouse, I can sense it.

And by sense, I mean I use one of my senses—sight—to spot her. Because I've been staring at the door for the last twelve minutes to make sure I can't possibly miss her.

"Hello, Ms. Fischer," I say, holding up a small, clear zipper bag. "I'm glad you could make it."

"Yeah, the snow's starting to come down, but it was still fine to drive in," she says. "What's the bag for?"

"You're not allowed to wear jewelry in the warehouse, so you can store your mom's earrings in here." She's never said they were her mom's, but her mom was wearing them in each of the social media pictures I've looked at. Even without seeing those, though, I had a hunch, considering I've yet to see her wear anything else.

She gives me a suspicious half smile. "You don't need to be quite so observant."

"I promise you I'm not with anyone else."

"Should I be flattered or scared?"

"Ask Jenna," I say as Liesel removes her earrings. "I didn't notice she cut her hair into a pixie cut between our first and second dates."

"Oh no," she laughs. "I wouldn't have given you a third date, either."

"I'm the one who didn't ask her out again." I hold open the bag, and Liesel slides the diamond earrings into it. I zip up the bag and put it in her outstretched palm, folding her fingers over it and holding her hand as long as she lets me. "I figured if I didn't notice she had a foot of hair missing, we weren't going to work out."

A small smile plays at her lips. She tucks the bag with her earrings into the back pocket of her jeans. I wrap a hairnet around her silky blonde hair, making sure my fingers skim across her cheeks and forehead way more than necessary, because I love the feel of her skin.

"Jenna's loss," she says quietly.

And those two words erupt like a volcano low in my gut.

"Does that mean it's Liesel's gain?" I ask, the need to kiss her crackling like a fire inside of me.

Liesel glances around us. This is a move I've gotten used to in the last few weeks. It's what she does when she wants to talk —wants to *flirt*—but isn't sure she should.

"You know, we probably shouldn't be seen together," she says. Her darting eyes drop to my mouth and then bounce back up to my eyes. "There are going to be a lot of photos at this event."

I pick up two Santa hats from a nearby table and fit one on her head and the other on mine. "They asked for no pictures on the warehouse floor." I keep my eyes on hers. If I look at her mouth, I'm going to kiss the heck out of it. "They'll take pictures at the end."

The pompom at the bottom of the hat falls in her face, and I move it to the side. "What about Doug?" she asks.

"His family left for Hawaii this morning."

"What about Juliet and Nate," a voice says from right next to me. I flinch and see Liesel's roommate wearing a hairnet and batting her eyes at us. Nate is standing behind her with a hairnet and an almost apologetic smile.

Liesel wrinkles her nose. "I forgot to tell you that Nate's the head of legal for the Cruz Foundation. And Feeding Futures is owned by the Cruz family."

"I'm starting to think *I* might be owned by the Cruz family," I grumble.

"Sorry," Nate says. I hold out my fist and he bumps his against mine. To Liesel, he says, "My family doesn't 'own' the charity, though. It's the charitable arm of our organization."

"What's the difference?" I ask.

"Semantics," Juliet says.

"It's not semantics. The distinction matters," Nate says.

"That's what rich people say when they don't want you to know they own everything," Juliet whispers.

Nate pinches her side, and then he and Juliet launch into a hushed debate while we join the throngs of volunteers to get instructions for the day's work.

Liesel's probably smart to be on the lookout for anyone who could snitch on us, but I can't seem to care. I stand closer than I should, bumping her arm with mine. I can't do the heavier routine activities, but I talked to the coordinator already and got assigned to a low-impact job.

When the coordinator finishes her explanation, she tells us that after every forty meals we box, she'll ring a bell. "So let's make those bells ring!" she says.

Everyone cheers and breaks for their different assignments. Liesel makes a move to follow Juliet, but I hook my arm around her shoulders and redirect her. "Actually, we're this way."

She grabs my hand on her shoulder, and for a second, I think she's going to hold it. But then she bumps me with her hip and spins out from under my arm. "Shouldn't I join my department?"

"Well, I can't do any scooping or lifting," I say, pointing to my scar. Her eyes tense when she looks at it. "So I've been assigned to label bags and boxes and organize volunteer stations."

"And what does that have to do with me?"

I put my arm back around her shoulders, moving past volunteers going another direction. This time, she lets me keep it there. "I explained that I would probably need to have someone on the team help, in case I overexert myself."

"How very responsible of you," she says.

"I volunteered you to help, because I figured you wouldn't trust anyone else to babysit me."

"No, I would not."

"See? I knew it. I'm sure your department will appreciate your sacrifice."

"If anything, I think they would want me to do everything I can to protect the team's investment."

"I hoped you'd see it that way."

When we get to our labeling station, there are chairs set up for two, and we get to work. Our arms bump into each other. Our thighs press against each other. We flirt and talk for the next three hours. Every once in a while, a worker rings a bell, signaling that another forty meals have been packaged. We cheer every time. The spirit in the warehouse is cheery and infectious, and Liesel is the happiest I've seen her since we met.

We've gotten to know each other well over the last few weeks of texting all night. Every new thing I learn deepens my feelings for her. I like that she loves cheesy disaster movies and considers *Die Hard* a Christmas movie. I love that she prefers the mountains to the beach (even if she's wrong). And when she tells me she can't fall asleep if her closet door is open, I feel an overwhelming urge to hold her.

"Let go," she says with a laugh when I try.

"Shh." I smooth her hairnet. "It's okay. I'm here now."

She shimmies out from around my arms and then adjusts her hairnet with a glare.

I love her glare. I want to pass it notes in class and ask if it will be my girlfriend.

Or Liesel could become my girlfriend. That works, too.

I peel a label from the sheet and put it on one of the sorting bags. "So is it a fear of the dark? Are we talking *Monsters, Inc* or *Dateline* level fear here?"

"It's never been as defined as all that. It's just one of the general fears I've always had."

"One of them?" The tenor of the conversation is shifting, but I can handle the direction. "Do you have a lot of fears?" She wrinkles her nose. "Like what?"

"Oh, gosh. I hate sleeping with my feet exposed. I'm still afraid of what could be under my bed. I refuse to look at mirrors at night. You name it."

"Falling? Collapsing while on an overpass?"

"No, not that kind of thing, oddly. More like the semi-irrational stuff."

"Do you still have these?"

"Yeah, but I force myself to confront them sometimes."

"To show you're stronger than your fears?"

"More to show myself that they're not real. Exposure therapy is the best treatment for anxiety." She grabs a new sheet of labels and a new stack of bags. "It was bad when I was little. My brothers got to share a room their whole lives. They'd claim they hated it, but I was in my own room across the hall. I kept my door open, and I could hear them talk every night. It made me lonely. I'm not saying loneliness *caused* my fears, but I never felt secure. I was the only person in the house who didn't share a room with someone, and it always felt like anything could happen to me and no one would even know."

"That's a heavy thought for a little kid."

"I know. I'd grown past the worst of it, but when I was thirteen and my mom got diagnosed, all those fears and superstitions came right back. I started wishing on the first star I would see every night—and it was pretty much always an airplane, because it's not like you can see the stars that well in the Chicago suburbs. I'd throw spilled salt over my shoulder, wouldn't step on cracks or walk underneath ladders."

Someone rings the bell, and we all stop and applaud for another forty meals.

A piece of her hair is peeking out of her hairnet, so I tuck it back under. "Little Liesel," I say.

She returns her attention to the label sheet, but her mouth is turned down into a slight frown that makes me want to protect her from everything that's ever scared her.

"How is it for you now?"

"Fine for the most part. But every once in a while, I'll just have this irrational fear hit me, or I'll spiral into anxiety, so I have to do some anxiety busting techniques."

"Oh, yeah. Love those techniques. I'm a big fan of progressive muscle relaxation."

"I can't do that one to save my life! The second I get past the top of my head, I'll realize my forehead is screwed up in concentration and I have to start over. It's all about the 5, 4, 3, 2, 1 for me."

"Grounding," I say. "Classic coping skill."

She smiles. "Do you have experience with anxiety?"

"I'll have anxious moments now and then, but I mostly learned about it by researching things to help my mom."

She nods slowly. "That's right. You told me she has social anxiety."

I nod. Michael Bublé serenades us over the drone of the

warehouse volunteers, singing about his dreams of a white Christmas. I've never dreamed of a white Christmas. I've dreamed about my mom leaving the house.

Don't think like that, I chastise myself. *You wouldn't feel that way if she were wheelchair bound. If she needed dialysis and couldn't leave the city. She hasn't found a treatment that worked. Don't you dare blame her for that.*

I move a stack of bags so I can label more. I should say something to Liesel, acknowledge her question. She's been so open about things with *her* mom, and she's the first woman I think I could talk to about my mom without it becoming a sob story, which I can't abide, or without her feeling upset with my mom, which I can tolerate even less.

I've never wanted to open up to a woman before. I've never told anyone a thing about my mom. Just mentioning the social anxiety is more than I've done with anyone else.

I want to tell Liesel.

But if I tell her, that's it for me. The first woman I tell about my mom is the last woman I plan to tell about my mom. Her condition isn't something to expose to speculation, anger, or ridicule.

I can't imagine any of those responses from Liesel. And that's one more reason I *want* to tell her.

Can I tell her already? After only three weeks?

We're both engaged in our tasks—peeling labels from the sheet and putting them on bags—but I've rarely felt so connected to someone else. Not just in this moment, but overall. Since our first exchange in the airport, I've been drawn to her. And since we called our truce and have become friends, I've felt an interest that defies explanation. I've dated famous, beautiful, interesting women. But none of them have held my interest like Liesel does.

I know that's easy to say. It's only been a few weeks.

It's tempting to think it's just infatuation. She's smart and funny and calls me on my crap, which I find maddeningly attractive. She's also stunning. Drop dead gorgeous. But infatuation is about only seeing an idealized version of someone, and nothing about my experience with Liesel has been ideal. I don't even *want* some glamorized Liesel. I like the messy one. The one wearing a hairnet and talking about having anxiety. The one who dry shampoos her hair for cocktail hour and still manages to look like the hottest thing since sunburn. The one who leaves flour on her face while she bakes in her sweats and big fuzzy socks.

I've seen so many glimpses of Liesel, but it's like seeing all the pieces of a puzzle and knowing the image they'll make versus actually seeing the complete picture.

I want the complete picture. Something tells me I won't get that if I don't open my mouth, though. My heart hammers at the thought, my pulse doubling just thinking of opening up, letting someone know how much I care.

If you don't care about anything, you can't get hurt by anything.

"We're out of labels," Liesel says. Her tight smile makes me think she agrees with my mental self-assessment: I should have opened up.

"I'll come with you to get more," I say, hoping she gets from this that I'm still willing to put forth some effort.

Even if that effort is going to an office ten yards away to get more sheets, bags, and boxes.

Yeah, that's weak even to me.

Everywhere, people are engaged in scooping ingredients into bags, boxing, and moving them. They smile and laugh, but they all work. Nate and Juliet look like they're in a rousing debate about something as they pack meals. They're both animated—Nate keeps spilling food back in the bins when he talks with his hands—and they look like there's nothing they'd rather be doing.

When we're back to our table, I ask Liesel, "So Nate and Juliet met last year because of … parking space wars?"

"Pretty much. Nate is our downstairs neighbor, and the old building gossip was always trying to set Juliet up with him. She never really knew him until they got stuck on our elevator during a blackout, though. Six hours and a near diabetic coma later, they went from hating each other's guts to falling pretty hard."

A chuckle sounds in my throat. "That sounds like some cheesy Christmas movie."

"Cheesy? No, that sounds like an *amazing* Christmas movie. And I hate Christmas movies."

I yank the label from her hand and put it on my bag, instead. "I think you *want* to hate Christmas because you're afraid of how it will feel if you admit that you love it."

She blinks several times at the bag in front of her. One hand reaches to spin her earrings, but she must remember they're in her back pocket, because she puts her hand down.

I meant what I said, but now I worry it was the wrong thing. Or too much of the right. I keep pushing her to open more and more while I'm not doing the same.

"So what is Nate like?" I ask, heading off whatever direction her thoughts were going. "I've only met a few billionaires before, but none of them would live in the Riviera Apartments in Pilsen. Or give their car to a friend just because hers was stolen."

"That's Nate for you. He's the most generous guy I know. He's also practically a doomsday prepper, so, you know, balance in the force."

I chuckle. "How so?"

"It's part of them having gotten stuck on the elevator. They're all about having Swiss Army knives and emergency supplies everywhere they go now, because they're both too afraid of losing each other. It's kind of romantic."

"And only slightly paranoid," I add.

She shrugs, looking at her smiling friend. "I think when you really love someone, you'll do anything to minimize the risks that could take them from you. No matter how paranoid."

"That's not how it works, though. No matter what you do, the other person still has agency. Or a condition that limits their agency. And that's to say nothing of accidents. You can do everything right, and something could still happen."

"That doesn't mean you don't try," she says.

I shake my head. "That way lies madness."

"It's not madness. It's love."

"It's overwhelming. You spend your whole life second-guessing yourself, constantly questioning every choice you make, worrying if you're responsible for other people's decisions, if you're at fault for every twist of fate. Hope turns into a fixation. Love becomes neurosis. It's too much pressure!"

Liesel gives me a sad look. "Is that how you felt? With your mom?"

I feel like I've just stripped naked and streaked across the stadium. "I don't know. I'm just saying."

"Ah, okay."

Stupid Cooper! Just open up!

A bell rings, and the volunteer coordinator calls us all back into the center of the warehouse.

"Looks like that's our call," I say.

She squeezes my hand and smiles. I smile back, all the way to my eyes.

So why does that make her frown?

CHAPTER SEVENTEEN

LIESEL

"Thanks to your efforts," the volunteer coordinator says. "We packed 400 meals for children and families this afternoon. Give yourselves a hand!"

We all cheer, and one of the coordinators rings a bell, adding some excitement to the feelings of love and warmth in the air.

The lights dim, and then a projector opposite us shows a video of the many communities the charity serves. We see kids eating the meals that have been provided, as well as artisans in those communities hand-making beautiful crafts. The crafts are bought by the charity and sold in the stores of every Feeding Futures warehouse to help further benefit those communities. Beaded wire-framed animals and wooden charcuterie boards from countries in Africa; ornaments from Costa Rica and Nicaragua; tea towels and threaded bracelets from Asia.

"My mom would love those," Coop says quietly.

"Which ones?"

"All of them," he says.

When the video is over, the coordinator gives us one last thanks.

"Two thousand years ago, the world was given the greatest of all gifts. Today, you have honored that gift by giving hope and joy to others. That is the true spirit of Christmas."

Juliet puts her head on Nate's shoulder, and he kisses her crown, and the feeling I've been ignoring since that dang cocktail party fights its way to the surface:

I want that.

And one look at Coop, with his crooked smile, tells me I want it with *him.*

The coordinator wraps up her message, and I grab my purse. "Hey, I'm going to freshen up quickly. I'm going straight to our *Christmas Adam* celebration from here."

"Is it weird that I wish I could come with you?" he asks.

"Always looking for a party, aren't you?"

His pinky brushes against mine, and then he locks them together. We're holding pinkies, and a snow flurry swirls in my belly.

"Not quite," he says.

I look left and right, but no one's paying attention to us. "You want to try my uncle's ribs that badly?"

"A man's gotta eat." His eyes are playful, but they don't hold their normal mischief. They spark more than twinkle, and it's the most dangerous look he's given me yet.

My eyes flit to his lips. "I'll be right back."

"I'll be here."

I run into a restroom and fix my hair. And by fix, I mean I pull it into a messy half-ponytail, half-bun, because that net did not do me any favors. I swap my volunteer shirt for a cute red cable-knit sweater. Mom's family always wears ugly Christmas sweaters, but I couldn't bring myself to wear one. This will have to do.

My mom would tut and tell me to celebrate. To live a little.

"You're allowed to have fun," she must have told me a hundred times.

"I *am* having fun," I'd tell her as I wrote the family calendar or made a grocery list with her input. "What could be better than hanging out with my mom?"

She would smile in her wheelchair. "You have to be the only teenager I know to ever say those words."

"Then other teenagers suck."

"Your brothers have never said that."

"My brothers suck."

And she'd laugh.

We had a variation of that conversation dozens of times. She would never have blamed me for going out with friends, but I knew even then I'd never regret the time I spent with her.

And I don't.

I miss every second.

I think about her as I leave the bathroom and walk to the market at the front of the Feeding Futures warehouse. I spot Coop checking out while I look at the ornament table. I may not like Christmas anymore, but I have a soft spot in my heart for ornaments. Mom collected them, but not in the "every ornament has special meaning" way as much as the "there can never be too many ornaments" way.

The idea of adding a new one makes my throat hurt.

Although, the ache doesn't throb quite as badly as usual.

"Can I also make a donation?" Coop asks the cashier. He's speaking quietly, but I'm close enough to overhear.

"Of course. You can input the amount on the screen."

I know I shouldn't look.

But I do.

Son of a nutcracker, that is a *lot* of zeroes.

I avert my gaze so he doesn't know I peeked, and my eyes land on an ornament that stops my heart. It's an exquisite recycled ceramic angel with beads and delicate wrought iron. Everything about the angel tugs at my heart, filling me with complicated emotions.

I loved working in Costa Rica. It was important for me to get away from my family personally and professionally. My time there was enriching, eye-opening, and humbling.

But now that I've had time to process, I can admit that last Christmas was by far the lowest point for me. I avoided coming home because I didn't want the pain of missing my mom. Instead, I got the pain of missing *everyone*.

I was alone with my grief, no matter how hard I tried to ignore it. The weight of it nearly suffocated me.

Somehow, this angel ties those feelings of loneliness, grief, and longing together, coupled with that humbling sense I got from my time there.

And, of course, it's an angel.

I run my finger along one of the wrought iron wings. The metal is cool and smooth, and as I follow the natural curves, I can feel the slight ridges from where the artisan painstakingly worked the material.

Coop joins me with a receipt and a large white bag. "Oh, is that one from Costa Rica?" he asks. "You should get it."

"The ornaments are gifts for donations," I say, putting it back. It almost hurts to let go of it. "I'll donate, but the top tier donations are a little out of my price range. This bead heart is beautiful, though." I pick up a red bead heart, also from Costa Rica.

"It is," he agrees.

"So, what did you get?" I look at his bag.

"Something from everywhere," he says. "I like getting my mom gifts from around the world. She'll love this stuff."

He smiles, and I wish he'd say something more. Elaborate. But he just smiles. It's not like he's shutting me out, but it's almost like he's pretending an entire wing of a mansion doesn't exist. And that tears my heart a little.

He told me he'd always be honest with me. He said I was tough enough to handle the truth.

So ... where's all that truth?

"Hey guys," someone from Firebirds management says. "The snow is hitting hard. The Feeding Futures people said they're closing so everyone can get home safely."

I check out quickly, making my donation and getting the pretty heart ornament from Costa Rica. And then we all head to the front doors. I see Juliet and Nate waiting for me.

"Hey, are you guys heading out?" Juliet asks.

"We drove separately, but yeah," Coop says.

"Be careful," Juliet says. Then she grabs my shoulders. "Do you still have the emergency supplies in your car?"

"Of course, Mom."

Juliet doesn't smile. "I mean it, Lee. Watch out, okay?"

"Okay," I say, and then I give her a hug. "You too."

"Nate drove the Hummer today. We'll be fine. See you back home."

Coop is talking to Nate. "Did they say anything about flights in and out of O'Hare?"

Nate shakes his head. "I didn't read anything about it. But if you need a flight, I'm happy to arrange for some help."

Coop snorts. "Don't tell me you own an airline."

"Don't be absurd. It's a single jet."

"My mistake," Coop says. Then he gives me a wide-eyed look, and I give him a pointed shrug that says *See? He can't help himself.*

We all bundle up, including putting on snow hats—toques, as my mom always said—and zipping up our thick coats. Then we brave the elements. The wind howls, and snow falls at a sharp angle.

"Bye!" Juliet and I call to each other. Coop and I run to our cars, which are parked on the same row, a few spots down from each other. He drives a gray Jeep Grand Cherokee, and the light is on. Did he already hit the unlock button?

"I wanted a better goodbye than this," he says when we reach my white Prius. "I'm going straight to the airport."

I throw my arms around him, hugging him tight. "Call me when you're taking off," I say.

"Can we go out when I get back?"

"Coop, I don't think we're supposed to—"

"I don't think I care."

My stomach flips. I'm not sure how much I care, either, but we're standing in the middle of a blizzard. "Call me and ask me out once you're home safe, okay?" I kiss his cheek, and he picks me up and lifts me so our cheeks are touching and my feet are dangling.

"I'm safe right now," he says in my ear.

I laugh and swat him. "I mean it." We let go and I give him my biggest smile. "Bye, Coop. Merry Christmas."

"It'd be a lot merrier if you said you'd go out with me!" he says as I unlock my Prius and climb in.

"You heard me!" I say. I close my door and then hold my thumb and pinky out like a phone and put them up to my ear, mouthing, *Call me.*

He mouths, *I will* and then runs to his Jeep.

I turn on my car, both happy and disappointed. I've engaged in so many different Christmas activities this month—the escape room, a work Christmas party, decorating cookies, and now a charity event (that I could do anytime of the year, but doing it at Christmas always feels more special)—and I was able to get through each without the pervasive loneliness that's plagued me since my mom died.

And it's because of Coop.

It's hard to believe how wrong I was about him.

He's not the selfish, cocky jerk I thought he was.

I'm about to back out when my phone rings with a call from Kayla Carville.

I put the car back in park to answer. "Kayla! Hey, how are you?"

"Liesel! I'm so glad you answered. I'm sorry to make this short, but I had to tell you the good news: I just offered a huge cash consideration for a trade I'm freaking out about, and I think the team's going to take it."

"That's cool! Who is it?"

"*Your brothers*! I'm getting them from the Nashville Outlaws, you know, the Firebirds' Triple-A team? Can you believe it?"

A chill sweeps over me. "You're acquiring my brothers?"

"Yes! I heard I needed to do everything I could to get great pitchers, so I'm offering an exorbitant amount of money to get them from their affiliate. I've had to talk to both owners, but apparently if you throw enough money at a problem, you can solve anything!" She laughs. "Isn't that exciting?"

"Uh … wow. My brothers are going to another minor league team! That's so unexpected!" I say with as much enthusiasm as I can feign. "How did you even hear about them?"

"Your friend!"

The chill becomes subarctic. "Cooper?"

"Who else? He put them on my radar the first time we talked, so *my* brothers looked into them, and they said he's spot on. Also, did you know we both have a brother named Logan?"

"You don't say?" My voice doesn't sound as weak as it feels, and I'm glad. Kayla hasn't done anything wrong.

Cooper Kellogg, on the other hand …

"Now you'll have a reason to visit me in *Mullet Ridge* next season. Go Mudflaps!" Kayla says. "And no, I can't believe I said the words 'mullet' and 'mudflaps' out loud, either."

My chuckle is faker than Cooper's 'honesty.' "That's … so crazy! I can't believe it." I say. "Listen, there's a big storm in Chicago, so I need to get on the road before it gets any worse.

But can we talk later? I really would love to chat when I have more time."

"Of course! I'll reach out after the holidays, and I'll definitely text you when the deal's done. Merry Christmas!"

"Thanks, Kayla. Merry Christmas to you, too."

I end the call and my anemic smile dies.

Coop told Kayla to acquire my brothers?

We had a plan! They were supposed to be added to the extended roster! They were going to have a rigorous training schedule this year so we could prepare them to get called up to the Firebirds! We agreed on it! We presented it to our GM! And he *immediately* went behind my back so he could get them out of the way. I guarantee if I call Doug right now, he'll tell me Betancourt—Coop's top pick—is signing papers.

The sense of betrayal is so deep, I feel like I've been hollowed out. Everything I thought about Coop over the last few weeks is a lie.

He's not thoughtful. He's not deeper and more considerate than I expected. He's simply a better actor than I ever imagined.

A knock on my window startles me. I put a hand on my heart and see the man himself, his face bright red from the cold.

I roll down my window a fraction of an inch. "What are you doing?"

"My Jeep died. I tried using the portable charger I keep in my car, but I must have left a light on, because it's too dead to even take a charge. Is there any chance you could take me to the airport?"

I want to say no so badly. I want to drive off, letting my tires spit snow and sludge in his face. Heck, I want to run him over. But as furious as I am—as hurt and betrayed and enraged as I am—I still have to work with this man for the next year.

And I need to give him a piece of my mind.

"Climb in."

CHAPTER EIGHTEEN

COOPER

Liesel's trunk is *packed*. She has a twenty-four pack of water bottles, a couple of boxes of protein bars, road flares, space blankets, a tent, flashlights, and I don't know what else, because there's also a full hiking backpack.

"It looks like you raided a Costco and a DICK'S Sporting Goods. What is all that?"

The roll of her eyes is the fluttering *give me strength* kind of eye roll, and it makes me feel like I'm missing something. "Juliet and Nate."

"Oh, right. The pipeline from the elevator to emergency preppers, right? That's kind of sweet that they're worried about you."

"They weren't worried about *me*. This was all in there when Nate gave me his Prius." She sounds almost hostile as she drives out of the parking lot. But of all the ways Nate has possibly overstepped her comfort level, at least this one is practical. Ish.

"It's nice that you have it, though. Aren't you the kind of girl who likes to be prepared for everything?"

"Of course I *want* to be prepared, but I don't know why I bother. No matter how much I prepare for something, I'm *always* blindsided."

Somewhere in the two minutes since our goodbye, Liesel has gone from hot enough to melt snow to frostier than an icicle. A pointed icicle.

I just don't know what the point *is.*

Or why it feels so *stabby.*

"It's cold in here," I say.

"We're in the middle of a blizzard."

"That's not what I mean," I tease.

We're stopped at a light. Liesel turns her head to me so slowly, it's something out of a horror movie. *Slay Bells Ring,* or *Slaying All the Way.*

I snort.

"Something funny?"

"I was just thinking of a good title for a vampire Christmas movie. Which is better: *Slay Bells Ring* or *Slaying All the Way?*"

"That's what you're thinking?"

"No good, huh?"

She exhales a word. "Unbelievable."

I look around me. "Did I miss something?"

"Nope." She pops the last syllable. Hard.

"I don't think that's true."

"What you think doesn't matter."

I keep looking around me. Have I entered the Twilight Zone? Has Liesel been body-snatched? "Are you okay?"

"Super."

"I can tell."

She does that breathy scoff again and gives a small shake of her head. Her eyes are fixed on the road. There's decent visibility, but the snow is coming sideways, and we're not even to the freeway yet. The way she's gnawing on the inside of her cheek makes me think she's debating something internally.

My phone buzzes with an alert from JetWays. My flight has been delayed. "Crap," I whisper. I'm putting my phone in my pocket, but then there's another buzz.

"Excuse me," I say to Liesel. "It's my mom."

MOM

Find a Friend tells me you're on your way to the airport!

COOPER

There's a flight delay, but yup. I'll be home before you know it.

MOM

I can't wait. It wouldn't be Christmas without you.

COOPER

Back at you. I made sugar cookies, melt-aways, and gingersnaps the other night. I blew my date away.

MOM

Date??

COOPER

Don't get too excited. I'm not sure she's speaking to me right now.

MOM

Well, if your cookies didn't win her over, she must have a frozen heart.

BTW, your dad and I have been watching your old games on my VR headset.

COOPER

You're loving VR, huh?

MOM

I am! I took a road trip from the couch the other day. Route 66!

I did not like driving through Texas.

Boring!

And we hit a deer.

I struggle swallowing. These experiences she thinks she's having aren't real. I can only imagine how hard the last twenty years have been for her, occasionally making progress just to backslide again.

This isn't progress.

It's a nail in the coffin of hopes and dreams I haven't let myself consider in years. Until now, I'm not sure I even realized they were still dwelling in the recesses of my mind. How do I respond to something she's excited about that's breaking my heart?

COOPER:

I'm glad VR is making you happy.

MOM

Oh, it is. I've loved all your games, especially that one against the Rockies. It felt like I was right there with you! Take that, Colton Spencer.

My thumbs hesitate over my keyboard. I don't hint at troubles in my life because I don't want to put more emotional burdens on her. I tell my dad, so it's not like I have no outlet, but Mom is safe from my regrets.

But a glance at Liesel and her flared nostrils makes me drop my filter. Whatever has upset her, it has *something* to do with me. And girl troubles require a mom's help.

COOPER

You know, not everyone liked me blowing him a kiss. Or the back flip at home plate.

MOM

Who cares what they think? You made that game so fun. You make baseball fun.

COOPER

Maybe I need to be more respectful.

MOM

To whom?

COOPER

Baseball? Fans?

MOM

What has you thinking this way? Did the team say something?

COOPER

No, just a friend.

MOM

Some friend.

COOPER

I'm serious. Maybe I need to stop being so showy.

MOM

You don't have to make yourself smaller for a sport that's been around for almost two hundred years. Baseball is big enough for you. If your "date" thinks otherwise, she's an idiot.

COOPER

She's not an idiot.

MOM

You're the best part about the game.

COOPER

You're nice, Mom.

Gotta run.

Love you.

MOM

Travel safely. I love you!

I put my phone away, feeling somehow even worse. I opened up the door a crack, looking for real advice, but my mom treats me like I can do no wrong, and I'm not sure it's always helped me. I used to worry so deeply that I'd caused her anxiety and agoraphobia. I would obsess over what I might have done wrong. Was it because I was such a turd in elementary that she always had to come down to the school to talk to the principal? Did all my trips to the hospital for possible concussions and stitches overwhelm her? Did my high energy simply drain the life out of her?

I sigh. I hate thinking about my old worries. If I'm not diligent, they'll flood back in, washing away my peaceful acceptance of my mom's condition.

I close my eyes and focus on regaining my "radical acceptance" of reality. Mom is sick. It isn't my fault. I can love her and accept her for how she is and not feel brokenhearted that she's living her life through a virtual reality set instead of making efforts to live it in the real world.

This is just how it goes.

It is what it is.

Whatever stupid, trite saying you can think of, insert it here.

My eyes open. Nothing is working.

"This sucks," I whisper to myself.

"Excuse me?" Liesel asks.

"Nothing. Just talking to myself."

"No, by all means, say it louder."

"It's nothing. My flight was delayed."

Her exhale speaks volumes. Unfortunately, it's in a language I don't understand.

"Do you wanna tell me what's going on?" I ask.

"Why don't *you* tell me?"

"Uh, I had a bad exchange with my mom?"

She makes a sound that's half scoff, half growl, and all contempt.

AM I TAKING CRAZY PILLS?

I splay my fingers, my forearms and hands so tense, they shake. Her irritation is like a contagion. But while hers feels sharp and focused, mine is broad and unspecified. Nothing but a huge, exasperated cloud of confusion. "What are you so mad about?"

"Like you don't know?"

"KNOW WHAT?"

She purses her lips, and her nostrils flare wide.

"Liesel! If something's going on, say it!"

"*You* say it."

The noise that issues from my throat is intelligible. It can only be expressed in special characters: ampersands, asterisks, and at signs.

And a crap ton of exclamation points.

"Why are you being so insufferably vague?" I say.

"I'M BEING INSUFFERABLE?"

"YES!"

"ME?" Her wipers are having to go so fast to clear the snow, they're almost a blur.

"OBVIOUSLY!"

"You *would* pretend you have no idea what's going on. Well, I only have two words for you, *Buddy*."

"That was like twenty words already."

Her glare is sharp enough to pierce armor. "Kayla. Carville."

I blink, wondering if I heard her right. "Huh?"

"Kayla. Carville."

"I'm gonna need more words."

"You know what?" she asks, gripping the steering wheel, her eyes on the taillights in front of us as we merge onto the freeway. "I'm glad this happened. I thought I had real feelings for you. I could have wasted months on you before realizing the truth."

"The truth of what?!"

"That you are *exactly* who I thought you were."

I bump my head on the dashboard. "Do I have a concussion?"

"Right. Blame everything except the obvious: you."

I snap upright. Her Prius is going maybe thirty miles an hour on the freeway due to the blizzard conditions. The storm outside can't compare to the storm in my brain.

"Liesel. I think it's pretty clear that I have no idea what you're talking about. If I've done something, do us both a favor and come out and say it."

"Fine, I'll say it. You got everything you wanted. You didn't want my brothers on the team, so you made sure Kayla Carville acquired them. You win."

"I repeat: huh?"

"Don't act dumb, Coop! You're a selfish tool, but you're not dumb. You orchestrated this whole thing so you could get what you wanted. We're probably not even signing Colt Spencer, are we?"

"No, we're not." Her mouth opens, like she's speechless. "But it's not what you're saying! I didn't tell Kayla to get your brothers! And it's not my fault we're not picking up Colt! The guy's an idiot, and all I did was show Doug—"

"You already talked to Doug? You are the most breathtakingly selfish man I've ever met! What was the point of us even spending that entire night working on the roster?"

"We were doing our job!"

"*I* was! *You* were playing me!"

"I wasn't playing you. And I still have no idea what's going on!"

She sputters. "I can't believe I thought we had something real. I can't believe I wanted to *kiss* you."

My ears perk up. "You wanted to kiss me? I knew it."

"How can you be cocky at a time like this?"

"Because I don't know what time it is!"

She shakes her head in tiny, rapid movements, breathing like she's trying to get her anxiety under control. I should feel sympathy for whatever she's going through, but I'm too confused, too annoyed, and too ... *angry*, frankly.

"I cannot get you to the airport fast enough," Liesel says.

"No, you can't," I agree.

"If I have to be stuck in this car with you for another minute, I'm going to scream."

She takes her eyes off the road for only a second, so I see the red taillights in front of us a split second before she does.

"Look out!" I yell.

Liesel slams on her brakes to keep from colliding with the other car. She skids, one tire hitting ice, the others gripping the road. The motion causes her to fishtail a few feet, but she manages to stop before crashing. She's at an odd angle, taking up most of the lane. But at least she stopped a few inches shy of the car in front of us.

"Nice save," I grumble.

Red brake lights stretch before us as far as the eye can see. The visibility isn't great, but it's enough to show me that all three lanes going our direction are at a total standstill.

"Look up the traffic on your phone," she says.

"Maybe don't tell me what to do," I say, even as I do as I'm told. But only because I was going to, anyway. I pull up my maps app and groan painfully.

"There's an accident up a half mile. The road is closed."

"WHAT?"

She throws the Prius in park and grabs my phone from me, reading the user-generated comments about the crash.

"'Multi-car pileup ahead. Expect a long wait.' 'All lanes blocked. Avoid if possible!' 'Just passed the scene. Looks like a semi jackknifed. At least 20 cars involved.' 'A bus is blocking the exit ramp—no way out!' 'It's going to be a cold night. Stay safe.'"

She drops my phone into my lap, looking shell shocked.

"Time to scream," I say.

"What?"

"You're going to be stuck in this car with me for a lot longer than a minute."

CHAPTER NINETEEN

LIESEL

"'*It's the most wonderful time—*'" I jab the button, turning the radio off. The stupid lying radio. This is far from the most wonderful time of the year. We've been stopped for thirty minutes, and the reports of the accident keep getting more disastrous.

"An ambulance got through, but the fire truck hit black ice and now they're stuck too," Cooper says.

"Enough," I say, covering my head with my hands. "I don't want to know anymore."

"Pretending nothing happened isn't going to help."

"Knowing what's happening isn't helping, either. It doesn't change anything."

"It helps us prepare. Plan ahead."

"Plan ahead for what?" I ask. I gesture around me. "We're stuck in the car!"

"Right, but for how long? Do you have any medical conditions you need help with?"

"No."

"Are you sure you didn't get bit by something? You seem pretty venomous."

"Wow. All that setup for a mean joke?"

"No, that just came to me." He says, holding his arm straight out and rotating his right wrist.

"Is *your* injury okay?"

"Just stiff."

My eye twitches. I want to say something scathing, something that stings worse than a jellyfish. But I'm not actually a mean person. Something about Coop brings out the worst in me. And, honestly, I thought he was also bringing out the best in me, but I was clearly mistaken. That disappointment is probably making me even nastier, and my guilt over it makes me feel like my heart is pumping acid instead of blood. "If you need me to turn the heat up in the car, let me know."

Cooper frowns but nods.

My leg starts bouncing. I text Juliet.

LIESEL

The freeway's at a standstill, and guess who's stuck on it?

JULIET

NO!

Are you okay? What do you need? I'll have Nate send a helicopter.

LIESEL

Do not have Nate send a helicopter!

JULIET

Of course I will! Literally, what is the point of being a billionaire if he doesn't help his friends?

"Juliet wants to have Nate send a helicopter to come get us," I tell Cooper, though I don't know why I do. It's not like he deserves to know.

(And yes, the rational part of my brain can acknowledge that he *does* deserve to know.)

With his arm still in front of him, he points his hand upward, then flexes it downward. "Then your car would block traffic once it starts back up again. That could lead to other accidents."

LIESEL

You can't do that. If we abandoned our car, it would lead to other accidents.

"Besides," he adds, "there's no way a helicopter could fly in this. It's too dangerous."

LIESEL

Besides, it's too dangerous for a helicopter to fly in this weather.

JULIET

Dang it. Nate agrees with you.

Leeee! What can we do?

LIESEL

Pray? Maybe Nate can help with the emergency services side of things?

JULIET

Maybe we could rent an ATV and go deliver food and water to people?

LIESEL

I'm not sure you could get through. And I'm not sure it's safe. You see how nasty this storm is.

JULIET

I hate feeling powerless.

And I hate that you're stuck alone.

LIESEL

I'm not alone. Cooper's with me. His car wouldn't start.

JULIET

Oh, I'm so relieved!

LIESEL

Don't be.

JULIET

??

LIESEL

He arranged for my brothers to get traded to another Triple-A team instead of being called up to the Majors.

JULIET

What? Why would he do that?

LIESEL

Because he didn't think they were ready.

JULIET

Ouch. What did he say when you called him on it?

LIESEL

He said he didn't do it. But Kayla Carville—the owner—told me he did.

JULIET

I hope there's more to that story. I liked him. But if he's sabotaging your bros, I'll roast him like chestnuts on an open fire.

LIESEL

Right there with you.

JULIET

Do you have everything you need? You kept all the supplies in the car, right? Do you have a full tank?

LIESEL

Yes, yes, and yes.

JULIET

Good. If something changes, we'll get an ATV and find you. Share your location, okay?

LIESEL

Okay. Thanks Jules.

JULIET

<3

You should talk to Cooper. At the very least, fighting will keep you both warm.

LIESEL

ha

I'll keep you posted.

"Are they okay?" Cooper asks.

A fresh wave of guilt pumps from my heart. I didn't even check with Juliet. "I don't know. She didn't say otherwise," I admit. "I should text her."

"She'd have told you," he says. "You can text her, but don't beat yourself up for being scared."

He can't know how much I needed to hear that. But it's hard to hate him when he says something so intuitively, unintentionally kind.

"I'm not scared," I say. It's mostly true. I'm nervous. I'm frustrated beyond belief. But I'm not *scared.* "They aren't sending a helicopter, by the way. But she said they'll rent an ATV and come help if we need them."

"Man, they're nice."

"They're the best."

"Have you told your family what's going on?" he asks.

"Obviously," I lie, pulling up my phone. I text my dad and brothers.

Lucas's response is swift and stupid, as expected.

LUCAS

But you have the cookies! Aunt Meredith is going to be so mad.

LOGAN

Lee, I knew you'd do anything to avoid Christmas Adam, but this is a little much even for you.

PAPA FISCH

I think she'll do anything to avoid you knuckleheads. How are you, Lee?

LIESEL

I'm safe and have supplies and a full tank of gas. I was driving a coworker to the airport, so I have company.

LUCAS

What friend?

PAPA FISCH

She didn't say it was a friend, she said it was a coworker.

Which coworker? Do we know her?

LIESEL

You guys have the subtlety of an atomic bomb.

I'm safe. Give my love to everyone. If this clears fast enough, I'll be there.

A few days ago, I would have been thrilled to avoid Christmas Adam with the family. As it is, I'm torn between relief and … regret.

I miss my mom like a drowning woman misses oxygen. But being around her siblings *and* mine doesn't sound like the worst way to cope.

Cooper keeps stretching, and I watch him from the corner of my eye. His movements are strangely graceful. For so long, I've hated the way he treats the sport I love, but there's no question he takes it seriously. It almost makes me hate him *more.* If he were a slacker, it would be so much easier to be upset at how he showboats. But he really does work as hard as he claims.

That doesn't make him a good person, though.

He's still appallingly selfish.

Yes, that's right. He's selfish. This isn't a bonding moment. We're not "in this together." We're in this at the same time and place. Independently.

"So, are we going to talk about whatever's bothering you?" Cooper asks.

"I already told you what's bothering me."

"No you didn't."

"You got my brothers traded to a different minor league team! Believe me: that's bothering me."

I lower the heat on the dashboard. For how freezing it is outside, it's a little too warm in here.

"I didn't get your brothers traded to another team."

"Then why did Kayla Carville tell me you put them on her radar? You may not have pulled the string, but you pushed the first domino that led to the others falling."

"While I appreciate the imagery and your faith in the power of my persuasion, I don't know what you're talking about. I met Kayla Carville one time, and all I told her was that she needed to get a great GM and great pitching, because the Mudflaps suck. That's it."

"So you're telling me you didn't mention my brothers at all? I find that hard to believe."

Cooper's tongue pushes against the inside of his cheek, making it pop out like a whack-a-mole I want to smack. "Okay, yeah, she asked me about getting good pitching, and I said something like, 'Don't ask me. I'm torn about the Fischer brothers.'"

"You planted it in her head!"

"I'm not a gardener!"

My laugh slips out before I can stop it. I clear my throat. "You planted it in her head. You mentioned my brothers because you didn't like the plan we agreed on."

He puts his head on the head rest. "You know exactly how I feel about your brothers. They're hotheads who act like they're already in the show when they need to focus more on getting there. But they *can* get there. That's not news."

"Then why did you mention my brothers to her at all?"

"Because we—" He stops and huffs.

"Yes?"

"Because we were talking about *you*."

"You and Kayla were talking about me? Why?"

He drops his arm, evidently too exhausted from our discussion to even continue his light stretching. "She caught me looking at you and made a comment about how pretty my 'girlfriend' was, and I said you wouldn't like being called that."

"Pretty or your girlfriend?"

He snorts. "That's exactly what she asked. The latter, for the record."

"Correct," I say.

He gives me a wary smile. "So when we talked about her dilemma as the new owner, I told her that I'd deny it if *you* asked me, but she should focus on pitchers over hitters."

"You're not wrong. Pitching wins championships."

"I know. So when she asked about how to get good pitching . . ."

"You made the comment about my brothers."

"Bingo."

It's not as nefarious as I thought. "You shouldn't have mentioned trade info like that," I say.

"Yeah, you're right. But it didn't occur to me she'd do anything about it. It's almost impossible for a Triple-A team to acquire players from another Triple-A team. They're not in the same organization." He's right. This acquisition is a testament to the powers of Kayla Carville. Also of money. "How did you two meet, anyway?"

"In the spa." I tsk, frowning. "Shoot. Did she orchestrate that whole meeting to get information from me?"

"I think Nate and Juliet's paranoia is coming out in you in unexpected ways."

I eye him. "I'm serious. I really liked her. If she was using me to get information, that hurts."

"I guess that's possible, but—and I don't want this to come off wrong—she's probably as rich as Nate. If she wants something, I don't think she needs a data analytics manager to get it."

"Just a star right fielder," I say sarcastically.

"I appreciate that you think I'm all-powerful, but I didn't *try* to get rid of your brothers. I think they'll be awesome."

"Eventually."

"Yeah."

"What do you have against them? They have almost the exact same numbers as your boy, Betancourt."

"I don't have anything against them."

"Then why do you look so annoyed anytime you talk about them?"

"Being annoyed by your brothers has nothing to do with why I think they're not ready."

I blink quickly. "You *are* annoyed with them. Of course that affects you not wanting them on the team!"

"For the love of Christmas," he mutters. "I agreed to trade for Colt Spencer. Believe me, nothing your brothers could do could compare to anything that jerk says or does."

"They *did* something?"

"No," he says. "It's not a big deal."

"Cooper Freaking Kellogg," I say in my most menacing tone.

"Fine." He leans his head back. "I met them last season and they were jerks, okay?"

"*My* brothers were jerks? To *you*?"

"I know, you assume that I'm such a massive tool, no one could ever be rude to me unprovoked, but even if I didn't know their dad—*your* dad—was an ump, I wouldn't just be rude to them out of nowhere," he says.

I laugh darkly. Like, really darkly.

"Wow, you won't believe anything I say, will you?"

"Oh, I believe it, all right. Not the part about you never being rude out of nowhere—that's patently false. But I definitely believe my brothers were jerks. And I'm going to kill them."

CHAPTER TWENTY

COOPER

"Come again?"

It's been over an hour at this point. I'm not hungry or thirsty, but I kind of need to pee. Not that I'll tell Liesel that anytime soon.

We're both bundled up in our huge winter coats. The idling car is keeping us warm, but it alternates between feeling too warm—like I'm sweating in my coat—and downright frosty.

Of course, that could be the mixed signals I'm getting from Liesel, too.

I get that she'd be mad about me getting her brothers traded *if* I'd done that. But I've thought about that conversation with Kayla over and over. I wasn't trying to get Liesel's brothers off the team. I wasn't thinking about *them* at all. I was thinking about Liesel and how hot she looked in that black dress.

But now that the cat's out of the bag, I can't deny that her brothers bug me. We met last year during Spring Training. The Firebirds' farm teams—minor league affiliates—trained at the

Pinnacle Peak Stadium where the Firebirds train for two weeks. I didn't interact with the players much, but their coach wanted to get them some tougher practice.

Lucas threw one right at me.

I assume, at any rate. Either that, or he has crappy control. Or he was nervous. But when I got out of the way and held my hands out in the universal "what the heck, bro?" gesture, he shrugged. Didn't even apologize. Just *shrugged*.

I sent one into the cheap seats. He threw his hat in the grass.

When it was his brother's turn, Logan tried a trick pitch—he throws a decent knuckleball—but I could tell something was coming, and I hit it to the warning track.

Most minor leaguers are excited to play against a major league player. Every other guy I encountered from their team was cool. I'm not saying Liesel's brothers should have been deferential, but we're part of the same organization. They should have at least been cool.

I talked to them after and said, "You guys have some real power." I'm the major leaguer, so I was determined to be the bigger man.

Do you know what those punks said? "Next time you step in the box against us, you're going down."

"Then it's a good thing you two are so predictable," I said. "Stop telegraphing your pitches, you amateurs."

Not gonna lie, I felt pretty good about that then.

Now? Honestly, still pretty good. Except the whole Liesel part.

Speaking of Liesel, she hasn't answered me yet. Not a word of explanation. She's sending what looks like a series of furious texts, judging by how fast and hard her thumbs are flying.

"Those arrogant, overprotective butt nuggets," she mumbles. She puts her phone down, looking fiery enough to melt the snow. "Tell me exactly what happened with my brothers."

"Are you sure?"

"Positive."

So I tell her everything from the near miss to the trick pitch. I tell her about their threat, too.

"They really said they'd drop you next time they faced you at the plate?" she asks.

"Yup."

"What did you say?"

"I told them that would never happen because they suck at disguising their pitches. And I may have called them amateurs."

To my utter shock and delight, Liesel laughs. "They had that coming."

"I kind of thought so," I say. "Any idea why they had it out for me?"

"I have a pretty solid working theory," she says. But instead of giving that theory, she climbs into the back of the car, pulls down the middle seat that separates the front of the car from the trunk, and the next thing I know, she's pulling out a couple of waters and protein bars. She hands me one of each.

I take both, but I only open the protein bar.

"You should drink, you know. Even though it's cold, you can still get dehydrated."

"I know. But … I don't want to drink anything yet."

"Why? Do you have to pee?" She snorts. I don't answer. "Oh no, you have to pee? What are you gonna do?"

"I'm going to wait until I'm ready to die, and then I'll run outside and pee."

"Ew."

"It's coming for you, too. Let's be honest."

"I peed before we left. I'm fine."

"Wait until that water catches up with you."

She takes a sip and screws the lid back on. "Good point."

We both open our protein bars. "Not so mad at Nate now, are you?" I ask.

"You really can't help saying the dumbest thing that pops into your head, can you?"

I laugh and take a bite. Each chew sends a pulse of pain into my head, and I realize I'm getting a headache. "What's the point of constantly censoring yourself?"

"Being polite."

"Overrated."

"You don't actually think that, do you?"

I chew. The bar is decent—it's a puffy, chewy bar that tastes a little too good to be that healthy. "I used to. I've had some experiences lately that have made me second guess my theory, though."

She raises an eyebrow at me. "I certainly hope so."

"Do you still hate me?"

"I'm not positive yet. You still haven't explained the Colt Spencer thing."

I pull up the video and show it to her. "Jake sent this to me a couple weeks ago."

She watches. And then winces. "He broke his hand?"

"And just had surgery. I sent the video to Doug. He may not even be healthy till the end of Spring Training, and then he could be rehabbing for a while in the minors. Doug doesn't like the idea of spending that much money for a dude who may wash out after his injury. Also, he agreed that Colt is a giant blowhard."

She turns toward me and tucks a leg under her, getting comfortable. "So let me guess: we're going to call up your boy Betancourt and keep Jessup for one more season."

"Not my call. But that's on the table, as *we* agreed, if you remember."

"I do remember," she says. She pinches the bridge of her nose.

"You okay?"

"Yeah, just a headache," she says.

"I kind of have one, too," I say. "Nothing like getting trapped on the freeway in a blizzard to give you a tension headache."

She sniffs. "Yeah, no kidding."

"So ... are we going to talk about the elephant in the room now?"

"What elephant?" she asks. I give her a level gaze. "What elephant?"

"The 'I can't believe I wanted to kiss you' elephant."

She pushes my shoulder. "You can't be serious!"

"As a heart attack! You said you wanted to kiss me! Frankly, I'm impressed by my own restraint. I thought you were trying a little harder to play hard to get."

"I wasn't playing hard to get."

"No, you *wish* you were. You're just like your brothers: you telegraph every move."

"How are you like this?"

"Like what? A ... classless, overpaid punk?"

She closes her eyes a bit hard, like she's feeling woozy. "I didn't mean it."

"Liese. You meant it."

"At the time, maybe." She shifts in her seat.

I like seeing her squirm. But, I also want to know how she really feels. "I've never been accused of being classy, but do you *really* think I'm overpaid?" My ego wasn't bruised when she said it in the airport—I've heard so much worse so many times, it's white noise. But the idea that she still may think that hurts. Don't get me wrong: if there's a flaw in my game I don't know about, I *want* to know, even if it hurts. But if the girl I like thinks I'm mediocre at the game we both love ...

"Overpaid isn't the right word," she says, her neck almost matching her red blouse.

"But not as good as Hideo Suzuki."

She puffs her cheeks full of air and blows. She's breathing a bit too hard. But then, so am I. "Um, you're a little better than Suzuki."

"A little? How little?" Her blush is all the way to her ears. "How do I show up on your all-seeing analytics program?"

"It's not all-seeing."

"Did you know I was gonna get injured? Is that why you were so mad?"

"No. I mean, yes, by the end of the regular season, we predicted with a high confidence level that you'd get injured, but that's not the reason I was upset we traded for you."

"Wait, you were upset the team traded for me in the first place? Liesel Fischer! What is so wrong with me? Is this because you're a traditionalist? Because I'm so brash?" Lee pulls the hood of her coat up, like she's trying to cover her face. "Sugar Plum?"

"ItsbecauseIhadacrushonyou."

"One more time, in English."

"It's because I had a crush on you!"

"WHAT?"

I say this so loud, people in neighboring cars can probably hear us. Liesel is fully covering her face with her hood now, curling in a ball in her seat.

I tug her hood down, getting my face right next to hers, my lips puffing against her ear in a way that zings against my lip. "Spill. Now."

She looks one glare away from an explosion. "I don't have a crush anymore, obviously."

I grin. "Obviously."

"It's when I was a teenager, okay? You were on the cover of every sports magazine, and I ... may have had a poster of you."

"But I was in high school. I didn't have any posters until I was drafted."

She is redder than Santa's sleigh. "So, it was kind of homemade."

I gape in utter delight. "You made a poster of me?!"

"My brothers did! I, uh, took one of the magazines you were on and I sort of had it in my room—"

"Oh my gosh, did you kiss it? Did you kiss the cover with my face on it?"

"NO! I was fifteen, not twelve. I wasn't kissing the cover."

"You just put the magazine right beside your bed and said goodnight to my face every night, didn't you? It's okay. You can admit it."

If looks could kill, I would be deader than last year's Christmas tree. "I knew I shouldn't have told you."

"You telling me is truly the greatest Christmas gift I've ever received."

"I think I'm back to hating you."

"It's okay now that I know you started with loving me. You'll come around."

"I didn't love you. I thought you were eye candy. And so my brothers thought it would be hilarious if they made a life-size cutout of you and put it on the back of my door."

I almost cackle. "Life-size? We've gone from a magazine cover to a poster to a *life-size cutout*? This is the best day of my life."

"Don't you want to know how I went from a crush to loathing you with every fiber of my being?"

My laughter stops. "Oh. Uh ..." Her challenging expression doesn't bode well. "Yes?"

"I met you."

"What? No way. I would remember meeting you."

She rolls her eyes. "Do you remember your first major league game?"

"Of course."

"My mom got our whole family tickets because she knew what a huge fan I was. My dad adjusted his schedule so he could fly out with us, and everything. You got a walk, hit a single, *and* hit a sac fly. It was incredible. Your bat speed was like nothing I'd ever seen. My brothers were almost as obsessed as I was. Even my dad was impressed. So after the game, we stuck around so I could ask you for your autograph."

It's my turn to wince. Hard. As exciting as that day was, it was also devastating.

My mom had made me a promise: when I played my first game in the majors—my lifelong dream—she would be there. She was working with a therapist and was ready. She swore up and down she would be there.

She wasn't.

To top it off, the hate I got from the opposing team and their fans was vicious. Heck, even some of my own teammates were hostile.

Being on the cover of Sports Illustrated at seventeen changed my life, but it also set the tone for how everyone else in baseball would approach me from that moment forward.

"You said, 'Get a life.'"

"No," I admit, my insides writhing, "I said 'get a life and stop ruining mine.'" I can't swallow. I'm feeling nauseous and even a little lightheaded. And I still need to pee.

"You remember?"

"Not *you*. I didn't even look you in the eyes. But yeah, I remember what I said. It's eaten away at me for the last, what, seven years?"

She gives a slow blink. "Why? Why has it eaten away at you? Why did you say it?"

Why *did* I say it?

No seriously. Why did I say it? I'm having a hard time remembering, but this is something I feel like I should know. I pinch my temples. My headache is getting worse, as is my nausea. Maybe that protein bar isn't sitting well with me. And my other ... bodily urge is getting too bad to handle.

Liesel closes her eyes, resting her head on the seat. It's late afternoon, but she looks tired.

She breathes deeply, almost painfully. "I feel off."

"I hear you," I say.

"It's probably stress, right?" she asks.

"Probably. I'm sorry to do this, but I have to go. Like *go* go. I hope you can still look at me when I get back."

She nods and waves her hand, not even looking up as she draws in another deep breath.

I grab the door handle, the movement almost tiring. How can grabbing a handle be so draining? I'm breathing way too heavy for an hour and half of doing nothing. I wonder if I'm coming down with something or if it's stress, like Liesel said.

I open the door, and a gust of icy wind slaps me in the face. My foot sinks into the snow drift that's already formed around the car. I shiver and plunge my other foot in. I try to leave as quickly as I can, but I hear Liesel moan.

"Cold!" she says.

I duck my head back in the car. "Sorry!"

"Close it!"

"On it." I close the door and then look around in the thick storm. The snow is thicker and wetter out here than I thought, and the cars stretch on in both directions for as far as I can see. I make my way over to the barrier, and the snow banks lessen the farther I get from the cars. It's been snowing all week, and the wind seems to be pushing the ground cover against the cars, creating the snow drift I stepped in. After I take care of business as fast as a human can, I weave around cars to get back to Liesel.

It's only been two minutes, and I'm freezing—my legs and hands are numb, and my face feels chapped from the snow—but my head already feels better. In fact, I don't feel quite as nauseated, either.

Huh. Maybe I just needed some fresh air. Or to get my blood pumping?

Somehow, I overshoot Liesel's white Prius. It's hard to get a clear enough view with the snow attacking me as it is. I keep my head down and at an angle, instead looking at my footsteps and a few feet around them. I follow them back to Liesel's car, and that's when I notice something odd.

Because she fishtailed when she slammed on her brakes, she stopped at a different angle than the other cars around us, and that angle is causing the snow to hit directly against the back of her car instead of the side.

Something doesn't look right.

I glance at the other cars. Snow dumps on them just like on Liesel's. The people in them are huddled against their heaters or talking or looking at something on their phones. Hot exhaust pipes from their cars just like—

"The exhaust!"

I sprint to Liesel's car and open the passenger door. "Your tailpipe is blocked!" I say.

"What?"

I can't explain more. I leave the door open to let in as much fresh air as possible and run around to the back, where dense snow has compacted and clogged the exhaust pipe. It's covering the tailpipe completely. I kick and swipe at the chunk until it's dislodged, and then I run back to the car. Liesel is shaking her head, breathing deeply.

"Are you okay?"

"My head hurts and I think I'm going to throw up," she says.

"That's the carbon monoxide. The angle of your car meant that the snow somehow got clogged up in the worst possible spot. Can you reverse and readjust your position?"

"I'm too dizzy. Can you do it?"

Liesel climbs over the console and into the passenger seat, and I slide into the driver's seat. We close both doors but open the windows to keep as much fresh air coming in as possible.

It's freezing. My face hurts. My hands are red and already

feel chapped. I back up a foot, move forward a foot, and repeat for the next thirty seconds until the Prius is in a safer spot.

"How's your head?" I ask Liesel.

"A little better. The nausea's not as bad, either."

"Do you want to call Juliet? She's a nurse, right?"

"No, Dr. Google will do just fine. If I call Jules, she'll send in a literal cavalry."

She looks up carbon monoxide poisoning on her phone, and a minute later, she says. "Turns out breathing oxygen is really good for recovering from carbon monoxide exposure. Who knew!"

I smile and close the windows, confident the frigid air is as fresh as it comes. Liesel opens her water bottle and guzzles. "I know I'll have to pee later, but water and staying calm are the only other things we can do. Drink up, pal."

I grab my water bottle, bump it against hers, and then we both chug.

When we've breathed deeply for a couple of minutes, she reclines her seat. The lights from the dashboard and other cars' brake lights are the only points of illumination in the otherwise bleak, dark evening.

"So, where were we before we were so rudely poisoned?"

"I think we were talking about your crush on me." I move the seat back as far as it can go. Liesel isn't short, but I'm a lot taller than she is.

"No. We're well past that. I think we were talking about what a huge jerk you were to me when I was a young, impressionable fan who only wanted an autograph."

"Right." I chew on my lip. "It's a long story."

"Since there's no place to go ..."

I nod. Here goes nothing.

CHAPTER TWENTY-ONE

COOPER

"You said I had a walk, hit a single, and …"

"Hit a sac fly," Liesel says. "It was incredible."

I nod. "Do you remember *how* I got walked? It was my very first at bat."

She shakes her head.

"I was hit. Chris Kirby drilled me. I'd never faced a pitch that fast and hard, and I barely turned enough to take it in the shoulder."

"Oof. Do you think it was intentional?"

"I *know* it was. He smiled at me as I ran to first. But that's not all."

"What else was there?"

"Do you remember what my team did?"

"I don't remember *anything*."

"Exactly. They saw an opposing pitcher target a rookie at his first appearance in the Majors, and they did nothing. No one stormed the mound for me. No one got outraged. My coach yelled something at the ump, but that's it. I was 20. I'm not saying I was a little kid, but I was the youngest person on the field by, what, four or five years? You called me a classless punk, but I wasn't mouthy in the minors. I wasn't some hotshot jerk looking for attention. I was hustling day in and day out to get to the Show, and the second I arrived, I was punished for being too good."

Her mouth twists to the side. "I didn't realize that."

"It's not like I could talk about it. I wasn't going to sit in interviews and complain about how everyone was out to get me. But I couldn't just act like Colt Spencer, either. I'm not him. I don't have that ability to be diplomatic or ... manipulative when I'm upset. And above anything, I couldn't let my mom find out that what they did to hurt me."

Liesel cocks her head to the side. "Your mom?"

"Yeah, my mom. She follows my career like a hawk, and she's a little overprotective of me."

"What did she say after the game?"

"I had six furious voicemails—"

"Voicemails?"

I swallow a pain almost as old as I am. "She didn't come to the game." I inhale, pausing just a second before admitting, "She's never been to a game."

Shock hits Liesel like a fastball to the helmet. "What?"

"I don't mean just MLB; I mean *ever*."

Tears spring to her eyes, and they're shedding before I can stop her. Before I can stop my own eyes from following her lead. My lips pull into a frown that I can't wipe away. "Her social anxiety became full blown agoraphobia when I was a kid. It's been bad my whole life. So much worse than bad." The wind howls outside of the car, an echo of the howling pain I've suppressed for so many years. "When I was little, she was always late getting me, and I found out later that she'd sit in the car for minutes that eventually became hours trying to psych herself up to leave our apartment complex or the parking lot. One day, she couldn't pick me up at all, and my dad—who used to be a long haul trucker—was miraculously home at the right time to get me before the school called the police."

"Coop." The word escapes her mouth like a sob.

"I didn't know what was going on. I was just a kid," I say, brushing tears from my face. "I thought there was something wrong with me, some flaw in my personality that made her not care. My dad put me in therapy for a few years after that happened, and I learned how to accept that her problem wasn't a reflection of me. But understanding that intellectually and feeling it emotionally aren't the same thing."

"Of course not," she says. She grabs my hand and holds it. Her hand is cold, so I cover it with mine. We've rolled the windows up and the heat is on, but Liesel still shivers. "Did your mom ever get help?"

"She did Telehealth for a while, but she wasn't at a place to be able to accept it. I don't think she ever has been. Every few years, she'll say she's going back to therapy, but it's never stuck. She'd be able to make a little progress—like walking up and down the stairwell, making it to the car or mailbox. But every time she made progress, something happened. Dad got into a fender bender. I got a black eye playing basketball with friends. A strange dog would run up to her. And she would spiral." The lump in my throat has dropped to my chest, a weight that keeps me more rooted to the seat than any blizzard could necessitate.

"The last time she seriously tried therapy was when I was drafted," I say. Liesel strokes my hand with her index finger. "She'd sworn up and down my whole life that nothing would keep her from getting to my first game in the Majors. I wanted so badly to believe her. I worked extra hard, thinking it would be enough incentive for her to finally get over the hump. She and my dad planned the drive from New Mexico to Phoenix. I was starting to hope for the first time in a long time. But she had a panic attack fifty miles outside of Las Cruces, and he had to turn around."

Liesel wipes her thumb across my cheek and peers into my eyes. "She's missed out on so much. So have you."

"Yes and no. I feel like a loser complaining about this when you'd do anything to have your mom here."

"Don't do that," she says firmly. "Don't dismiss your feelings. My pain has nothing to do with yours. You can't stop yourself from hurting because you think someone else is hurting worse. What you're describing sounds really hard."

"It is." Guilt hits me for saying that. "But it isn't, too. My mom is *amazing*. She celebrated every win, every hit, every play with me the second I got home. She asked me to recount every second of every game, and she would laugh, boo, and cheer like it was happening for the first time. Everyday life was a reason to celebrate for her. She bent over backwards to make sure I felt like the most special kid in the world. I can't blame her for being sick. I'm in awe of her for making the best of it."

"But it still hurts."

"Yeah, but her intentions matter. No one could have tried harder than my parents to give me a happy life. I refuse to fault her for trying her best."

"Your friend said he saw her in the grocery store. Could she—"

"No." I shake my head hard. "No way. I can't believe it, and I can't go back to hoping and being disappointed all the time. I love my mom and I accept her for who she is. I won't let unfair expectations hurt me or my relationship with her."

Our hands are clasped over the center console. Her hands are both warm now, and that warmth spreads up my arms and into my chest. I've only ever planned to talk about this to one woman.

I'm glad it's Liesel.

That tells me everything I need to know about her.

"Well, crap," she says.

"What?" I ask.

"My crush is officially back."

My lips stretch extra wide, and my chest swells. "You say that like it's a bad thing."

"It *is* a bad thing! You're a tough guy to resist, Cooper Kellogg. All that emotional depth and maturity, and a perfectly good reason for that cocky persona? Ugh. How could I not feel something?"

"You forgot the jaw. I have a great jaw."

"I take back the cocky part. It's not a persona."

"Fair." I chuckle. "I *am* cocky."

"But you're not the jerk I made you out to be. You had a choice between being emotionally vulnerable on camera—"

"You mean whiny."

"Whiny on camera," she corrects with a glint in her eye, "and being devil-may-care, and you chose the one that would make your mom happiest. So I repeat: crap."

I squeeze her hands. "Because liking me is so horrible."

"Kind of. Now we have to figure out what to do about Doug and my family." She leans forward, and a lock of her hair loosens from her clip and spills down her neck. I sweep it aside, my finger skimming her neck and cheek as I tuck it behind her ear.

"We? You're so sure there's a *we*, huh?"

Her eyes widen and she yanks her hands from mine to cover her face. "Oh my gosh, do you not like me? Did I misread this whole thing?"

"No! I like you!" I tug her hands back to mine, threading my fingers through her delicate ones. "I very much like you. You didn't misread anything."

Then she grins knowingly. "Sucker."

I chuckle. "That was a meaningless crime if I've ever seen one."

"Not for me, it wasn't. What if you hadn't protested strongly enough?"

"What, you would have kicked me to the curb to face the storm alone."

"Alone? Pfft. You're a famous athlete. Someone would have let you in their car."

I grit my teeth playfully. "You are something, Liesel Fischer."

"I am, aren't I?"

"So, now that we've established that we both like each other, is that kiss back on the table?"

"No. My nausea hasn't subsided *that* much."

"Ouch."

She laughs. "You know what I mean."

"I do."

Liesel leans forward and bumps her head against mine. She reaches her hand up to fiddle with her earring, but then she drops it. "My earrings!"

"They were in the pocket of your jeans," I say. "Remember?"

She checks her pockets, and then her eyes go wider in panic. "They're not here! Where could they be?" She pulls her bag from the backseat, careful not to disturb the Christmas cookies she was supposed to transport to her family's Christmas Adam party. She rummages quickly, throwing her volunteer shirt out and inspecting everything inside. But there's nothing. I find myself holding my breath that they're there and not sitting in a bag on the bathroom floor of Feeding Futures, where an unobservant custodian could throw them out.

And then it hits me. "You climbed over the seat! In the car, when we switched spots!"

We both spin in our seats and look around the gear selector and cup holders. Our hands dart down to that dead zone between the seat and center console. Liesel flips in her chair and feels something, and she gasps. Then her hand snakes deeper under her seat and comes out triumphantly. "Got it!"

She pulls the small baggie out and fumbles as she tries to open it. I put a hand on her elbow. "Can I help?"

"Please."

Her voice is so small. I take extra care opening the bag, and I give her one earring at a time. When she slides the last one into her ear, she exhales loudly.

"I can't believe I almost lost them."

"You didn't, though. You misplaced them for a minute, but they were always there."

She climbs back into the passenger seat, dropping like the weight of her fear has exhausted her.

"The earrings were a 'push present' from my dad to my mom when my brothers and I were five."

"A push present? Isn't that for when women give birth?"

"Yes, it is." She sniffs. "They used to joke about that a lot. But he said that, in his uninformed opinion, raising triplets was way harder than giving birth to them, and it was the least he could do."

"The very least," I say with a snort.

"That's what she always said." Liesel's smile is wistful. "She wore them everyday. When she couldn't put them in by herself anymore, the home health nurse or I did it."

"They look as good on you as they did on her."

"Thanks."

I reach an arm around her shoulders, and she leans into me over the center console. "Tell me about her. What are your favorite memories with her?"

She twists her earring and tells me story after story. Bumps and bruises her mom took care of, bedtime stories, watching baseball together as a family. So many Christmas traditions. The longer Liesel talks, the more I fall in love with her mom.

And the more I listen, the more I fall for Liesel, too.

CHAPTER TWENTY-TWO

LIESEL

I wake up disoriented. I feel an arm around my shoulders and look over to see Coop asleep, his head at an awkward angle that's definitely going to leave him with a kink. And the arm around me is his injured arm, too. I try to right his head carefully, but it drops back to the side.

I grab my phone and take a picture.

I don't know when we fell asleep, but it was sometime after eleven p.m. It's midnight now, which means we've been stranded together for almost eight hours. And we've covered a lot of ground. We've had conversations and confessions I avoid with everyone, including my family and even Juliet. I don't keep her in the dark on purpose, but some things are too hard to talk about.

Somehow, Coop makes them easier. More manageable.

I peek out the window and see that the snowfall has lightened up, but I'm still parked in a sea of cars. I get onto my navigation app and look at the comments for any insight.

Trapper4: Emergency services finally made it through!

It's dated an hour ago. They only got through an hour ago? That means this could stretch on until early morning still!

I stifle a groan, instead looking at the other comments. And then my throat catches.

MommaBird22: Does anyone have food or water? I have three kids, including an infant, and 911 said they can't guarantee when someone will be here. I'm a hundred yards from the N Kimball Ave exit in a blue Dodge minivan. Please help!

LeeFisch: I'm close! I'll bring supplies to you.

Her response is immediate.

MommaBird22: OH MY GOSH THANK YOU!!

I nudge Coop awake. He blinks and yawns, then he pulls me close and kisses my temple.

Um, swoon.

"Is the accident clearing?"

"No," I say. "We have an urgent mission from the North Pole."

I show him the message, and he smiles. "Good thing we still have our Santa hats."

* * *

Ten minutes later, we're trekking through the snow with a crate of waters, protein bars, dried apples, cookies, and more. Coop and I both stuffed bags full of supplies, and we're waving at drivers and offering goods as we go. One couple takes two waters and four protein bars. Someone else takes a jar of peanut butter and a plastic spoon. Another person takes a blanket and several of the sugar cookies Coop and I made the other night.

And each one of them says a variation of the same thing: "Thank you!"

"Bless you!"

"God bless you!"

And every time, Coop and I say, "Merry Christmas."

We're running out of supplies, so we trek the last bit without giving anything out, making sure we have enough for the mom and her kids. When we get to the blue minivan, we hear a baby screaming at the top of its little lungs.

Coop knocks on the window, and the mom whips her head around. When she sees us holding up supplies, she starts sobbing and throws open the door. "Thank you! Thank you so much! Bless you!" She pulls me into a hug with one arm. The snow is still falling viciously enough that she ushers us into the van. Coop climbs into the far back of the van, where a boy of around eight is studying him. I kneel in between the two car seats in the middle row

The mom looks at me. "Can you hold my baby while I make her bottle? We had some water, but my toddler accidentally spilled it while he was drinking. My baby's so hungry. They all are."

The little boy in question bursts into tears. "Sorry, Momma! I so sorry!"

"It's okay, baby!" the mom cries. "You're being so brave, Tristan!"

Tears spill down my cheeks as I remove my wet coat so I can hold the sobbing baby. I shiver, even though the van is warm. The mom mixes the water and formula quickly. "My milk never came in—"

"You do *not* have to justify how you feed your baby!" I say, bouncing and shushing the little baby the way my aunts did when they had little ones. "You're doing exactly what you should do." The baby is so tiny in my arms, and she's crying hard enough that her face is beet red.

The mom shakes the formula and adds a couple of drops of something milky. "Gas drops," she explains. "May I?"

"Of course." I hand the baby back to her in the front seat, and she puts the bottle up to her frantic baby's mouth. The baby makes an urgent, desperate sound and then latches onto it hard and fast. Little hiccups escape her throat, and she does double breaths as she drinks. Her mom whispers, "You're safe. I love you and you're safe."

I don't know what makes me look at Coop when she says this. But when I do, his eyes are already on mine, and the bravado I've gotten so accustomed to is nowhere to be seen. Instead, he looks open, stripped down, laid bare.

In that moment, a frisson of warmth travels from his heart to mine so surely, I can feel it.

And when he pulls his gaze away to talk to the insistent toddler, the feeling remains.

The little boy rummages through Coop's bag, foregoing the beef sticks and peanut butter crackers for two sugar cookies. His brother takes two more.

"Should we ask your mom?" Coop asks.

"No," the little boy says, stuffing his mouth with one cookie and then the other.

Coop laughs and gives both boys water bottles. The smaller boy drinks half of it while Coop helps hold the bottle so it doesn't spill.

"I'm Liesel, by the way," I say to the mom. "And this is Coop."

The mom looks up from her baby. "Coop? Holy cow, you're Cooper Kellogg!"

"Cooper Kellogg works for Santa?" the oldest boy asks, looking awestruck.

"Only when he's nice instead of naughty," I say with a wink.

Coop smiles at me before looking at the others. "It's good to meet you guys. I'm sorry we didn't see your message before this."

"I can't believe you'd risk walking in this storm to help a stranger," she says, crying again.

"Don't tell anyone this or it'll destroy his reputation," I say, "but he's actually a really amazing guy."

"That's right," Coop says. "We can't do anything to shatter my precious reputation."

I stick my tongue out at him, and the little toddler boy laughs and jams another cookie into his mouth.

"I'm Heather," she says. "This little angel is Shannon, and the boys are Forrest and Tristan."

"Where were you guys headed?" Coop asks.

"Rockford. We live in the city, but my parents are there."

"And what about their dad?" I ask.

"He's not with us."

"Oh, I'm so sorry!"

Heather laughs. "No, not like that! He's deployed. He's an Air Force doctor, but he's safe right now."

"Have you checked in with your parents?"

"Oh yeah. They're calling every twenty minutes for an update."

"What can we help you with?" I ask.

"Food and water is all I need. I still have about half a tank of gas. Now if the kids can just sleep, we'll wait until someone honks and then we can get on our way."

"Are you sure?"

"I'd take an autograph," the oldest boy, Forrest, says.

"I'll do you one better than that," Coop says. "If your mom gives Liesel her number, I'll get you guys season tickets. *And* an autograph."

Forrest's mouth drops and he starts crying. "This is the best Christmas present ever!"

When Coop catches my eye, we both smile.

We stay with Heather and her family for another thirty minutes, or so, with Coop talking to the boys and me talking to Heather. Shannon falls asleep almost immediately after being burped, so Heather has me put her in her carseat and buckle her back up. Then Heather smiles.

"You two are angels. You know that? Literal angels."

"I don't know about that, but I'm glad we could help."

"You did more than help," Heather says, choked up. "You saved us tonight."

I give her a watery smile. "It looks like your boys are almost asleep, so we'll head out. But you have my number. Text me if you need anything."

"I will," she promises. "Bless you. Bless you both."

* * *

On our way back to the Prius, I feel like I'm floating. I can tell Coop does, too. He's grinning and waving at everyone he passes, his goofy Santa hat bobbing on his head over his thick winter hat. We pass out the few remaining supplies we have, but not before Coop saves two gingersnaps.

"You haven't lived till you've tried these," he says when we get back into the Prius. I sit in the driver's seat, and he's back in the passenger seat. He hands me one cookie and eats the other.

I take a bite, and I'm hit with molasses and ginger. It's soft and chewy, and I bet it would be amazing warm.

"We like to put pumpkin ice cream in the middle of two cookies and make an ice cream sandwich."

"Mmm," I say, chewing and swallowing. "I want that next time."

"Next Christmas," he says.

"It's a date."

That sends his lips into an epic, impish grin. "Speaking of dates," he says, getting closer to me. "We've probably had the equivalent of, I don't know, six tonight. Plus the charity, so really seven. Oh, and that's not counting the escape room. We're basically eight dates in. Is that enough for a kiss?"

He's staring into my eyes, leaning toward me, and my own eyes drop to his mouth. I've never paid so much attention to a guy's mouth as Coop's. And I'll take this secret to my grave, but while I never kissed his magazine cover as a fifteen year-old, I definitely kissed the life-sized cutout of him.

I thought my feelings for him were intense then, but they're nothing compared to what I feel for the real thing. The complex man who holds space for his mom to manage her illness while loving her with his whole heart. The man who performs casual acts of kindness when it doesn't benefit him in any worldly way. The guy who makes me laugh and lets me grieve but also pushes me to see that more is possible.

I stare at his lips, consumed with a need to know what they feel like. How they taste. "I think you've earned it," I whisper.

Coop's lips pull into a wide grin. "I was hoping you'd say that."

Our faces are close enough to taste the cookie on his breath, and suddenly, I know without question that gingersnaps will be my favorite cookie for the rest of my life.

My eyelids flutter closed, and our noses brush. I hear his breath pick up, and my heart beats faster than a drum. His lips pause in front of mine, and the anticipation is worse than having to wait for your parents to wake up on Christmas morning. Then I feel the lightest touch—a skim—and I put my hands to his cheeks and pull him closer.

But he doesn't yield. Instead, his lips are like a whisper against mine, touching but without kissing.

"What are you doing?" I ask.

"Your breath smells amazing."

I laugh, my eyes closed, my cheeks bumping against his. "You're smelling my breath?"

"I wouldn't normally, but you don't know how much I love these cookies."

"I think I know what you mean."

Our noses and cheeks are touching, and our lips graze every time we speak. As much as I want to make out with Coop, there's something deliciously intimate about this … conversation.

But it's time to move this kiss along, dang it.

I jut my bottom lip out, flapping his with mine. Coop stills, so I do it again, this time letting it linger just below his bottom lip.

And then I tug his lip between mine, and it

Is

On.

HONK! HONK! HONK!

I open my eyes and see lights moving. I moan against Coop's mouth. "Of all the lousy timing."

He makes an aggravated growl and pulls back from me just enough to brush my hair out of my face. Then he presses his lips to mine softly, holding it there long enough to earn another honk. We break apart. His lips are the slightest bit chapped, and I make a mental note to put lip balm on before we kiss again.

"This conversation isn't over," he says. He sits and buckles up, and I mope but do the same. "Would it have killed emergency services to wait another hour or two?"

"Just an hour or two, huh?" I ask, biting my lower lip.

His eyes burn, and I catch fire. "Sugar Plum, that's what I'd need to warm up. I could kiss you for days."

"I guess we should schedule our next date, then," I say. "When do you get back?"

Coop grimaces. "Shoot. I forgot to check in with my parents. And my phone goes on do not disturb mode automatically at night. She's probably losing her mind."

The traffic is moving slowly, as we all funnel down into two lanes. The accident is almost a half mile ahead, but we're moving steadily enough now. "What's the flight situation?"

He closes his eyes. "Canceled."

"How about Midway?"

His fingers are a blur on his phone keyboard. He waits and I watch the road. We're creeping toward the accident, but once we pass, we'll need to have a decision quickly about where we go—the airport or … not.

"First available flight is the day after Christmas."

"Can you fly into another city and rent a car? Or … you could take a bus to another city so you can get some sleep and then drive straight—"

"How did that work out for the mom in *Home Alone?*"

"I'm serious, Coop! There has to be a way to get you home for Christmas!"

"It's over 20 hours of nonstop driving. I already checked the Greyhound schedule, and it's full."

"Take Nate up on the offer to use his jet!"

"I'm not using Nate's jet."

"But it's already Christmas Eve!"

He hesitates, and I grab my phone from the console and give it to him. "Check with Nate."

He sighs and holds my phone up to my face to unlock it, and then he opens a text and shoots off the request. Nate has to already be asleep, what with it being almost two a.m., yet Coop gets a response within a few minutes, before we've even reached the accident.

"No go. His pilot is sick."

"But maybe he'll get better in time!"

Coop rubs my cheek with the back of his hand. His warmth makes me incline my head toward him. "Liese, I promise I'll be okay. And my mom will be, too. You haven't had a Christmas with your mom in two years, and you're handling it better than

I ever could. So I'm a couple of days late for Christmas with mine. It's not the end of the world."

"It's not the same," I cry. "If I could spend time with my mom, I would."

"Yeah, me too. But I've spent *years* hoping for miracles. Just because they haven't come in the way I wanted, doesn't mean they haven't come at all. I have a mom who loves me, and I'm happy with that. I can't keep killing myself to make things happen when they aren't in the cards. I've done what I could to get home. It didn't work out."

He keeps his hand on my face, drawing circles on my cheek with his fingertip. It's somehow comforting and new and exciting, all at once.

"Well, you're not going to be alone on Christmas."

I pull my eyes from the taillights in front of me long enough to see confusion on his brow. "But I can't go home."

"I know. But I can."

He backs up. "You don't mean what I think you mean."

"I sure do. Get ready for a Fischer Family Christmas."

CHAPTER TWENTY-THREE

COOPER

I'm not sure if I'd rather have frozen to death in the car or if I'd rather be impaled by one of the enormous icicles hanging from the house. Either fate is better than what awaits me in this house.

"Well, it's been nice knowing you," I mutter as Liesel enters the code to her dad's garage.

"Nothing's going to happen to you," she says in a hushed voice as the garage door raises. "Come in."

It's almost 4 a.m., and I'm toting our bags as I walk between her dad's Audi A8 and Toyota Tundra. Parked in the winding driveway are a Jeep and a Bronco. Her brothers' vehicles, I'm sure.

"We both know that's not true. Your dad is going to kill me."

"He won't kill you."

"Yes, he will. I'm doing a walk of shame with his only daughter in the *Home Alone* house."

"Stop. The *Home Alone* house was two blocks over. And this isn't a walk of shame."

She opens the garage door, and immediately, there's a loud beeping.

"Crap! The alarm!" She rushes into an entry room with white lockers and a matching bench with slate tile. She enters a code into a wall keypad while I panic, looking past the dark room for signs of life.

And by life, I mean my imminent death.

"Alarm off," a creepy robot voice says.

And a dog growls.

"You have a guard dog??" I whisper yell.

"That's just Bear," she says, removing her coat and hanging it up in one of the lockers.

Great. Bear. He's probably a pit bull or German Shepherd. Something bred for fierce loyalty, protection, and eating punks named Cooper Kellogg.

I brace myself as the growling grows louder. The house is dark, and with all that beeping and now a *freaking guard dog*, I'm counting my final moments.

I open one of the lockers and try to fit inside of it, but I'm too big, so I hide behind the door, instead.

I did not want to go out like this!

The growling reaches a frenzy. I'm forcibly reminded of that movie with Leonardo DiCaprio where he gets attacked by a grizzly.

But Leo got off easy only getting mangled and shredded like that. Papa Bear—or his dog surrogate—is going to end me.

There's a loud sniff, and then Liesel says, "There's my big boy." Next thing I know, my locker door is pulled from in front of me, and I see Liesel and ... a purse pet.

It's an actual Teacup Yorkie, dark brown, from what I can tell from the built in wall lighting.

"Give him a kiss," Liesel says, holding up the dog—Bear.

"I'm not giving him a kiss."

"I wasn't talking to you," she says. She shoves Bear into my face, and I turn my head so the dog's cold nose hits my cheek. Then she snuggles the tiny creature and sets him down. After he gives my shoe a couple of sniffs, he returns back to wherever he came from.

"So that was Bruce Fischer's dog. How old is he?" He has to have belonged to Liesel's mom, right?

"One."

"One? I assumed—"

"That he was my mom's?"

"Yeah."

"My brothers got him for Dad last Christmas."

"And your dad kept him? *Your* dad?"

"My dad's a sweetheart!"

"Your dad could beat The Rock in an arm wrestle."

Liesel grins. "Are we going to stay in the mudroom all night?"

"Yes. This is the closest exit."

"Come with me," she says with a quiet laugh. She grabs her purse, I grab my suitcase, and I let her tug me through a spacious kitchen, a formal dining room, a living room of some kind and into a …

Bedroom.

"I'm not sleeping here," I say.

"I know you're not, goofball. *I* am. I'm getting the spare linens from the closet so you can sleep on the couch."

I want to protest. I'd rather try my luck in the garage or the gazebo I spotted through the kitchen's bay windows. But I'm exhausted and my elbow hurts, and I need the sleep.

Liesel takes me through the dark house and into a family room with a long, low electric fireplace and a recessed niche above it where a wall mounted TV hangs. Across from it is a big plush sectional. I put a sheet down and she tosses a pillow and quilt on top of it.

Then she leans into me, bats those gorgeous baby blues up at me, and I sigh and wrap her in my arms.

Her hair is falling out of her ponytail, her mascara is smudged, and her lids are heavy. Her red blouse is wrinkled from wearing a parka over it all night.

She's gorgeous.

She could be covered in slime and would still be objectively hot. Any dummy with eyes could see that. But she's so much more than a pretty face and great legs. She's sharp and quick-witted, and she cares about people with her whole heart.

And somehow, I'm one of those people.

Me.

I'm crazy about her. This woman who sees through me like glass and who laughs with me in spite of herself. This woman who would risk upsetting our boss, her dad, her brothers …

She angles her head up at me and her eyes flutter closed as she rises to her tiptoes.

"What are you doing?" I whisper.

"Mistletoe."

I glance up.

"There's no mistlet—"

Her lips land on my jaw, soft yet tantalizingly firm. My eyes start to close of their own accord, but something in the back of my head tries to force them back open.

Why is something in the back of my head trying to force my eyes open? I'm with a gorgeous, spunky girl I'm insanely into, and we're about to make out. This is all green lights.

Her kisses trail up my jawline, and as much as I try to think, I can't. Not with her warm breath against my skin, not with those *lips*. Her kisses get closer to my mouth. Man, I really want Liesel's mouth on my mouth. When her bottom lip flaps against my own, my brain turns to mush and instinct—pure, unadulterated instinct—takes over. I put my mouth on hers and kiss her with a dizzying intensity.

Her splayed hands tug my hair between each finger, and that sends a wave of sensation from the tip of my head down my ears and cheeks and right to my mouth, where it meets hers.

This kiss.

How did I try to fight this?

Why?

No, seriously, why.

I hear a creak, and in a flash, my brain restores itself and I jump back with a hiss, almost tripping over the coffee table. "Devil woman!"

Shock drops her jaw. "What?"

"Are you *trying* to get me killed?" I whisper. "Get thee hence, Temptress!"

Her eyes pop. "Excuse me?"

"I will not kiss you in your dad's house!"

"Stop!" She giggles. "It's not like you've pressed me up against the counter in the middle of the kitchen." She catches her bottom lip between her teeth, giving me a sly look, and if there's anything I can't resist, it's this buttoned up woman wearing mischief as confidently as she wears my jersey. "Besides, you know you want to."

"Of course I want to." I cross my fingers at her like she's a vampire. "But I also want to breathe. And, you know, survive Christmas."

She swipes playfully at my hands, giving a breathy laugh. Then she takes a saucy step toward me. "Coop-er."

"No!" I back up, and this time, I fall onto the couch.

She sits on my lap.

"Liesel Bratty Brat Fischer. No."

I pick her up and remove her from my lap, and she pouts.

"I like you," she says. Then she leans down and kisses my cheek.

"I like you more." I grab her hips, spin her around, and then plant my socked foot to her butt and give her a small shove. "Now get away from me. And stop looking so cute."

She beams, blows me a kiss, and vanishes.

I'm asleep as my head hits the pillow.

* * *

I awake to a pillow hitting my head.

Hard.

"What in the name of Father Christmas are you doing on our couch?"

I'm bleary eyed, my head is throbbing (from a headache, though the pillow didn't help), and my arm aches like the dickens. But all of that pales in comparison to the feeling of dread as I look up at Logan and Lucas Fischer. Not even the Christmas tree in the background can make this feel anything less than intimidating.

But I'm me, so I yawn and prop myself up on my good elbow. "What's up, Fischer Bros? How's it going?"

Logan scowls while Lucas stands with his arms folded. They're both tan and athletic with windswept blond hair, although Lucas's is longer than mine and Logan's is shorter. They look like they could be extras in a Point Break remake ... that takes place at Christmas.

Because they're wearing full length, white and blue abominable snowman footie pajamas. Complete with the fuzzy tummy.

"I got here in your sister's car. And I *was* sleeping."

Lucas lunges for me, and Logan barely manages to stop him. My pulse is already elevated from the abrupt awakening, but it hammers extra hard at the violence in the Fischer Brothers' eyes.

"Chill," Logan says.

Lucas sneers, and I grin. "And here I thought you two would be happy to see me."

"You absolute piece of—"

"Dude," Logan says to Lucas. "Enough." Logan sits on the coffee table, which has been pulled back a few feet. He rests his elbows on his knees and fixes his pale blue eyes on me. "Why did Lee bring you here?"

Her brothers' eyes are a bit lighter than Liesel's, but they resemble hers enough that I let some of my bravado slip. I sit up and rub my face. I'm wearing the same clothes I fell asleep in last night—jeans and a volunteer t-shirt. I point at the shirt. "The battery in my car died after we did Feeding Futures yesterday, so she offered to drive me to the airport. And then the storm hit. All flights out of Chicago have been canceled."

Logan nods. Lucas stands behind him, arms still folded, looking like a bouncer at a yeti-themed bar.

"She should have left you on the side of the road," Lucas says.

Logan's eyes close in annoyance, and I bite back a smirk. "What's your plan?" he asks me.

"I don't know. Get an Uber to drive me to my place in Hindale?"

"Start walking," Lucas says.

Logan and I both ignore him.

"The roads south are closed. You're not going anywhere." Logan looks like he wants to spit the words, but he's doing an admirable job of, well, *not.*

It's my turn to close my eyes in annoyance. As much as I want more time with Liesel, I don't want it like this, in front of the menacing males in her life.

For the record, I could take either of her brothers in a fair fight, but I'm pretty sure they're not the type to fight fair.

Also, her dad could snap me like a candy cane.

The cushions on either side of me sink heavily, and my eyes fly open to show Logan on one side of me and Lucas on the other. Lucas pulls the coffee table close while Logan turns on the TV.

"Uh, what are we doing, guys?"

"*Home Alone* marathon," Logan says. He puts his arm around me and grins like a wolf. "And don't even think about finding our sister."

"Can I go to the bathroom?"

"You can go outside," Lucas says.

I scoff. "Are you serious?" I point to the windows, where the glare of the sun from the thick snow is blinding. And it's still snowing.

"I can escort you to the bathroom," Logan says.

"I don't need to go that badly."

Lucas and Logan both smile and lean back into the couch. And because Logan's muscled arm is around me, I lean back with them.

So, this is Christmas Eve.

CHAPTER TWENTY-FOUR

LIESEL

I must still be dreaming.

There's no other explanation for why Coop is sitting in between my brothers on our plush cream couch watching *Home Alone* and eating Canadian Smarties from a candy dish at nine a.m.

Hope explodes in my chest like fireworks on New Year's. Are they ... getting along?

I take a step further into the room—still far enough away that they can't see me—and excitement bursts in me again as they laugh at one of Kevin's pranks on the big screen.

My brothers—my big, obnoxiously overprotective brothers who hate Coop as much as I ever thought I did—are laughing with him like they're old friends.

As nervous as Coop was last night, it's nothing to how I've felt. I've never liked someone enough to bring him home. The storm forced it on us, but it felt inevitable after last night, anyway. Our roads have converged. The path would have led us here eventually.

And my brothers are getting along with him!

Joy makes me tear up …

And it's then that Coop tries to stand up, and both my brothers grab a shoulder and push him back down.

"Where do you think you're going?" Logan asks.

"I was hoping to use the bathroom again," Coop says.

"I already escorted you to the bathroom. You mean you were hoping to find our sister," Logan says. His voice is as sharp as the nail Marv's about to step on in the movie. The hope in my chest fizzles out like a dud.

"Guys, come on. I just want a shower. Do you really think I'm gonna … canoodle?" he asks.

Lucas snorts, and Logan shoots him a look. "Sorry," Lucas says. "Canoodle's a great word."

Logan's nostrils flare at Lucas. Then he pats Coop's back. "It's not that we think you're dumb enough to try something with Lee while we're here. It's that somehow, you've tricked her into thinking you're not the guy we all know you are. And we can't let you keep that up."

"You don't know anything about me."

"We know enough, and we don't like it," Logan says, and I wish I could curl back up in bed.

Lucas watches the TV as he talks. "Listen, man, you're stuck here, so we'll let you live. But not if you go anywhere near Lee."

Coop shakes his head. "I'm not staying away unless *she* wants me to."

"No, that won't do," Logan says.

"You'll have to live with it," Coop says. "I like her too much to let you scare me away."

The big fireworks may have died, but his words light a sparkler in me. One of the big, long ones that lasts forever.

I'm torn between wanting to hug Coop (and then some) and wanting to strangle my menacing brothers. I watch them go silent as they get back into the movie, and then all three of them laugh again. An urgent sense of *want* fills me. Not just my feelings for Coop. I want *them* to get to know each other. To get along. I want my brothers to know all of the things that make Coop special, from the lengths he's gone to for his mom to the small ways he's looked after *me*. And I want him to get to know them, too! They're so much more than the brats they're portraying themselves as. They have big hearts and care deeply about the people they love.

They would all love each other if they could get their machismo out of the way.

I walk the rest of the way into the room, catching more of the scene with every step. Coop's thick, wavy brown hair sticks out at all angles while my brothers' permanently windswept blond hair would make entire boybands jealous. But then my eyes rove around the big, cozy room, and I spot all of Mom's favorite decorations, including a wooden Rudolph in one corner, her collection of Nativities on the mantle below the TV, and twinkle lights running along the ceiling and entry. I see candlesticks, nutcrackers, stockings, and pillows. And all of the regular pictures and paintings have been replaced with holiday ones—Joy to the World and Deck the Halls signs. Pictures of us in matching pajamas over the years.

And the Christmas tree …

All of her ornaments are on it, arranged as well as a man missing his better half possibly could.

This must have taken my family *hours*.

My eyes grow warm and wet thinking of my dad and brothers decorating the house by themselves. Without Mom.

Without *me*.

I should have been here. I shouldn't have stayed away. I rush my brothers, throwing myself onto Logan, then Lucas.

"You doofuses!" I say, tears welling in my eyes and laughing at their stupid matching onesie pajamas. "I missed you!"

"Get off of him!" Lucas yells, pushing me off Coop. I almost fall to my butt, but Coop throws an arm around my waist and catches me.

"Don't push her!" he says.

Lucas punches Coop's arm. "Don't touch her!"

"Don't spill the candy, you bozos!" Logan sets the dish on the coffee table. And then he slugs Coop's other arm. "And don't touch her."

I laugh, and Coop gives my waist a squeeze that makes my stomach flutter.

"You smell nice," he mumbles in my ear.

Logan shoves me to my feet as Lucas makes a ruckus behind me.

"Don't smell her!" Lucas says. I turn in time to see him elbow Coop in the gut, causing Coop to wince. "And she doesn't smell good. She has road trip stink."

Logan looks at me, and I'm aware I never washed my face last night. My waterproof mascara has probably caked my eyelashes together and left flecks all around my eyes. "What happened to you? You look like you were rode hard and put away wet."

Coop punches Logan's thigh. "Don't talk about her like that!"

Lucas flicks Coop's ear. "Don't punch him!"

Coop gives me a tight-lipped smile that screams "it's been a long morning." I hold back a smile. Because the way they're fighting sets off a new wave of fireworks. They're fighting with Coop the way they fight with *each other.*

They don't know it yet, but they're going to be best friends.

"You need a shower," Lucas says. "You *both* do."

"You can go first," I tell Coop. I take the curved seat on the sectional, separated from Coop by an arm rest and one annoying brother.

"Not gonna happen. The Bash Brothers here have informed me that if I need to use any facilities, it'll be with an escort."

"Dudes!" I say.

Logan shrugs. "We said he could go outside."

"To shower?" I ask, my words as cold as frostbite.

"He could use the hose." Lucas looks past me to the TV, where the wet bandits are taking paint cans to the face. Lucas snickers.

"That's, what, concussion number four?" Coop asks.

"No, six?" Lucas says.

"You don't know if slipping on the ice would give him a concussion," Logan says, grabbing the chocolate Smarties and throwing the last handful into his mouth.

Coop peeks past Logan at me, but Logan shoulder-checks him.

"No looking."

Coop looks down at his lap, grinning.

"No smiling." Lucas slaps Coop's leg.

"Hey! I'm watching a funny movie! I'm allowed to smile."

"Not that smile, you're not. Eyes on the screen, bubs."

Coop rolls his lips together, and by the way he's holding his body so tightly, I think he's trying not to laugh.

I smile and fling my legs across the arm rest so they're practically in Logan's face.

"Ew," Logan says. "Get your stinky feet off me." He knocks my feet away.

Anger flashes across Coop's face, and he shoves Logan. "Don't hit her."

"Don't hit *him*," Lucas says, pushing Coop.

I laugh, watching Tweedle Dumb, Tweedle Dumber, and Tweedle Dead Sexy get into a push fight over me.

"Coop, you can go shower. I'll stay here with the boys."

"Hear that?" Lucas snorts. "She'll stay here with the *boys*. What does that say about you, Coop?"

He pushes off my brothers to stand. "It says I'm a man, Lukie."

Lucas tries to kick Coop, but he skirts past my brother too fast. Coop rounds the sectional and leans down to kiss my cheek before my brothers can stop him. "Good morning, Sugar Plum," he says softly.

"NO CANOODLING!" my brothers yell.

I pull up the collar of my pajama top to cover my smile.

* * *

Twenty minutes (and probably three concussions for Marv and Harry) later, my brothers and I are laughing at the TV.

"I forgot to ask how Christmas Adam was last night," I say, picking out the pink Smarties, which taste the best even though they're all the same flavor.

"It was canceled," Lucas says. "Everyone's at Uncle Paul's, but the roads were too bad to drive on."

"So Mom's whole family is still in town?"

Lucas nods. "If the roads are good enough, we're planning to try again on Boxing Day."

Lucas pushes me with his foot. "You can't skip out this time."

I eat another pink Smartie. "That's okay. I think I can handle going."

From the corner of my eye, I see my brothers trade looks.

A few minutes later, Coop comes back into the family room looking fresh and freakishly hot. His wet, wavy hair is slicked back, and all I want to do is run my hands through it.

And kiss him. I really, really want to kiss him.

"You're up, Stinky," Logan says, hitting my foot with his pajamaed one.

"And no touching her while you pass. This isn't some star-crossed love scene, you creep," Lucas says. Coop and I swap smiles with matching wide eyes as we walk past each other.

I head into the guest bathroom and shower as fast as I can. I could have slept in my old room last night. Could have used my old shower. But I knew if I went upstairs, I'd run the risk that Dad would hear me.

The fact that he's not up yet is something of a miracle. He's an early riser, so he must have slept poorly worrying about me to not be up and grilling Coop now.

The mere thought makes me cut my shower short—no shaved legs for this girl—and I don't even bother putting makeup on. I twirl my hair into a towel wrap, throw on my favorite (and only) cashmere lounge set, and run out to the family room.

Where Coop is missing.

"What did you do?" I ask my brothers.

"Nothing!" Lucas says.

Logan rolls his eyes. Bear is curled on his lap, and Logan absentmindedly pets him. "Dad came downstairs after his workout and saw Coop—"

"You let him take Coop? After a workout? He's gonna kill him."

"Your boyfriend asked *him* if they could talk." Logan cracks open a tin of mixed nuts.

I rush to the coffee table, getting between my brothers and the TV. "Tell me everything."

Lucas waves me away. "What's to tell? Dad came downstairs, saw Coop, looked like an enraged bull, and Coop asked if they could talk."

"Where are they?"

"Outside."

I throw my hands over my face. "If Dad kills Coop, I'm calling the cops on all three of you."

CHAPTER TWENTY-FIVE

COOPER

I never expected to find myself sitting on a snowplow made for two with Bruce Fischer as we clear his driveway on Christmas Eve.

But here we are.

At least he hasn't run me over with the thing.

Of course, considering he told *me* to drive, maybe he should be lucky I haven't run *him* over yet.

The sun is covered by clouds, but it's still bright enough reflecting off the snow that I have to squint to see. The frigid air bites at my cheeks, and I cinch my hood around my ears and use the UTV's joystick controller to shovel.

"Bruce, I—"

"How do you know how to use this? Have you plowed snow before?"

"No. My dad worked for Builder's Bench and he taught me how to drive some of the machines."

"Builder's Bench? The hardware store? What, does he own all of the franchises along the West Coast?" he scoffs.

"No, but before he retired, he was the warehouse supervisor at the store in Las Cruces," I say proudly. "He's the hardest working guy I've ever known. And my hero." I feel Bruce's eyes on me. "But would it matter if he were wealthy? You're not doing too bad for yourself."

"I learned a long time ago what it's like to sacrifice."

I could clap back and make him eat his words, but I don't. I toggle the joystick and push a huge mound of snow out of his winding driveway until he stops me at what must be his lawn. I throw the machine into reverse over the path I just cleared.

"Liesel told me some about your wife. I'm sorry," I say. "That must have been hard."

"*Hard?*" Bruce echoes in disbelief. "You have no idea." He pauses long enough for me to plow another strip across his driveway and another. "It was so much more than hard. It was ..." He pauses. "It was an *honor*. It was a privilege to get to help her, to get to *serve* her every day until she took her last breath. You can't know what that's like."

The heavy emotion in his voice squeezes some of the air out of my lungs, and I'm reminded of a brutal playoff loss when I was twelve. I came home to one of my mom's parties, like usual. I wanted to throw my glove—I wanted to *break* something after how badly my team played—but the nervousness on her face made me pull myself together.

"So?" she asked.

"You win some, you lose some," I shrugged, stuffing down my indignation and turning my showmanship up to eleven. "But you should have seen Braden tonight. He was a beast on the mound, wasn't he, Dad?"

"He was on fire. If everyone on the team had played as well as you two, you'd have a championship trophy."

I told Mom a couple of stories, giving her the few highlights and some dramatic lowlights, but no matter how hard I tried, my heart wasn't in it.

My mom reacted the way she always did—elation, frustration, and everything in between. And in the end, I braced myself for her inevitable question: "So, is it cake time?"

I'd never told her this, but I *hated* eating cake when I lost. Big losses took my appetite with them—still do.

So I braced myself for her to ask the same question she'd asked dozens of times in the past. But she surprised me.

"I gotta say," she said. "I know we always eat cake after your games, but I want to ... smash it more than I want to eat it. I can keep a piece aside for you, but—"

"Let's smash it," my dad and I said it in unison.

The three of us went into the tiny apartment kitchen, and instead of cutting the beautifully decorated cake she spent hours on— a cake in the shape of a baseball, complete with stitching—she slapped it.

A glob of frosting exploded on her face, and I started laughing so hard, snot bubbled from my nose. And that made my parents crack up. Dad took the next swing, smashing his fist down on it. And then it was my turn.

I punched the edible baseball player on top of the cake. My fist sunk into the thick frosting in the most satisfying way, so I punched it again, and soon, they both joined in. My parents and I pulverized that thing, and by the end, we were laughing so hard, we were in tears. We licked the cake from our hands, and Dad sent us both to hit the showers while he cleaned it up.

That was the start of a new tradition: winners eat the cake, losers beat the cake.

Bruce doesn't think I know anything about sacrifice.

He doesn't know my family.

"I told you to stay away from her, Coop," Bruce says. "I can't understand why a guy as smart as you would do something so stupid."

"Maybe it's because you're not the only person who knows what it's like to sacrifice for someone you love."

"You don't love my daughter."

"No, we're not there yet, but I care about her, Bruce. I care about her more than I've cared about anyone outside of *my* parents. Ever."

"If you really cared about her, you'd leave her to find someone worthy of her."

I laugh and flex out my fingers. The cold is already making them stiff, even through the gloves. "Who? Who could be worthy of someone like Liesel? Do you think there's a guy out there who wakes up thinking of ways to make her laugh more than I do? Do you think there's a guy who looks at her broken pieces and wants to help her put them back together more than me? Do you really believe there's a man who loves the things she loves more than I do but whom she can't steamroll with her intelligence?"

"She's way smarter than you."

"No argument here. But I'm just overconfident enough to challenge her, anyway. And she likes that. She doesn't want a guy who worships at her altar. She wants someone she can tease. Someone she can laugh with and cry with and dream with. Someone who isn't intimidated by her intensely overbearing family. If you know a guy who can do that better than me, I'll step aside." Bruce doesn't answer. "I know I'll never be good enough for her. Why should that stop me from trying?"

Bruce's jaw grinds like he's chewing boulders. "That's the first intelligent thing I've heard you say in eight years."

I move the toggle, shifting more snow as the frosty air bites my cheeks. "You've officiated, what, maybe ten, twelve games per season since I came up? Do you think that's enough to get to know a person?"

"I think your little nickname for me is."

I groan. "Bruce, come on. It was a dumb joke in a heated moment. Can't we move on?"

Bruce grunts.

I've always been respectful with umps. My GM is right: you don't mess with the guys who can call a game against you. But when I first hit the pros, everyone had noticed that Bruce Fischer had pulled a Barry Bonds—he'd gone from being an athletic guy to going full WWE wrestler size over the course of only a couple seasons. The jokes started about him being on steroids. On juice.

Bruce doesn't miss much on the plate, but in a particularly tense game, he called a strike on me that I thought should have been a ball, and like the idiot I am, I said, "Is that what we're doing today, Juice?"

It was one time. One stupid slip of the tongue early in my career, and evidently, it's stuck with him all these years.

I really have a habit of saying dumb crap in front of the Fischer family.

"My wife weighed a hundred and sixty pounds when she was diagnosed with ALS. She weighed a lot less at the end of her life, but she was sick for ten years," Bruce says, his voice low but piercing. I don't like where this is going. Bruce is shaking his head, staring at the snow, but I can tell his thoughts are far from here. Dread and regret gurgle in my stomach. "Do you know how she showered? How she was transported in and out of vehicles? To and from beds and chairs and up and down stairs? *Me*. So yes, I spent a lot more time at the gym, because I wasn't going to be the reason my wife missed a single moment in our kids' lives."

I stop the UTV. I feel like I'm gonna be sick. "I didn't know. I'm so sorry, Bruce. I didn't know."

"You didn't care."

"I do now." I look at him, dropping every hint of bravado I have left in me. "We don't know each other well, but please believe me when I tell you that I'm sorry. I shouldn't have said it, regardless, but I *never* would have said something so callous if I'd known."

"You disagreed with me on a call and threw my sacrifices in my face. That's a punk move, but it's not the reason I dislike you."

I wince. "I know. Liesel told me about the game. I don't have any excuse for what I said, but I do have reasons."

"I know better than most how hard that first season must have been for you, but you have to understand that I can't let someone near my daughter who can't control himself when he's upset about the game."

"I would never have acted like that over a game."

"You *did*."

"No. That's not the real reason I snapped at Liesel that day."

Bruce squints through his sunglasses. "Why should I believe you?"

"Because my parents raised me better than that. My mom ..." My lips purse as I clear my throat. "My mom has been sick most of my life. With mental illness, not physical, but it's just as real." I stare at the snow and start driving again. Some conversations are easier when in motion. "She had a big set back that day, and I didn't deal with it like I should have."

The plow stops where I dump the snow, and I should reverse, but I can't. Bruce's silence is giving me space to admit things I've only ever told one other person: Liesel.

"You'd like my dad. He's a lot like you. Strong enough to carry every burden his family needs him to carry. He quit a higher paying job for one that gave him the flexibility he'd need to take care of my mom *and* me. He sacrificed to take me to games, get me on club teams, help me get to and from tournaments, and all while making sure my mom was taken care of, too."

Bruce nods. I risk a glance at him, and his brow is creased.

Then he looks back at me. "He sounds like too good of a guy to have a dope for a son."

"He is. You two have more in common than you'd think."

His lip twitches. "Apart from the dopey sons?"

I laugh before I can stop myself. "Uh, yeah, actually."

Bruce's snort sounds like a grunt. "Tell me more about your mom. She must be a saint to put up with you."

I laugh again. And that's how I find myself telling Bruce Fischer about my family.

All about my family.

CHAPTER TWENTY-SIX

COOPER

After we plow the Fischer's driveway, I ask Bruce if he has any neighbors who need their driveways plowed. He seems surprised by the question, but he directs me to a few of the houses in the neighborhood, including that of a sweet old widow and a family that's out of town for the week. Fortunately, none of the driveways are as long as Bruce's, so we're done after only a couple of hours.

A couple of hours with Bruce Fischer, and I'm somehow still alive. And feeling lighter than I have in years.

"I used to make fun of Canada as much as the next guy," Bruce says when we get into the house. He's been talking about his wife—Claire—and somehow, that's shifted to us talking about her home country. We shake off our hats, coats, and boots in the mudroom, and then Bruce takes my coat from me and hangs it on one of the hooks in his locker. "But anyone who hates *poutine* is trying too hard. It's fries with gravy and melted cheese. How could that be bad?"

"I hear you. I get it every time we play in Toronto."

"The food's the best part about officiating there. I brought home boxes of Claire's favorite chocolate and chips every time I worked a series in the MotherLand, as she called it."

"Liese was telling me about her favorite Christmas snack being Canadian—nuts and bolts?"

Bruce looks at me like I've dropped a bombshell. "She talked to you about Christmas?"

"A lot, actually."

His dark blue eyes seem to lighten a shade and he claps my back.

Honestly, it kind of hurts.

"I hope you're as handy in the kitchen as you claim," Bruce says. "We have some baking to do."

He leaves the mudroom and almost runs smack into his daughter.

Liesel is folding her arms and tapping a slippered foot as she glares at her dad. "What did you do to him? He looks half frozen!"

"We had a chat," Bruce says, giving his daughter a big hug. "And we came to an understanding."

When he lets go, she eyes him. "Is that some kind of a threat?"

He chuckles and walks past her into the kitchen, while I smile and take her hand. I don't bother looking at Bruce to see if this bugs him, because I imagine he'd do a pile driver on me if it did, and there's nothing I could do to stop him. "We're okay. We talked, and I apologized for being dumb, and he decided he approves—"

"Doesn't disapprove," Bruce corrects me, opening one of several boxes of Canadian cereals sitting on the counter.

"He doesn't disapprove," I say to Liesel.

And that's enough to make her break into a smile that steals my breath.

"What have you been up to?" she asks, her eyes searching mine. A small, disbelieving smile tugs at the corner of her lips. She's not wearing any makeup, and she's braided her hair, which is still damp from the shower a couple of hours ago.

I've never wanted to kiss her so badly.

"Snowplowing."

"You and my dad?"

"Yup. And now we're making nuts and bolts. You want to help?"

"I don't trust my family with you, so yeah, I'm not letting you out of my sight." She shifts her hand so our fingers are interlaced, and I immediately feel grounded. The rightness of holding her hand, of being here with her and her family on Christmas Eve when I can't be home roots me in place.

But … it weighs on me that I can't be home. No matter how right it feels to be here, there's a hollow spot in my heart, a gnawing emptiness that can't be filled without my mom's smile or my dad's teasing. There have been countless events in my life my mom couldn't make, so Christmas has become sacrosanct. We've never been apart for the holidays.

"Are you okay?" Liesel asks. "And don't do the fake smile. I can read it like a spreadsheet."

"What fake smile?"

She pokes me in the stomach. "The one where your eyes crinkle. It's so fake."

"No it's not! Smiles make everyone's eyes crinkle."

"Not yours. Your cocky smile is all teeth. Your fake smile is all eyes. Your *real* smile is your whole face."

"Wow. How much *have* you studied me?" My mouth spreads, and I realize she's right: my cocky smile *is* all teeth.

She swats my abs. "Coop. Be real."

Bruce is busy dumping a box of "Shreddies" into a huge metal mixing bowl, and he doesn't seem concerned with what we're doing. I'm not sure if it's an act or if our chat really did change things for him the way it did for me. Regardless, I don't need an audience.

I pull Liesel back a few feet into the mudroom and sit on the bench. I tug her down to sit on my lap, and she puts her arms around my neck.

"I'm thinking about my parents. It's hard imagining my mom cooped up in the house on Christmas without me."

"Cooped up without the Coop," she says with a wry smile.

"Yeah," I breathe. "I don't know. Part of me wants to call Nate again and see if we can bend heaven and earth to make it to her. But the other part of me is …" I shake my head. "Resigned. But also tired. I would never ask her to push herself into a panic attack, but it's hard. It's been hard for a long time." I rest my head on her shoulder. "I've already accepted all of this. Why is it resurfacing now?"

She runs her hand through my hair, and the sensation makes me shiver. "It sounds like you need to let yourself mourn."

I shift my hands on her lower back. "What's to mourn? My mom's alive. I can see her in a few days."

"Maybe that's not the right word, because you're so accepting. The stories you've told me make it sound like you went straight from being left in a parking lot to seeing your mom in the car and promising yourself you'd never be the reason she cried again. You jumped straight to acceptance, but you never let yourself process the other steps of grief." She looks at her hand in my hair rather than my eyes, almost like she's trying to let me process her words without an audience.

I've never processed *anything* without an audience.

"Mourning the loss of expectations doesn't mean you don't love your mom, only that you're acknowledging that this wasn't the way you thought things would go. It's not a betrayal of her. It's letting go of what might have been so you can better accept what is."

I don't know how I feel about what she's saying. She kisses

my forehead, and I close my eyes and melt into the feeling. Then she hops off of my lap, throws on a coat, and stomps into some boots.

I look at her quizzically.

"Come with me," she says.

* * *

We're standing outside in her large, winter wonderland of a backyard. Fat snowflakes fall lazily from the sky, and the world has gone quiet in that way only thick blankets of snow can accomplish. We've passed the gazebo and have stepped into a small copse of naked oak and willow trees. Liesel and I are holding hands in front of a willow tree. Its skinny tendril-like branches dangle down on us, tickling our faces.

She puts an arm around my waist and leans into me.

"What are we looking at?" I ask.

"Do you see the trunk?"

I look at the gray bark with its deep cracks and peeling strips. And then Liesel points out a part of the trunk that has been gouged out. "Yikes. It looks like someone took an axe to it."

"Because they did. Lucas got in trouble for something he said to a teacher at school when we were nine or ten. He got really upset about it, took my dad's axe out of his toolbox, and started wailing on the tree because he knew how much my mom loved it. The tree was a lot smaller then, and when Mom saw him through the kitchen window, she flipped. She ran out, took the axe, and grounded him. She was afraid he'd just killed the tree."

"It's a massive gouge. I'm surprised he *didn't*."

"I know."

I kiss her forehead through her beanie. "What are you getting at here, Liese?"

"I'm a stats nerd. I have no idea what I'm getting at. But it feels significant, doesn't it?"

"The tree isn't mad at your brothers. It accepts what happened, marshaled its little tree resources, and moved on."

"Yeah. That's one of way of looking at it."

"What's the other?"

"Maybe if the tree could have told my brother it was hurting, something could have changed."

I move my head back to look at her. "I'm not telling my mom I'm hurting to try to change her. That's manipulation."

She pulls away from me, looking horrified. "I would *never* suggest that. Ever." Her eyebrows thread together. "But … Lucas was hurting when he attacked the tree. Our teacher was always putting him down and comparing him to me, and that hurt his feelings. He never told my mom about it, and I bet she'd have felt awful if she'd known what was really going on with him."

"But I'm not attacking anything. I'm not lashing out. The pain stays with me."

"What if *you're* the one you're hurting? What if not letting her know you're disappointed is hurting you? What if it's hurting *her*?" Liesel looks at the tree, and I watch her eyes water. "I've stayed away from my family for the last two years, and I thought it was only hurting me. But I think it may have hurt all of us. Grieving alone is a lot more painful than grieving together. It's not like she doesn't know she's sick. Maybe acting like nothing's wrong is hard for *her*, too."

I pull Liesel back into a hug and hold her close. I roll my lips together to keep back my frown. But no. I shouldn't keep back my frown, should I? Isn't that what Liesel's saying? My eyes squeeze closed, and I think about the pivotal moments of my life—wins and losses, graduations and performances. I think about the smaller ones, too. Church parties. Haunted houses. Sledding down a hill the first time I ever saw snow in Las Cruces. Getting a milkshake with Dad. Getting to see a Spring

Training game after one of my Little League tournaments in Phoenix.

And the tears roll down my cheeks.

"I miss my mom," I whisper.

"Me too."

"No hugging!" a voice yells from behind us.

And then a snowball pegs me in the back of the head.

Hard.

CHAPTER TWENTY-SEVEN

COOPER

One totally unfair snowball fight later (I had to throw left-handed! And Liesel's brothers are both pitchers!), the four of us are red faced, smiling, and drinking hot cocoa on the couch while we all watch *Home Alone 4.*

"Can't we go back and watch *Home Alone 2*?" I ask Liesel. We're on the loveseat end of the sectional. "I missed the whole thing when I was plowing snow."

"Nope. Sorry," Lucas says.

"But this one's ... not awesome."

"We watch every *Home Alone* movie on Christmas Eve," Logan says.

"It's tradition," Liesel says.

"So was giving naughty children coal," I mutter. "Not all traditions are created equal."

Liesel laughs, and I grab her legs and sling them over mine. I rub the gray cashmere, and she smiles and takes a long drink of hot cocoa.

How have we only known each other for a couple of weeks when it feels like we've been doing this forever?

"No canoodling!" Lucas says. I turn just quickly enough to see him throwing a Canadian Smartie at me. I catch it in my mouth.

"Enough," Logan says, kicking Lucas across the couch. "They're gonna canoodle."

Bruce enters from the kitchen. "All right. Drain the hot chocolate and let's finish the nuts and bolts, already."

"Yes sir," I say. I set down my mug and remove Liesel's legs from mine. When I stand, I hold my hand out to pull her up. Her brothers stare at me from the couch. "What?"

"'*Yes sir?*'" Lucas repeats.

"Are you trying to make us look bad?" Logan asks.

I smirk. "You're doing that all on your own."

Liesel puts her hands on my shoulders, and instinctively, I hold my arms open for her to jump on my back.

"No piggybacks!" Lucas yells as we go into the kitchen.

"Bro, chill," Logan mumbles.

Liesel laughs in my ear.

Nuts and bolts are a cinch to make, but they bake in the oven for hours and require frequent mixing, so when everyone goes back into the family room to watch the movie, I take a break in the kitchen under the guise of helping. But really, I'm back to looking for earlier flights home.

And messaging my parents.

I haven't talked to them all day, only texted. The fact that neither of them will answer their phones bothers me. They keep texting that everything's okay, but it's suspicious, to say the least. My mom is homebound! Has she become addicted to her VR headset? Is she so caught up in "experiencing" the world that she's forgotten about me?

She can't have. She loves me. I know she loves me.

But in my lowest moments, that fear has a way of resurfacing. That day I waited in the office at school while the admin staff called her over and over again left a mark. The secretary said something to another admin that I've never quite been able to shake: "How little do you have to care about your own kid to just forget him?"

In spite of what I told Liesel about my radical acceptance, I can't stop looking for flights. So when I get an alert of a seat opening up, I text my parents immediately.

COOP

Good news! I found a flight that's leaving earlier. I've booked a red eye leaving Christmas night, so I'll be there when you guys wake up the day after Christmas. I'm just sorry I can't get anything earlier! Stupid storm.

DAD

Don't worry about it, son. These things happen. We'll see you when we see you.

MOM

Is the ticket refundable?

COOP

...

...

What do you mean?

MOM

Nothing! I saw on the news there's another storm coming in. I'd hate for you to waste that money if it gets canceled again.

COOP

If they cancel it, I get refunded. But that won't happen. I'll be there, Mom.

MOM

Don't stress about it, sweetie. We understand.

Mom has an over-the-top personality. I get it from her.

She is *not* being over-the-top. She's not saying how much she misses me. She's not expressing regret the way she always does for not being able to come to me. Her responses are almost nonchalant.

How little do you have to care about your own kid to just forget him?

Is that what's happening?

It can't be. She never wanted to leave me at school or miss milestones. She loves me. If she's gotten into this headset, maybe it's her way of coping with *her* pain. Liesel could be right that just being open about how I feel might allow us to have conversations that help both of us be more authentic.

I don't want to do this through text, though, and they won't answer my calls, so I pull up a face messaging app.

I look at the image of me on my phone. I'm wearing a navy and red Firebirds hoodie, and my hair is a bit wild from being stuffed under a beanie for hours outside. I don't look sad, but I don't look happy, either. I *always* look happy when I send messages to my parents.

My finger hesitates over the record button. And keeps hesitating.

"What are you doing?" Liesel asks, coming up behind me.

I put the phone down on the counter and rub my face with my hands. "I don't know. Trying to work up the nerve to send a message to my parents."

Liesel sits on the stool next to me and puts her hand on mine. She runs her fingers lightly over my skin, but I shift my hand so our fingers are interlocking. As much as I love the feeling of her touch, I need something more solid. More grounding.

"They're still not answering the phone?" she asks.

"No. And they don't seem to care that I'm not there."

"Of course they care," she says. "Your mom is probably too upset to talk. She could be beating herself up."

"I don't know. Maybe. Or maybe she's on that stupid headset."

She spins in the stool so one of her knees is in between mine. "I'm sorry this is so hard. What can I do?"

The timer rings, and we both get up and cross around the island to take the nuts and bolts out of the oven and stir them. The Shreddies, Crispix, pretzels, peanuts, and Cheerios shift around, and the smells of garlic, butter, Worcestershire sauce, and a few other seasonings fill my nose. It smells delicious and like a nice change from all the chocolate and candy we've eaten today.

"Want to press record when I send the message?"

"Whatever you need," she says. She puts both pans back in the oven and we return to the stools.

"Ready?" she asks. I nod.

The phone is propped on the counter facing me, and I watch Liesel's finger hit the button. I automatically smile, but I see what Liesel means instantly: the smile is in my eyes, but I don't look happy.

Not really.

Does my mom know that?

"Hey guys." I sigh and drop the smile. "I miss you. I don't know why you haven't been answering today, and honestly, I'm bummed. We've never been apart on Christmas Eve. It feels wrong. And I'm sad about it." I pull my eyes from the screen and look at the kitchen without really taking anything in. "I'm having fun, though, and I feel kind of guilty about that. Kind of relieved, too." Then I look up at Liesel, whose mouth is pulled to the side like she's trying not to cry. "Want to meet my … is it too early to call you my girlfriend?" I ask. "I don't want to date anyone but you."

Her eyes pop. "Uh, neither do I."

I feel the smile overtake my face, but I don't look at the image of me on the screen. I watch Liesel, instead. Because she's biting her lip like she's trying to bite back her smile, and that only makes my grin widen. "Then it's official." I grab the phone and duck my head so it's next to hers. "Mom, Dad, this is Liesel Fischer. My *girlfriend.* Bet you never thought you'd hear those words out of my mouth, huh? I guess some Christmas miracles really do come true." She rolls her eyes with clear affection and then turns to face the screen.

"Hi Mr. and Mrs. Kellogg. I wish we could meet in person, but I promise my family will take good care of Coop until he can get home to you."

"Don't believe her. Her brothers and dad all tried to kill me."

"It was light maiming," she says, looking at me. "And you probably had it coming."

"I definitely had it coming," I say. She looks at me while I watch her face on the screen. "Oh, and Mom, the face tattoo was a stroke of genius. Liesel and I met in the airport, and she didn't recognize me. She *works for the Firebirds.*"

"That idea came from your mom?" Liesel throws her head back and laughs at the ceiling, and the view of her long neck makes me want to kiss it. But not on camera. "It was a Rudolph face tattoo! No one can look someone in the eye if they have a face tattoo. Brilliant idea, Mrs. Kellogg."

"But it's okay. Turns out Liese has had a crush on me for like ten years."

She shakes her head, laughing. "He may be a brat, but you've raised a great guy," Liesel says. "I hope you both have a Merry Christmas."

I sigh as Liesel backs out of the screen, leaving me with my parents. Sort of. "I wish I could be there with you guys," I say. But even as I say it, I know that's not true. That's not what I want to say. I look at my hands in my lap, and Liesel's hand slips into mine. I look up at her, smile sadly, and then look at the screen. What I want to say is *I wish* you *were* here. But I can't say that. I won't. I can be honest without being hurtful. "I wish we could be together on Christmas. Love you guys. Call me when you can."

I hit stop. And the message sends.

Liesel gives me a tight hug, and I breathe into her hair. "Thanks for helping me," I whisper, "Girlfriend."

"Thanks for letting me be a part of it. Boyfriend." She moves her face so she can kiss my head, then my cheek, then my lips, and when we part, she smiles. "I'm proud of you."

I breathe out heavily. "Can we watch *Elf* now?"

"Oh, sweet, sweet boy. The fifth movie just ended. They've turned on the sixth."

"No."

"Yes."

"But the first two are so good! Why would you even watch the others?"

"Tradition."

"But my family has a tradition of *not* watching dumb movies on Christmas Eve."

"Embrace the Fischer way." She stands up, and I follow suit, but instead of walking into the family room, I grab her, spin her around, and kiss her.

I kiss her *good*.

Her mouth is warm and inviting, and while her body initially is stiff in surprise, she quickly folds her arms around me, and my hands clutch her back. In the background, there's a dinging sound, but my thoughts are too focused on Liesel for anything else. I love the way she tugs gently on my hair. It makes every kiss and movement electric. She turns her head and deepens the kiss, and I moan—

"NO MOANING!"

We pull back and I'm almost dizzy with want. We're still holding each other, but my eyes catch on Liesel's stupid, interfering brothers looking at us with their arms out in a universal "What the heck?" stance.

They'd be intimidating if they weren't wearing abominable snowman footie pajamas.

"Dude, just because we're letting you live doesn't mean you can make out with our sister," Logan says.

"Not cool," Lucas says.

The dinging is still going on, and her brothers pass us—both with a punch to my shoulder—and go around the kitchen to the oven, where they take the nuts and bolts out, turn off the timer, and let them sit on the stove top to cool.

When they come back around, Logan grabs me by the shoulders while Lucas grabs Liesel. "Back to the movies, guys," Logan says.

I whimper.

"Can we *please* watch *Elf*?"

"Not a chance, Buddy."

CHAPTER TWENTY-EIGHT

LIESEL

It's Christmas morning. We moved Coop into the guest room last night, so I'm waking up in my childhood bedroom.

To Coop's face.

A gasp escapes my lips, and then I clutch my chest, breathing hard.

The life-size cutout of Coop is right next to my bed.

My brothers kept it?

Just when I thought I couldn't hate them more …

I'm this close to marching into their room and jumping on their dumb faces to wake them up when I think better of it. If they're awake, they make trouble.

Besides, a quick check of my phone tells me it's not even 7 a.m., and we aren't allowed to wait on the stairs until 7:30.

Not even at twenty-five years old.

I open my phone to check my messages and see a text from Juliet from only a few minutes ago. We talked last night, and she was as happy for Coop and me as she was sad for Coop and his family.

JULIET

Merry Christmas! Did your family kill Coop in his sleep?

LIESEL

I don't think so.

She responds right away.

JULIET

You didn't check?? Lee!

LIESEL

They're getting along! We played like five board games last night, and they barely even fought.

JULIET

Well deck the halls and call me Santa.

LIESEL

I know!

JULIET

How are you? First Christmas at home, and all that. <3

LIESEL

It's actually nice being home. I miss Mom, but it hurts less being with everyone. It almost feels like she's here.

JULIET

I'm so glad. Keep me posted on how the day goes. Love you, friend!

LIESEL

Love you too! Give Nate a hug for me.

I put my phone back down on the bedside table and stretch like a cat. Then I look around my room. I redecorated it in high school, with Mom overseeing it. The light sage green of the walls has always felt calming to me. Bookshelves surround my desk—a time capsule devoted to my love of sci-fi, fantasy, and awesomeness—and high shelves line the walls. Unlike the shelves in my brothers' room, which are full of trophies, mine are full of memories. Bobbleheads from baseball games. Seashells from beach vacations. Honor roll certificates and perfect attendance awards. And the angels my mom started to collect after *her* mom died, only a year before my mom first got sick.

For a while, I collected them with her. I stopped when she passed, but I've never stopped loving them.

I miss my mom.

I miss her so much.

This hollow spot in my heart will never heal, but after the last few weeks with Coop, I feel a little like the tree outside. I can grow around the wound. It will never be gone, but what I can become is all the more unique—more beautiful—because of it.

I open my closet and pull down a box from the top shelf. My mom bought and wrapped Christmas sweaters for us for the next … I don't know how many years. Dad gave the boys theirs the day after Thanksgiving, but I skipped out. Just like I skipped out on decorating the tree and the house and going to see Christmas lights. And just like I missed Christmas Adam with Mom's family. At least I can blame the storm for that one.

But I don't want to miss out on anything else. That's not what she'd want for any of us. Nothing made Mom happier than being with her family. I felt the same way once, and I felt it again yesterday.

Nothing makes me happier than being with my family.

The fact that Coop was also here …

I can't think that far ahead. The very possibility sets off an excited flurry in my chest.

I unwrap the gorgeous red and white twine bow and kraft paper Mom always put around our presents. The idea of her making sure we always have new Christmas sweaters makes me smile. I can imagine her lovingly picking each out. Making sure they were all carefully, beautifully wrapped. Gift after gift after gift.

But … my mom didn't wrap this. She couldn't have. She wasn't able to wrap for years.

This was my dad.

My heart grows three sizes thinking of my big, beefy dad, of his huge hands doing such delicate work, and all because of his love for his wife. For his kids. For *me.*

I am so lucky.

I pull the twine, open the crisp white Kraft paper, and then look at the simple *"Love, Mom"* note that my dad copied from a card she wrote one of us years ago.

I pull the tissue paper off the sweater and laugh in shock.

LIESEL

YOU WILL NEVER GUESS WHAT CHRISTMAS SWEATER MY MOM GOT ME!

I snap a picture, laughing with tears streaming down my face. It's an ugly gray sweatshirt featuring a calico kitten sitting in a stocking wearing a Santa hat. Beneath the kitten in a festive script, it reads "The stockings were hung by the chimney with cats."

It's Juliet's sweater!

Her response is immediate:

JULIET

Lee! *sob face emoji*

angel emoji

Twin emoji

I hold the sweater to my chest and laugh, letting happy tears pour down my face. How can Mom be gone and still be with me?

I put the sweater on over my pajamas and look at my reflection in the closet mirror. My hair's a mess and I have no makeup on, but my smile …

I look happy.

I *feel* happy.

How it's possible to miss her so much and be so happy is a mystery I don't know if I'll ever solve. But maybe it has something to do with gratitude. Gratitude that she loved me so much.

I hug my arms tightly around myself.

"Thanks, Mom," I whisper. "I love it."

I check the time. It's 7:12 a.m. I tiptoe out of my room and downstairs. My brothers probably set their alarm for 7:30 on the dot, because they like sleep, but they're also basically big, dumb children. My slippers land softly on the floor as I pass Dad's office and stop at the cracked door to the guest room. The sun is just about to peek over the horizon, and it's letting in enough light through the blinds to show that Coop isn't in bed. The light is off in the guest bathroom, too.

I pad through the house, looking in each room until I find him.

On the bench at the bay window in the family room, he's looking out at the snow-covered front yard while he pulls on a therapy band, working out his arm. The room is still dark enough in the early morning sun that the lights twinkling from the tree and from where they line the ceiling cast a cozy glow on him. In a pair of green and cream flannel pajama pants and a cream waffle knit top, he looks Christmasy without being embarrassing (unlike my brothers). The look reflects the other side of his personality that I've gotten to know and love. Not everything about Coop is showy. So much of him is sincere and real. All of him is pretty wonderful.

A creak in the hardwood floor gives me away, and Coop spins to see me. He stands and smiles, but when his eyes catch my sweatshirt, a wide-mouthed gape replaces it. "Where did you get it?"

"It's the Christmas sweater my mom left for me this year."

I meet him in front of the Christmas tree, and he holds me close. "She's even more awesome than I thought." He kisses my temple, and his hand fiddles with the collar of the sweatshirt. At first, it feels like he's just playing with the skin at the nape of my neck. But then he angles his head, and I feel the thick cotton pull from the back of my neck.

I push away with big eyes. "Are you checking the size?"

"Just seeing if it's big enough to fit me!"

"You're not stealing my sweatshirt."

"You stole mine."

"I *won* yours. In a bet," I say.

"We tied."

"First place is first place."

"I want the sweatshirt." Coop tugs on the bottom of it and I push him away with a laugh. "Take it off."

His hands grip the bottom of the sweatshirt, and he tugs me against him. "I'm not taking it off."

His hands pinch my sides, and he grits his teeth in that playful manner that makes me want to squeal. "I guess I'll have to stick around for a while, Sugar Plum."

I smile, stretching up enough that he kisses the tip of my nose. "Oh yeah? How long is that?"

My eyes close as he kisses one eyelid and then the other. "How long will it take you to let your guard down?"

"Long. Like, super long. Years. Maybe decades."

His lips are roaming my face, pressing softly against the skin of my forehead, cheeks, chin, and jaw. Then I feel his breath against my mouth and the softest brush of his lips against mine. "I'm good with that," he says.

I smile as he kisses me. I'm kissing Cooper Kellogg in front of a Christmas tree in my childhood home. I have a life-size cutout of him upstairs in my bedroom. But the real thing down here is so much better.

He gives me another soft kiss and then rests his forehead against mine. I open my eyes to see that he's smiling.

"Have you heard from your parents?" I ask.

"I got a 'Merry Christmas! We love you' text about fifteen minutes ago."

"Did you try calling them again?"

His lips pull to the side the way they do when he's holding back emotion. "No. They'll call me when they have time."

Hurt and defeat war on his face, while outrage burns in my chest. He loves his parents with his whole heart, and they sound like amazing people. But how are they not beside themselves trying to get in touch with him? What excuse could they possibly have?

"I'm sorry," I say. Upstairs, my brothers' alarm goes off. "We need to go sit on the stairs before the Tweebs find us."

We get up, and he puts his arm around my shoulders as we walk to the stairs. "Tweebs?"

"Twin dweebs. I stole it from a TV show when I was a kid."

"But you're triplets."

"Technically, they're identical twins and I'm a fraternal triplet."

We sit at the foot of the stairs, and a moment later, my brothers lumber down the stairs, yawning. I rest my head on Coop's shoulder.

"Does that mean I really *can* call them the Fischer Twins?"

"No," I say immediately. "You can call them Tweedle Dumb and Tweedle Dumber. Tweebs. Dorkwads. Twerps. Jagweeds—" Lucas flicks the back of my head.

"Don't hit her!" Coop says, turning to slap Lucas's hand.

"Kids, that's enough," Dad says from the top of the stairs. All four of us turn to see him wearing a Santa hat, red and white checked pajama pants, and no shirt, although he's holding one in his hand. He's all giant pecs and chiseled abs.

Coop gawks. "Cover those things up, bro. There are children present!"

He stuffs an arm into the hole of his white shirt and then the other as he walks down the stairs.

My dad is disgustingly ripped. Honestly, he's pretty much ruined muscles for me. So while I appreciate that Coop is toned and athletic, it's also kind of a snooze fest. His cocky smirk, on the other hand, makes me weak in the knees.

Not that he's smirking now. He's almost cowering as my dad pulls the shirt over his head on his descent. The four of us separate like Moses parting the Red Sea, and when Dad passes, Coop stares in awe.

"Your dad is terrifying."

"I know."

My brothers push past us next, and then Coop and I stand. "I'm taller, though."

I give him a peck on his cheek. "And you should be very proud."

We spend the morning opening presents, most of which are things like books, socks, See's Candy, and special salts for smoking meat. Dad gets me a dainty gold satellite chain and smiles when I put it on.

"I thought it would look good with your mom's earrings," he says.

I jump up and hug him, careful not to disturb a sleeping Bear on his lap. "I love it. Thanks, Daddy."

"Coop, sorry we didn't have more for you," Dad says, even though he most definitely took a couple of name tags off of my brothers' gifts and gave them to Coop.

"Right, like that hoodie wasn't meant for me?" Logan grumbles.

"You have plenty of hoodies," Lucas says. "He got my Redmond Real Salts. How am I supposed to grill now?"

"Those were mine, too," Logan says, pointing. "Yours are right there."

"Score!" Lucas says.

"Sorry, boys," Dad says with a chuckle.

"I'll make it up to you," Coop says. "I'm sorry I couldn't get you guys anything. But, I do have something for Liese." He pulls a gift bag from the bench where he was sitting this morning. I give him a quizzical look and pull out the gift wrap and then take out a Firebirds jersey. It has Coop's name on it.

I snort. "Seriously?"

"What? You look hot with my name on your back." My brothers, Dad, and I all groan. "Put it on."

I'm wearing pajamas under my cat sweatshirt, so I peel off the sweatshirt and put on the jersey. It's one of the *really* nice ones that players wear, though this one's too small for Coop. It's roomy without being too baggy, and it maintains its structure when I tuck the front into my pajama bottoms. It will look amazing with some leggings or jeans, and the idea of Coop's hungry eyes on me makes me flush. I hope my family thinks I'm just embarrassed. "There. Happy now?"

"Very," he says suggestively. Then he rips the cat sweatshirt from my hands and throws it on. "No take backs! Merry Christmas!"

I laugh and roll my eyes. "I will pry that off your dead body."

"I'm not dead."

"You will be."

He grins and looks at the bag. "There's one more thing in there."

My forehead wrinkles as I look at the bottom of the bag to see …

The gorgeous wrought iron and ceramic angel ornament from Feeding Futures.

"Coop," I breathe. I hug him and he wraps his arms around me tightly. "It's beautiful. Thank you."

"You're welcome," he says.

"That's nice," Dad says. I hang the ornament carefully on the tree and pause to look at it among all my mom's favorites. It's beautiful.

Then I grab a box from under the tree and turn back to Coop.

"I got you something, too."

"You mean in addition to the sweatshirt, right?" he asks.

"No chance." I hand him the box.

He opens it up and then grins. It's a sweatshirt with Buddy the Elf on it ... but with Coop's face on it instead of Will Ferrell's.

He laughs and hugs me again.

"Ugh, you two are disgusting. I hope you break up soon," Lucas says.

Dad throws a pillow at his head at the same time that Coop says, "We're not breaking up." He holds me tighter when he says this, and it feels final. Like he's putting a stamp on this relationship.

Coop and Liesel.

Done.

I grin.

"Well, then, I guess we should show you *our* present, Coop," Logan says with a sigh. He and Lucas swap mischievous glances.

"You guys got him a present?" I ask skeptically. "If it's a flaming bag of dog poop—"

"Dude! We're grown men. We're not pulling some dumb prank on the guy. Chill," Lucas says.

"We'll be right back," Logan says.

The two run for the stairs, and based on the pounding, they're taking them two at a time.

"I have a terrible feeling about this," I say.

"Me too," Coop says.

"Not me," Dad says, leaning back on the armchair in a way that makes his guns look even more massive. He grins at Coop, and the feeling of foreboding intensifies.

My brothers run down the stairs like a herd of elephants, and a moment later, they appear with something behind their backs.

Or someone—

"NO!" I scream, rushing them. "No way!"

Logan holds me back while Lucas pulls the life-size Coop cutout from behind his back. Every part of Coop opens up in gleeful delight. His eyes, his mouth, his arms. He looks at me and says, "YOU LOVE ME!" Then he bursts out laughing. And so do my brothers and Dad. They all laugh themselves to tears, while I stand there and punch my brothers' shoulders as hard as I can.

Dad gets up and tries to pull me off of the tweebs, but he's laughing too hard to keep a hold of me. Coop succeeds where he fails. "Why are you mad? This is the best gift I've ever been given."

"I hate all of you. I'm running away from home."

"Don't go, Lee!" Logan says through his stupid streaming laugh-tears.

"We love you!" Lucas says, clutching his stomach.

I punch the Coop cutout in the face before the real Coop can stop me, and that only makes everyone laugh harder.

Including me.

"I guess you really did get everything you wanted for Christmas," Coop says.

"I hate you."

"Nope. I have proof. You love me," he says, folding me in his arms and rocking us back and forth. "Or you will soon enough."

The cockiness on this guy!

Dad sets Bear down and starts picking up wrapping paper and putting it into a large black garbage bag, and the rest of us quickly chip in. When Coop tosses his wrapping paper in the bag, I hear my dad ask, "What does your family do Christmas morning?"

"We watch Christmas movies while we do a gingerbread house competition every year."

"That sounds fun. I'm sorry we don't have any kits."

"They definitely do *not* use kits. Am I right?" I say to Coop.

He nods, a wistful smile on his face. "We homemake the gingerbread."

Dad slaps him on the back and Coop falls forward. "All right! Looks like we have a new tradition, kids! Coop, show us how it's done."

I watch as my dad takes Coop into the kitchen and my brothers follow. My heart thumps in time with their steps. But there's an ache there, too, and this time it's not because I miss my mom. It's because I know how much Coop misses his.

My family has rallied around him. They're not just accommodating him, they're making him feel at home. That can't change the fact that it's not *his* home, though. And the song is exactly right: there really is no place like home for the holidays.

CHAPTER TWENTY-NINE

LIESEL

We're piping frosting on our houses when I get a text from Kayla Carville.

KAYLA

Liesel! Your brothers are about to get a phone call that I hope makes you all very happy! Merry Christmas!

I adore Kayla. She can't know that the idea of my brothers being traded to another Triple-A team is a gut punch of epic proportions. They were about to be put on the extended roster for one of the top teams in baseball. *My team!* They were practically guaranteed a shot in the Majors this year.

Now, it's all out of my control.

As much as I thought I was tired of worrying about their fates, I realize now that I'd be sad to see them anywhere else but with me.

Coop nudges me with his foot, and I show him the text while

my dad and brothers work on their gingerbread houses. His tight-lipped smile shows more than sympathy. I get the feeling this hurts him, too.

A minute or two later, my brothers get the call from their agent.

Who makes deals on Christmas Day, for Santa's sake? Sports agents, that's who.

Logan frowns at the phone, but Lucas's eyes light up. He answers and switches it to speaker as the two walk through the dining room and down the hall to Dad's office.

"How are you, Glen?" Logan says just before the door closes.

We don't hear the rest, but I worry my lip while Coop and I look at each other. He takes my hand under the table, and his warmth stops me from going cold.

Dad's eyes jump between Coop and me, and I know he knows *we* know.

"What's going on?" he asks.

"We'll find out soon enough," I say.

"Or," Dad says, piping frosting on a wall of his house. He's been working on that same wall for minutes. "We could find out now, considering you two clearly know something."

"I tried, Dad," I say, guilt thick in my throat.

"Tried what?"

"To get them called up."

"They just hit their stride last season. They have time." Confusion tugs his threaded eyebrows up into concern. "Did you think that was your job?"

I frown. "I wanted to watch out for them like Mom said. You were there. We were watching the draft, and she made me promise to watch out for them."

Dad puts his frosting bag down and trains his eyes on me. "Lee, honey, you've always put too much pressure on yourself. You were so worried about them missing out on anything when your mom was sick that you made it your mission to help them however you could. But they didn't need that."

"I didn't do it for them. I did it for *her*. I saw how hard it was for her to not be involved, so I took over and brought her into every discussion and decision. I wanted her to feel ..." I stop, at a loss for words.

"Useful?" Coop asks. His brown eyes swim with empathy.

"Yeah." I nod. "She loved being a baseball mom. She took so much pride in being the kind of mom who didn't complain about lugging kids to and from practices and living at the baseball field. And then, it was taken from her. I didn't want her to feel like she was missing out on even more."

Dad gets up, rounds the table, and hugs me. "You brought her so much joy." His words hit my heart like a bass drum. "She would be so proud of you. But you know it was never your responsibility to create training programs for them. All she wanted was for you to use that big brain and heart of yours to keep them from daring each other to jump out of a plane without a parachute. She never expected you to help them make the pros. That's on them."

"I know," I say, even though I don't know anything of the sort.

"Lee," Dad says gently, backing up. "Believe me. She would be more than proud of all you've done for them. But she'd also be the first person to tell you you've done more than enough. It's time to let them worry about their futures."

Coop clears his throat, and my dad winces like Coop kicked him.

"And ...I recognize I'm guilty of holding on too hard, myself." Dad says, dropping his eyes. "I shouldn't have come to your presentation, sweetie. Or called all the teams you interviewed with. Or gotten background checks on the guys you've dated—"

"WHAT?"

He scratches his forehead sheepishly. "I've overstepped, and I'm sorry. You're an impressive young woman. You don't need your dad in the stands cheering you on."

"Daddy," I say, affection squeezing out the annoyance in my chest as I hug him "I'll always need you in the stands cheering me on! But maybe you could watch from the cheap seats next time. And with fewer threats to guys I like."

"Or none," Coop says. "None's a good number."

"No, some is okay," I say, peeking around my dad to smile at Coop.

Dad's laugh rumbles against me.

My brothers come back right as Dad sits back down.

"Well, well, well," Lucas says, "you're looking at the newest star pitchers of the Mullet Ridge Mudflaps, baby!" Lucas pops the collar of his Christmas tree camo pajamas.

"Mullet Ridge?" Dad asks. "The Triple-A team out of South Carolina? They're a Rockies affiliate." Dad asks.

"They *were*."

"What?" Coop and I both ask.

"Turns out, the Rockies owner doesn't like Kayla Carville's style, and it's a contract year for both the Mudflaps and the Firebirds' Triple-A team. So Kayla proposed a swap … as long as the Fischer bros were part of the deal," Logan says.

"WHAT?" I almost scream.

"That's right," Lucas says. "She said she wanted the Fischer bros, and she managed to convince the Rockies that they *don't* want to be in the Mudflaps business and the Firebirds that they *do*. Oh, and we've been placed on the Firebirds' extended roster!"

"AAAHHH!" I jump up and hug my brothers, stomping my feet excitedly and squeezing them for dear life. "I'm so happy for you guys!"

When I let go, I give Coop a shocked look, and he just smiles.

Lucas grabs a handful of nuts and bolts and throws them in his mouth while he sits back down at the table.

But Coop's eyes move to Logan's.

"What do you think, Logan?" he asks. "Are you upset?"

"No, I'm worried," he says. "I'm worried I'm not there yet."

"You'll get there," Coop says.

"You said I telegraph my pitches."

"You do."

"I've watched tape on myself. What do you see that I don't?"

"It's your curveball."

"I have one of the best curveballs in the minors."

"Yeah, but you pause when your left knee is up during windup. You're probably checking your grip, or something, but it's just long enough. And minor leagues don't have pitch readers on staff, but the majors do. A pitch reader will be able to call that out every time."

Logan sniffs, and Lucas laughs at him. "You pause."

"I *pause*?" Logan asks. "Coop ... would you ... mind ... helping ... me?"

Coop laughs. "Was that really so painful?"

"Yes," Logan says.

"I'm happy to," Coop says.

Logan looks relieved, but Lucas is still snorting.

"Yuk it up," Logan says, getting back to his gingerbread house. "He said we *both* telegraph our pitches."

Lucas sits straighter. "What? What do I do?"

"I told you this last season," I say. "You raise your glove too high on your slider."

"And you keep your glove at your chest on your changeup," Coop says. "It's a dead giveaway to anyone who can read a pitch."

"If it's so obvious, how come no one has ever mentioned this?" Lucas says.

"I said it!" I protest. "You just didn't believe me. You guys *never* believe me when it comes to baseball."

Logan frowns, putting a Skittle on his poorly frosted roof. "We believe you, we just ..." The tweebs look at each other. "Mom told us we needed to look out for *you*. She made us promise that we wouldn't let you spend all your time behind a desk or computer screen mapping out our futures," Lucas says.

She what? My tone softens as I think of my mom thinking of *me*. "So why wouldn't you believe me?"

"We didn't want managing our careers to feel like your job. We have trainers and analysts for that. We just wanted you to feel free to be our sister," Logan says.

"But you guys can't even make cookies without me!"

Logan rolls his eyes. "Of course we can. Lucas's Oreo cake pops are insane. Uncle Paul ate like twenty last year."

"You told me you brought Costco cookies!"

"We lied!" Lucas says, frosting the roof of his house until it caves in. "Dang it."

"Why did you lie?" I ask.

"Because we miss you," Logan says. He meets my gaze, and when his eyes start welling, mine mirror them. "Being around you makes it hurt less."

I start crying. "You guys are such freaking turds."

Logan and Lucas both pull me to my feet into another bear hug that makes Dad's dog yap his little face off.

When we all sit back down, Coop bumps his leg into mine beneath the table, and I don't care who's watching. I lean my forehead into his shoulder.

Dad chuckles and glances at a family picture on the wall. It's from a few years after Mom got her diagnosis, when she was still able to use a walker. She was so pretty. It always feels odd when people say how much I look like her, but it's an honor, too. "I hope you'll all keep looking out for each other, but I think you've done your duty to your mom. You're all old enough to take care of yourselves."

"Mostly," Logan says. "Lucas still has trouble untying his cleats when he does a double knot."

"That was one time! And none of the rest of the team could untie it, either."

Dad is drinking eggnog, and he snorts it out of his nose, making us all bust up. "All right," he says, wiping his face. "Lee and Logan, you two watch out for Lucas. Lukie, you get a pass."

Lucas throws candy at all of us.

* * *

After more decorating (Coop is building a mansion while the rest of us are working on shacks), Coop takes a break to get water in the kitchen. He's still not back after a couple of minutes, so I go into the kitchen and find him staring at his texts.

"Any word?" I ask.

He puts his phone into his pajama pants pocket. "Mom responded to the video message."

"Oh, let me see!"

"She responded with a note, not a video. She said they miss me and will call me when they can." He holds his arms out for me, and I slide into the hug, wanting to cry.

"How are you?"

"Fine," he says, but I know he's lying. "I'm not going to yell at a brick wall for being immovable."

His mom being immovable is one thing. Her not spending every second trying to see his face on the screen she has access to is another.

"I'm sorry."

"Thanks." He kisses my forehead. "How are *you* feeling? How is your first Christmas at home without your mom?"

"Better than I thought it would be."

"Because I'm here, right? I knew it."

"Shut it, you," I say. But he's not wrong. Not at all.

"I noticed you guys don't have mistletoe up anywhere. We're going to need that if we're going to make out in front of your family with impunity."

I laugh against his chest. "We're not making out in front of my family."

"But you'll at least admit in front of them that you're madly in love with me, right?"

"Not today, I won't."

"That is wildly disappointing."

I kiss him just long enough to take some of the disappointment away, and then I pull him back into the dining room to finish our gingerbread houses.

And I think about his question as I watch him with my dad and brothers. A few weeks ago, I could hardly stomach admitting that I was *working* with Coop. Now, I'm stealing kisses.

And he's totally stolen my heart.

CHAPTER THIRTY

COOPER

I win.

It's not even close, although Liesel and Logan both did okay on their gingerbread houses. Lucas's was an embarrassment, and Bruce couldn't even get his to stay up. He kept blaming his "big meat hook hands."

"How are you so good at making a gingerbread house?" Logan asks. We've moved on to putting together a puzzle on the coffee table while *Elf* plays in the background. Puzzles are a Christmas tradition *both* our families share.

"My mom's a pro. Not technically, but she could be. She's an incredible baker."

"You should see the cakes she made Coop when he was growing up," Liesel says, smiling at me over the puzzle. It's a sad smile, though. It's late afternoon on Christmas Day, and while they've sent plenty of texts, I haven't received a single phone call, FaceTime, or video message.

As much as I try to keep the pain at bay, I haven't hurt this much since elementary, not that I'll ever let her know that. I thought maybe Liesel was right, that telling her would be cathartic, but it wasn't. It didn't backfire. It did *nothing*.

But my mom loves me, and she's always done the best she could.

It's enough. It has to be.

"What about the cakes?" Logan is asking Liesel.

Liesel pulls up her Instagram, giving me a questioning look, like she's asking permission to show him. I shrug. It's sweet of her to want to be my mom's hype woman. It feels like she's defending my mom even to *me*, not that she needs defending.

"Whoa, your mom made that? How?"

"Which one is it?" I ask. Liese shows me a picture of a three-tiered cake with pin stripes and buttons on the bottom tier, baseball glove stitching on the middle tier, and a baseball cap as the top tier.

"That's nothing," Liesel says. "You should see the stadium cake!"

I watch how sweet Liesel's being, how cool her brothers are acting, and it pinches my heart. I don't know how I could possibly feel so comfortable here after only a day and a half, but I do. It's mostly because of Liesel, but I feel a camaraderie with her brothers and Dad, too. It makes me excited to think that I'll be playing with them this year, because with a little coaching, I'm positive they'll get called up.

Oh, and I hope Doug won't kill me for going behind his back and dating the *heck* out of Liesel anyway.

Speaking of which …

"Bruce," I say as he connects an edge piece to the winter wonderland scene. "What's gonna happen the season after next? When I'm playing again and dating Liesel and you're officiating?"

Bruce raises his eyebrows like he's understanding the significance of what I'm asking. That's almost a year and a half away.

"I'll be put on a different rotation. If you have a personal connection to a player, the Umpires Association keeps you from officiating games for those teams. It'll be the same thing whenever the boys get called up."

"Does Doug know this?"

Bruce chuckles. "Yes, but I'll reassure him he doesn't need to worry."

I almost slump in relief. "Maybe we could do a conference call and make sure he knows that we're all on the same page and that I didn't seduce Liesel with my masculine wiles."

Fists punch my shoulders before I can even say I'm joking.

When the tweebs sit back down, we all look around the table.

Everyone is smiling.

And that causes a bittersweet pang in my heart. I like Liesel's family. Heck, I love them. I never would have imagined being so happy on Christmas Day without my parents.

But no matter how much I'm enjoying being here, the more the day goes on, the more it hurts that my parents aren't even trying to talk to me.

Anyone can text, "I miss you."

It's different to see it on their faces or hear it in their voices. I excuse myself to go to the bathroom, and I close the toilet lid and sit on it. I try to FaceTime my parents *again.*

It rings.

They don't answer.

A moment later, I get a text.

MOM

Can't talk right now, but we love you! How are you?

My anger and hurt bubble up to the surface, and I do something I've never in my life done.

I get mad at my mom.

COOP

What the heck, Mom? What is so important that you can't take my call on Christmas Day?

This hurts.

I'm immediately racked with guilt. She's coping the best she can. She's not some negligent parent who doesn't care about me. I try to unsend the messages, but it's too late. They've been delivered. Read.

I pinch my temples, feeling sick and sad and … forgotten.

And when she doesn't immediately reply, I dash angry tears from my cheeks.

I'm done. Not forever, but for now. The pain of this disappointment and hurt have cut through layers I thought had healed years ago, and I'm left with a seeping wound that I have to stop poking at.

I flip my phone to do not disturb. I've never held a grudge against her, and I don't know that I even do now.

But I can't pretend this doesn't affect me. It's one thing that we can't see each other today. That's no one's fault. It's another that she's shutting me out, refusing to talk to me, choosing something over me.

The axe has cut deeply into my trunk, and it's going to take time to heal.

I splash cold water on my face and leave the bathroom. The Fischers are all getting on their winter coats, boots, and hats.

"What's going on?" I ask.

"Another Fischer family tradition," Liesel says, smiling. "Come on."

* * *

It's freezing cold, the snow is up to our knees, and the tweebs have made hundreds of snowballs. The yard is probably half an acre—plenty of space to throw a ball around—but we're not hurling more snowballs at each other.

We're hitting them with baseball bats.

Logan and Lucas have cleared a space big enough for them to stand in, and Liesel, Bruce, and I have all done the same. And Bruce tromps a path large enough to look like a crude baseball diamond for the fun of it.

The three of us—Bruce, Liesel, and me—are holding bats, standing at imaginary plates, as Logan and Lucas throw them past us.

I'm hitting left-handed, for the record. And they are *not* going easy on me.

"Who throws a brushback pitch to a dude who had Tommy John's surgery?" I say to Lucas, kicking the snow and trying to square up. I'm careful not to use my right arm at all, which means Lucas is smoking me.

"Winners, that's who."

"It was a strike," Bruce says, even as he pulverizes a snowball Logan threw to him.

"You're not even behind the plate!" I cry. "Nepotism." Lucas pegs me with a snowball, and I laugh. "You suck."

"No, you suck," Lucas says, throwing another pitch, this time to Liesel. She smacks it and then another, laughing all the way.

When it's my turn to hit again, I square up and crush it. The ball explodes in a cloud of white powder that makes me laugh. "That's how it's done, boys," I say, dropping my bat and trudging around the makeshift diamond. The tweebs boo me while Liesel cheers, and when I make it back around to Liesel—my home base—she jumps into my arms and kisses me.

Her brothers and Dad all throw snowballs at us, and I spin and shield her from the worst of it while she laughs.

But someone else claps.

Liesel senses it the same moment I do. I whip around, still holding her, to find the source of the clap.

A couple has come into the backyard from the plowed driveway. The man is about my height, with a handsome, weathered face from years of hard work. The dark eyed woman has beautiful ivory skin that hasn't seen the sun in decades and that makes her look younger than she is. Her smile is warmer than a fireplace.

"Mom?" I whisper. "Dad?"

Mom starts laughing, holding her hands over her mouth, tears streaming down her face. Dad's hands are on her shoulders, but he's crying, too.

"I've never seen you hit a ball before," Mom says. "You're so talented!"

I run at full speed to them, almost tackling my mom when I dive into her arms. I sob in a way I haven't in years, breaking down uncontrollably. The three of us hold each other tightly, and I don't care that Liesel's family is seeing this. I don't care about anything else in the world.

"You're here! How are you here?" I ask through my tears.

"We drove," Dad says, sniffing back tears of his own. "I told you I was getting a Winnebago. Your mom's gotten really comfortable in it over the last few months."

"I've been practicing," Mom says in my ear. The three of us are all still hugging, and I can't let Mom go. She's shaking like a leaf, and while I'm sure some of that is happiness at seeing me, I know there has to be real fear and anxiety to it, too. "I found a new therapist last year. I've been doing exposure therapy. I'd hoped I could make the playoffs, but I wasn't ready." She frowns, and tears gush out. "I'm so sorry I wasn't ready."

"I don't care!" I cry. "You're here now!"

"I'm here," she says, trembling and squeezing me. "I love you and I'm finally here."

"This is why we couldn't take your calls," Dad explains with an apologetic, watery smile. "We knew you'd hear the Winnebago in the background."

"I'm so sorry you were hurting, sweetie," Mom says. "I had to do this. When my therapist recommended that silly VR headset, it opened the world to me. It was terrifying at first, but also … life changing. It showed me that there's so much beauty in the world that I've missed. But it was when I started watching your games that I realized I couldn't go on like this anymore. I couldn't stand to live another moment missing *you live yours*." Her tears are freezing against my face, and I couldn't care less.

"How did you know where I was?" I sniff when Mom and I finally break apart.

"Find A Friend," Dad says with a chuckle. He looks past me to talk to Liesel's family. "I hope you don't mind us crashing."

"Not at all!" Liesel says.

"It's our pleasure," Bruce says.

I wave Liesel over and tuck her underneath my arm as I introduce her to my parents. "You guys saw my message, didn't you?" They nod. "This is Liesel."

"We're so happy to meet you," Mom says, hugging Liesel.

Dad hugs her next. "I never thought I'd see the day when Coop introduced us to a girl. He's never cared about anyone enough to even tell us about a date."

Mom gives Liesel a full smile. I get my smile from my mom, and while mine is a little too cocksure, Mom's makes people feel like they're the only person in the room. In the world, maybe. "He clearly cares a lot about you," Mom says.

I take Liesel's hand. She looks up at me with so much joy on her face, I can't believe I told her dad we weren't in love yet.

Of course I'm in love with her.

"Yes, he does," I say of myself. "He cares a *lot* about her."

One of Liesel's brothers groans. "Talking about yourself in the third person, are you, Coop?"

I chuckle and wave the rest of Liesel's family over to make introductions. My mom has to be overwhelmed—she doesn't meet new people often, and never outside of her environment.

But she smiles and shakes hands and jokes with Liesel's dad and brothers like they're old friends.

And all I can do is watch in awe and … gratitude. Humility, maybe. I don't know what the right word is, but the feeling is all encompassing and makes my soul hum with a contentment I've never known.

I have spent so many years doing everything I could to bring happiness to my family. Always making accommodations and meeting my mom where she was.

Today is unlike any day I've ever had.

My mom came for me.

She came for me.

CHAPTER THIRTY-ONE

LIESEL

We're all teary when Coop introduces us to his family, even my big, dumb brothers. If they had any lingering doubts about what a great guy Coop is before this, they're gone now. Seeing him with his mom could thaw anyone's heart.

He's holding his mom, tears rolling down his cheeks, and beaming brighter than the setting sun against the snow.

"Michelle, John," my dad says after they're introduced, "would you want to come inside?"

Coop's mom's eyes flit around the backyard and I can almost see the moment the panic sets in.

"Or is there space for all of us in your RV?" I ask. "I've always wanted to see one."

The look of gratitude on Coop's face is mirrored by his dad's.

"There's plenty of space," Coop's dad says. "Come on in."

We all stomp through the snow and out to the driveway,

where a huge RV is parked. My dad and brothers go in after Mr. and Mrs. Kellogg, and then Coop and I join them.

Coop's parents are sitting on one side of a dinette table, while my dad is sitting across from them. My brothers are at a small sofa. Coop is about to sit in the driver's seat when he looks at the roof and his eyes light up.

I laugh. "Mistletoe?"

"That's what I'm talking about!" Coop says, dropping me into a dip. "Now we can make out with impunity."

"You really can't," my dad says.

"Not the wisest move, son," Coop's dad agrees.

Coop's mom is laughing at all of us, and the happiness on her face makes me feel like I'm glowing from within.

Coop pecks my cheek, and I laugh. "We should let you guys celebrate together," I say.

"Oh, please stay," Coop's mom says. "The three of us have spent enough Christmases alone. I didn't come all this way to go back to where we were. Of course, you're welcome to go into your house, and we can go to—"

"You're welcome to park here and use our facilities. And we're happy to hang out as long as you can put up with us," Dad says. Then he smiles. "You've raised a fine young man."

"No take backs!" Coop says, pointing at my dad.

"He's okay," Coop's dad says. "A bit of a punk sometimes."

Everyone laughs except Coop's mom, who defends his honor and then pulls out some games. Coop's dad turns on a football game on the TV in the background.

"Why don't I go grab snacks?" I offer.

"I'll come help," Coop offers.

We head outside to see that the snow has started falling again, but the flakes are soft and fluffy and take forever to melt when they land on my eyelashes. When we get into the mudroom, I start shaking off, but Coop stops me.

"What—" He puts his hands on both sides of my face, pulling

me toward him, and then his mouth fuses into mine. His kiss is hot enough to melt us together. All of our tension—our constant push and pull—syncs up perfectly in an intricate dance of kissing, nibbling, smiling, and laughing. I feel his cheeks lift in a grin as he slides his hand up my cheek and into my hair, knocking off my hat. Fingertips press against my scalp, making me sigh and fall into him, as happy as I can remember being in a long time.

I don't beat myself up for feeling happy. The fact that I've gotten to this point at all is a miracle nearly as big as Coop's mom being here.

It's Christmas, and my mom's gone, but I can still be happy. It's not betraying her to enjoy the things we loved together; it's honoring her. Every laugh is a tribute to the legacy she left me and my family. And it's taken Coop to help me see that.

"You're amazing, you know that?" I say.

"I do," he says. "But feel free to list all the reasons you think so."

"I should let my brothers beat you up a little," I laugh.

"Only if you promise to kiss me better."

"I can do that."

He drops his face and kisses me again, slowly, his lips lingering tenderly on mine. "I need to say something, and I want you not to freak out."

My eyes fly open to see his closed ones. "Okay ..."

"I think I love you."

I smile and close my eyes again, letting my lips brush against his. "Oh, that? Tell me something I don't know."

"Why don't you?"

"Why don't I what?" I ask, our breath mingling together in puffs of warm mist.

"Tell me something I don't know."

"The circumference of the earth is twenty-four—"

"Something else."

"A cloud weighs around a million—"

"Liesel."

"Yes, Coop?"

"Tell me you love me."

"You're not the boss of me."

"LIESEL SUGAR PLUM FISCHER."

"Yes?" I ask, my lips very much on his.

"If you love me, kiss me."

I kiss him.

He grins. "I knew it." I kiss him again. "Oh, wow. You love me a *lot*," he says.

"Nah, I just thought it would finally shut you up."

"Never," he says.

Then our voices stop but our lips keep moving in a conversation all on their own.

And I love every word.

EPILOGUE

SIX WEEKS LATER

COOPER

It's Nate and Juliet's wedding day, and I'm sitting in a beautiful white barn in Sugar Maple, South Carolina watching my girlfriend walk down the aisle in her sexy bridesmaid's dress while her dad and brothers sit next to me.

Lucas elbows my gut. "No ogling."

"When are we gonna be past that, man?" I say through clenched teeth.

"Never," Logan mutters on my other side.

"She's my girlfriend," I whisper.

Lucas inclines his head toward me as the music changes to the Wedding March. "You could be celebrating your twentieth wedding anniversary, and we're gonna punch you if you kiss her for too long."

"She'll always be our sister first," Logan says.

"Tweebs," I grumble, even though we've become good friends in the six weeks since Christmas. I watch Nate's the moment he sees Juliet walking down the aisle with her dad. The way his eyes widen and his mouth parts like he's trying to catch his breath—he looks like he's in awe of her. Like he can't believe that someone so magnificent could really be his.

My eyes find Liesel's.

I know the feeling.

The wedding is beautiful and goes off without a hitch, as does the family dinner. During the toasts, Juliet's identical twin sister stands up and speaks glowingly of her sister and of the way that Nate changed their family's lives for the better.

"Nate, you helped us realize how dangerous it is to put people in a box and keep them there. I had done this to my own sister, and I almost lost her. But because of you, we're closer than ever. I'm so happy I can now call you my brother," the sister says, and I don't know why I'm crying, but it's a wedding, and that's what you do.

Liesel's tribute to Juliet is beautiful, funny, and heartfelt.

"It's crazy how things that seem like a disaster on the outset can turn into your biggest blessings," Liesel says. "Like parking space wars and a dumb white Prius."

"White Prius!" Juliet says loudly, shaking her fist at the sky. I understand the joke now—it was Juliet's nickname for Nate before they got stuck on the elevator—but it's one of those things that's funniest for the people who lived it.

"That car is the best thing that ever happened to you, too," Nate says to Liesel from his seat, and she blushes and looks at me. "Stop pretending you two won't be here in a few months."

I grin when Liesel's flush deepens prettily. "Be that as it may," Liesel says. "I'm thankful that something as small as a car parked in a covered spot could be the means of bringing you two together. Juliet, I've seen you come into yourself because of Nate's acceptance and love. Nate, you are getting the most incredible woman in the world. Be good to her or I'll sic my dad on you."

Laughs circle the room, as everyone has noticed Bruce. He laughs along with them.

She ends the toast with a few more heartwarming words, and we all raise our glasses.

I'm at a table with Liesel's dad and brothers and Kayla Carville, of all people, who happens to be a friend of Nate's from their Harvard undergrad days. She's here with her fiancé, who looks and smells like old money, with his actual wristwatch —not smart watch—and that easy confidence that comes from knowing you could buy everyone here.

Except for Nate and Kayla.

Also, his name is Aldridge Sinclair. What does a guy even do with a name like that?

He's not funny. He's not particularly engaged in the wedding. But he's extremely attentive to Kayla.

And by the looks of it, she's sick of it.

She keeps trying to talk to the Fischer brothers, but her fiancé stops her every time, trying to draw her attention back to him.

Bruce shoots me a look that I'm sure I accurately interpret: how the heck are these two together?

"It's one thing for your father to buy you a team in a place called *Mullet Ridge*," Aldridge says in a rich New England accent. "It's another to keep it. It's embarrassing."

"It was sweet," she says, even though I know she doesn't care about baseball. "And I'm starting to like it."

"Are you really going to stay in that *town* while you find your little workers?"

The "workers" he's talking about are the coach and GM.

Her smile is exhausted and nothing like the one I've seen from her in other circumstances. "Tripp said I can stay at his place in Sugar Maple while I figure things out with it." She looks at the rest of us. "My cousin, Tripp, owns this farm and has some beautiful places to stay here. Bruce, you'll have to stay in one of the cottages when you come out to see your boys play."

Bruce nods, but he looks as sympathetic as I think the rest of us feel.

Aldridge Sinclair is an emotional leech, and how he landed Kayla is a mystery.

But it's not one I care to solve. The only thing I care about is getting Liesel back in my arms.

The dinner ends and it's finally time for the reception and dance. I'm eager to hold the woman I love. Her thick blonde hair is pulled into a side ponytail, her sleek, silky sage green dress is doing incredible things for her curves, and the small, secretive smile she's flashed me a dozen times tonight needs to be kissed off those sexy lips of hers.

Lucas and Logan chat up a couple of Juliet's cousins, and Bruce sits down to talk to Juliet's gran, who is the cutest little old woman alive. She and I sat together while Nate and Juliet were taking pictures, and she showed me all her favorite GIFS.

It was odd, but totally awesome.

Liesel saunters over to me in a way that makes her hips look like lethal weapons. "Want to dance, hotshot?" She pulls me up by my tie.

"More than anything," I say.

We walk over to the farthest side of the dance floor from her meddling family, and I wrap one arm around her waist and a hand around one of hers. Her hand around my neck plays with my hair. "You know," I tell her, gazing into the gorgeous blue of her eyes, "you lied in your toast."

"How do you figure?" she asks.

"You said Nate is getting the most incredible woman in the world. But that's not true, because she's currently mine."

"Currently?" she tugs on my hair.

"Now and always." I kiss her temple, and I feel her eyelids

flutter against my cheek in a butterfly kiss that sends a wave of goosebumps over me.

"Oh, it's always now, is it?" she teases as we sway.

"I'm not letting you go," I say in her ear. "I haven't gotten that Christmas sweater yet."

A laugh bursts out of her, and she leans closer to me. "In that case, I guess I'll have to keep it forever."

"In that case," I echo. "I guess I'll have to keep *you* forever."

Liesel's heels are at least four inches, and it erases enough of our height difference that I can feel the ball of her cheek against my chin as she smiles.

"I love you," she whispers.

"Tell me something I don't know," I tease.

"That, you glorious dumb jock" she says, kissing my neck with each word, "could take all day."

"Since there's no place to go ..."

"Actually, the correct lyric is 'we've—'" she starts, but I kiss the words and the laugh from her mouth, grateful we have all the time in the world together.

Because I want every second.

Curious what happened when Nate and Juliet got trapped in an elevator together? Read all about it in Single All the Way!

And read on for a BONUS EPILOGUE featuring Kayla Carville.

BONUS EPILOGUE

KAYLA

I hate my engagement ring.

Am I allowed to say that?

I'm with my fiancé at a wedding for an old college friend, and instead of us staring at each other with moony eyes on the dance floor, he's staring at me—I can *feel* his eyes—while I stare at my very shiny, very gaudy ring.

The bride's ring is *stunning*. It's a five carat round brilliant cut, pure, simple, and unadorned. The ring speaks for itself, bold but not overbearing, confident yet not cocky.

It will age as beautifully as their love for each other.

"What are you thinking about, Beautiful?" Aldridge asks me. He tucks my auburn hair behind my ear, and I'm reminded forcibly of a gnat I want to swat at.

What is wrong with me?

I tear my eyes from my ring and smile at my fiancé's handsome face. "This will be us soon," I say.

"I can't wait," he says, putting his arm around me as he

watches Nate and Juliet dance. After six years together, I've memorized his every micro-expression. Unlike a favorite book, though, I'm tired of reading these expressions. The boredom in his eyes, the judgment in his lips.

That's not boredom, I chide myself. *That's contentment. You know the difference.*

His boredom comes with a sneer, and he's not sneering. He's *smiling.*

And that's even worse.

Aldridge loves me. He loves me so much, I'm suffocating on his attention. The more he dotes, the more I feel myself pushing away. He's the exact same man he's always been, though, so these feelings aren't an indictment on him but on me.

I want an excuse. I want an out.

No! I'm being absurd.

After six years, never has he given me reason to doubt his commitment. We're getting married in less than a month!

This is simply cold feet.

Even if said feet are sweating in these heels.

"Hey, cuz," a low Southern voice says. I look up and smile at my hulking cousin, Tripp. "Mind if I steal her, Aldridge?"

Tripp and Aldridge shake hands, and Aldridge goes the extra step of patting Tripp's hand with his free one. "What are you two going to talk about?" Aldridge asks.

I smile at my fiancé, hoping it hides the irritation making my cheeks quiver. "Nothing exciting, sweetheart," I say. "Unless you care about agricultural distribution as much as we do."

"Can't say that I do," Aldridge says, but the uncertainty in his brow makes him look like a little kid worried everyone is having fun but him. Except to Aldridge, "everyone" is a party of one:

Me.

The feeling of slowly suffocating hits me anew as I look at

him, and it isn't until Tripp pulls me to my feet that I can take a real breath.

"You okay?" Tripp asks as we walk through the gorgeous wedding grounds on his farm. It used to be our grandfather's farm, but when he passed, he split his massive holdings into the original family farm, which went to Tripp, and Carville Industries, which went to my father and our family. Tripp has more of a passion for agriculture than I do, but I love business and enjoy working for my dad and with my brothers.

Oh, and owning a baseball team. I've thrown myself into learning the sport over the last several weeks, and the challenge has become almost exciting. Something to look forward to after work. Something to think about instead of wedding planning.

Or marriage.

"I'm doing better than you are," I tell my cousin. The twinkling lights overhead illuminate a red stain on his dress shirt. "You spilled cocktail sauce."

He clicks his tongue and directs us over to the open bar. "Sean," Tripp says to a man with a thick black beard and slick hair, "could you get me a club soda and a cloth?"

The bartender nods and ducks his head behind the long wrap-around counter. A moment later, he pops up, and I flush when his blue eyes land on me for a split second before they move to Tripp. My reaction isn't because he's an attractive man —although he is—but because of how deeply his eyes peer. If I were the type to hide things, I wouldn't want this man near me.

"Here you go," the bartender says, handing Tripp the cloth and club soda. Tripp pours the liquid onto the stain, dabbing at it.

"Can I get you anything?" the man asks me in a low voice I probably shouldn't be able to hear over the music. His face matches his build—broad, strong, and a bit imposing, with just a hint of softness to his lips that catches me off guard. I tuck my hair behind my ear.

"Nothing, but thank you."

"Wow," he says, looking at my hand and leaning back a few inches. "That is a statement."

I follow his gaze to my ring, and I find myself sticking my hand behind my back with a shake of my head. "Oh, that. I know. It's silly."

"I don't think *silly* is the word I'd use."

Tripp snorts.

"Oh, stop," I say to my cousin. "Like Jane's wedding ring isn't big?" It's also a tasteful three carat princess cut that isn't trying too hard to prove itself to the world.

"I'm not sayin' anything," Tripp says. He looks at Sean. "But her fiancé is, ain't he?"

The bartender—Sean—nods, his thick brown eyebrows raising. I can't disagree, so I shrug and plant my elbows on the counter beside Tripp.

"Kayla, this is Sean. Sean owns a bar with his brother and is the captain of the local minor league hockey team. Sean, this is my cousin, Kayla, the new owner of the Mudflaps."

"Pleasure," Sean says, taking my hand in his thick one and shaking it. His hands are so thick and muscled, I look down at our clasped hands. I don't know why his hands throw me. It's not like Aldridge's hands are dainty. "So, Kayla, what's your vision for the Mudflaps?" he asks me, his blue eyes steady and piercing. "Are you sticking with the playbook or fixin' to go off script Savannah Bananas style?"

I smile. "It's adorable that you think I have any idea what you're talking about."

This earns a laugh from Sean and Tripp. "Don't listen to her," Tripp says. "She may still be learnin', but Kayla has a business sense to rival Elon Musk."

"It's adorable that you think I have any idea what you're talking about," Sean says, and it's my turn to laugh.

"What are you doin' here tonight, anyway?" Tripp asks Sean. "Shouldn't you be on the road?"

"We have a homestand," Sean says in the same accent as Tripp. I grew up in Atlanta, but I have no accent to speak of. "I could have asked another bartender to come, but your wife and the women running this wedding insisted they needed the best." With that, he grabs an open bottle, flips it behind his back without spilling a drop, and then pours a glass for a nearby guest.

I clap, and Tripp elbows me. "You really need to get out more if you think this is impressive. You should see what this guy used to do on the ice."

"Used to do?" Sean asks.

Tripp grins. "You're getting old, man."

Sean shakes his head and moves on to help another wedding guest.

Tripp and I turn around to look at the dance floor. His wife and a few of her friends are dancing with Juliet and my new friend, Liesel. I'm not sure how they all know each other, but they have an easy camaraderie that makes me smile. Female friendships can be hard to develop, and seeing so many women come together makes my heart sing.

"That's the first time I've seen you actually smile tonight," Tripp says.

"Stop," I say.

"I'm serious. Your smile throughout the wedding looked like it was recycled."

"How dare you?" I tease. "I have a fabulous smile. It's a universal fact about me."

Behind me, I hear a soft snort, and I turn my head and raise an eyebrow at Tripp's bartender friend, who's pouring a Coke for a guest. "You disagree?"

"Don't mind me," he says. "I wouldn't know."

I unleash my full Julia Roberts smile on him and then drop it just as fast. "See?"

Sean looks at Tripp. "It's a pretty good smile."

Tripp and I go back to looking at the guests. "I know you *can* smile. But you haven't smiled like *that* all night. What's goin' on with you and Aldridge?"

"Nothing," I say truthfully. "We're the exact same as we've always been."

"I think you two are missin' the 'growing' part of 'growing old together.'"

I roll my lips together in thought. "We've been together for a long time. We never fight. We like most of the same things. Everything about us makes sense. What is there to *grow* into?"

"If you ain't growing together, you're growing apart," Tripp says.

"Is this an intervention or a Ted Talk? I can't remember which one I requested when I RSVP'd."

I hear another soft laugh behind me, but I purposefully do *not* look at Sean. He's probably drying a wine glass or buffing the counter while he laughs at me.

No, *with* me. The timing of that quiet laugh was definitely in my favor, not Tripp's.

"I want to make sure you know what you're doing, that's all."

"With the team?" I ask, purposefully misunderstanding him. "Not at all. Who would have thought finding a coach would be so hard? Also, when did you start talking like Grandpa Tag? You sound like an old man."

"You're two years older than me."

"Yes, but I make it sound so much cooler."

Sean fully laughs this time, and the warm, easy rumble makes me grin.

I love laughing. I love funny people who can get the humor in a situation or comment without it becoming mean. With my eyes on the dance floor, I see plenty of laughter. Cooper and Liesel are dancing together, and judging by their gleaming eyes, they're engaged in their unique brand of playful banter. Nate and Juliet are dancing again, and I can tell she's teasing him about something based on her wide, batting eyes and the way he's trying not to laugh.

What would it be like to tease and be teased? To have the man I love say something that makes me throw my head back so my laugh reaches all the way up to the stars? To love so fervently that just looking away from the object of my affection is painful? To love so confidently that dancing with friends isn't a sign of escape but of empowerment?

I can only imagine.

Tripp's wife, Jane, is beckoning to him from the dance floor. She's giving her husband a *come hither* look I've never made to Aldridge.

"Go dance with your wife. We'll catch up later."

Tripp eyes me uncertainly, but I wave him away.

"We'll talk later," I tell Tripp. "Go dance with your wife while she can still put up with you."

"I'll be back," he says before heading out to dance with his wife.

I turn away from the dance floor toward the bar. I close my eyes and take a slow, deep breath.

"You okay?" My eyes open to see Sean standing opposite me, his hands on the counter, his expression as open as it is nonjudgmental.

"What do people usually say when the answer is no but they don't want to *say* no?" I ask.

"Not that."

I chuckle and then sigh. "You know the old cliché of a girl finding out that her fiancé is having an affair days before the wedding?"

Sean's demeanor shifts in an instant. The muscles all over his body seem to go on high alert. Tendons pop out in his forearms when he balls his hands into fists. Veins pop out in his neck. Even his beard shifts when he flexes his jaw. It's so *menacing*. "Is that what happened to you?"

"Only in my dreams."

His head snaps back. "You're saying you *wish* he'd cheated?"

"Not in so many words."

Sean laughs to himself. "Sounds like you're looking for a reason to leave him."

I shrug my thin shoulders.

He pours someone a drink but manages to keep talking to me. "The way I see it, wishing you had a reason to leave him is all the reason you need."

I lean forward. The bass of the dance song playing over the speakers thumps hard in my heart. "We make so much sense on paper."

"That's a relief for future readers, I guess. Not sure it works too well for you, though."

I laugh. "That's a clever way of putting it."

"What do you want to happen?" Sean asks.

"That wasn't clear from my wish? You'd make a terrible genie."

Sean's mouth spreads in a wry smile. "Let me rephrase: what are you going to *make* happen?"

It's at that moment I turn my head and spot Aldridge staring at me.

How long has he been watching me? I stifle a groan. "I guess we'll find out," I say, because Aldridge is making his way over.

Plenty of women stare at him as he saunters toward me. He's a beautiful man, and he knows how to captivate a room. If only I'd realized before we got engaged that he doesn't captivate *me*.

"Good luck," Sean says quietly moments before Aldridge holds his hand out to me.

I put my hand in his but turn back to Sean. "Thanks for the chat."

Sean holds Tripp's club soda toward me in salute. And, if I'm not mistaken, in support.

Aldridge leads me to the dance floor, and soon, we're dancing to a pretty slow song about a woman who doesn't want to live with regret.

It's a little *on the nose* for my taste.

"Did you two have a good talk?" Aldridge asks. His lips are near my ear, and I feel like it should make me shiver, not itch.

"The bartender?" I ask. Does he think something was going on there?

Because there absolutely was. Nothing flirty or untoward, but I told the guy I wished my fiancé would cheat on me so I could get out of marrying him! That's some top shelf bartender therapy.

"No, Tripp," Aldridge says.

"Yes, catching up with him was nice. He and Jane seem so happy together."

"That will be us soon enough," he murmurs against my cheek. He wraps his hands more firmly around me, and our bodies press together.

And I feel nothing.

Absolutely nothing.

My body doesn't care that he's acting like the hero of a romance novel. The night is cool enough that I should feel goosebumps from the light breeze, if not from the way his breath stirs the tiny hairs on my cheek and neck.

But I feel *nothing.*

"You know," he continues, "I didn't like letting go of you tonight even for a few minutes. I can't wait until you're all mine."

"I know."

I should say more. I should agree with him, at the very least. I can't, though. Because Sean's question is like a shot through my heart.

What are you going to make happen?

I might be bold, but I'm not brave. I can navigate a boardroom or negotiation with my eyes closed. There's a code in how to act in business. There are expectations and rules of engagement.

There are no rules when it comes to the heart.

I look back at the bartender and watch him maneuver with that casual ease he showed when talking to me. His gaze drifts to mine, and I see the question that lingers there.

What are you going to make happen?

The words have an edge to them now. Not a sharp, cutting edge; more like the edge of a puzzle—the last piece snapping into place, the picture complete. The question is what to do with that finished puzzle. Do I frame it and display it somewhere, the mystery and thrill completely gone, but the picture-perfect image preserved for all to admire?

Or do I put it in a box and try my hand at a new puzzle? A harder one—one that doesn't come with a reference image, one I get to make all on my own.

What are you going to make happen?

His question should cause panic in me, but it doesn't, because this sense of doubt means something. Until tonight, my path has been set, my course determined. If I don't know what comes next, that means, for the first time in years, I'm confronting the *possibility of possibility.*

What are you going to make happen?

I have no idea.

And that exhilarates me.

Kayla and Sean's story is coming soon, but in the meantime, check out Tripp and Jane's sizzling enemies-to-lovers banter in Strawberry Fields for Never.

ACKNOWLEDGMENTS

My first Christmas book was truly heaven-sent. This one has felt the same. While I spent a great deal of effort writing it, I also felt a quiet reassurance that it would work out. In fact, I even prayed for help getting it done by a certain deadline, and for the first time since last Christmas, I met that deadline without a single setback.

God is good.

My dear friends Kaylee Baldwin, Raneé S. Clark, and Gracie Ruth Mitchell aren't too bad, themselves. Thanks for critiquing, ladies. And thanks to my friends Jen Atkinson and Susan Henshaw for their input, to Jane Litherland for beta reading, to Crystal Nelson for polishing this beauty up, and to Sarah Carner for helping me keep my ship afloat. ARC readers and Bookstagrammers: thank you all!

My brothers inspired every punch from Logan and Lucas, and then some.

Elsie, Hugo, Archie, and Etta—I love you dearly. Jeffy, you're better than any book boyfriend. Dare I say I love you truly, madly, deeply?

Oh, darn it. I should have saved that for the next book.

ABOUT THE AUTHOR

Kate Watson is a Top 50 Amazon Bestselling author of cheeky closed door romantic comedies. Originally from Canada, she attended college in the States and holds a BA in Philosophy from Brigham Young University. A lover of travel, speaking in accents, and experiencing new cultures, she has also lived in Israel, Brazil, the American South, and she now calls Arizona home.

She started writing at six years old and sold her first book, "The Heart People," for $0.25 to her parents. It received rave reviews. Since then, she's written many books, including Single All the Way, a Top 50 Amazon Bestseller. She writes stories full of heart, humor, and happily-ever-afters.

She is currently living her own happily-ever-after with her super cute husband and their four wild and wonderful kids. She runs on caffeine, swoons, and Jesus.

ALSO BY KATE WATSON

Sweet as Sugar Maple Series:

Strawberry Fields for Never

Baby Llama Drama

It's Always Sonny

Don't Go Faking My Heart

Truly Medley Deeply

Christmas:

Single All the Way

Made in the USA
Middletown, DE
05 December 2024

66230610R00191